Contested Politics in Tunisia

Several thousand new civil society organisations were legally established in Tunisia following the 2010–2011 uprising that forced the long-serving dictator, Zine El Abidine Ben Ali, from office. These organisations had different visions for a new Tunisia, and divisive issues such as the status of women, homosexuality and human rights became highly contested. For some actors the transition from authoritarian rule allowed them to have a strong voice that was previously muted under the former regimes. For others, the conflicts that emerged between the different groups brought new repressions and exclusions – this time not from the regime, but from 'civil society'. Vulnerable populations and the organisations working with them soon found themselves operating on uncertain terrain where providing support to marginalised and routinely criminalised communities brought unexpected challenges. Here, Edwige Fortier explores this remarkable period of transformation and the effects of the opening up of public space in this way.

EDWIGE FORTIER is a research associate in the Department of Development Studies, SOAS, University of London. Formerly a Civil Society Advisor with the Global Fund to Fight AIDS, Tuberculosis and Malaria, she has worked for more than twenty years as a development practitioner to strengthen the involvement, care and support of vulnerable communities affected by HIV/AIDS.

Contested Politics in Tunisia

Civil Society in a Post-Authoritarian State

EDWIGE FORTIER
SOAS, University of London

CAMBRIDGE
UNIVERSITY PRESS

University Printing House, Cambridge CB2 8BS, United Kingdom

One Liberty Plaza, 20th Floor, New York, NY 10006, USA

477 Williamstown Road, Port Melbourne, VIC 3207, Australia

314-321, 3rd Floor, Plot 3, Splendor Forum, Jasola District Centre, New Delhi - 110025, India

79 Anson Road, #06-04/06, Singapore 079906

Cambridge University Press is part of the University of Cambridge.

It furthers the University's mission by disseminating knowledge in the pursuit of education, learning and research at the highest international levels of excellence.

www.cambridge.org
Information on this title: www.cambridge.org/9781108441858
DOI: 10.1017/9781108348386

© Edwige Fortier 2019

This publication is in copyright. Subject to statutory exception and to the provisions of relevant collective licensing agreements, no reproduction of any part may take place without the written permission of Cambridge University Press.

First published 2019
First paperback edition 2020

A catalogue record for this publication is available from the British Library

ISBN 978-1-108-42532-2 Hardback
ISBN 978-1-108-44185-8 Paperback

Cambridge University Press has no responsibility for the persistence or accuracy of URLs for external or third-party internet websites referred to in this publication, and does not guarantee that any content on such websites is, or will remain, accurate or appropriate.

For Loretta

Contents

Preface		page ix
1	Introduction: In the Pursuit of Dignity and Freedom	1
	The Downfall of a Dictator and the Resurgence of Civil Society	3
	Tunisia in Transition: A Critical Approach	12
	Structure of the Book	22
2	Situating Civil Society: Emancipation or Liberalisation	27
	Locating Civil Society Following the Emergence of Capitalism	30
	Bringing Civil Society Back in: Neoliberal Policy and 'Liberal' Democracy	40
	The Institutionalisation of Civil Society and the Spaces in between	48
	Conclusion	54
3	The Consolidation of the Tunisian State	57
	Situating the Tunisian State	58
	The Consolidation of Civil Society	73
	Manipulating the Rules of the Game: Moving through an Authoritarian Regime	81
	Conclusion	92
4	Civil Society and the Opening Up of the Public Space	95
	Political Liberalisation and the Expansion of Space	97
	The Resurrection of Civil Society	109
	Past Meets Present: Historic Actors and New Spaces	114
	The Emergence of the New	122
	Conclusion	132
5	Social Divisions and the Re-Manifestation of Social Islam	136
	The Making of a Counter-Public	137
	Social Islam: Claiming New Spaces	147
	Contestation from the Periphery: Growing Cleavages among Civil Society	154
	Conclusion	160

6	Consensus and Marginalisation: The Mapping of Priorities in Post-Uprising Tunisia	164
	Abandoning Consensus	165
	Whose Voice Matters: The Recovery of Personal Dignity	168
	The Expansion of Space for Marginalised Communities?	173
	Contracting Spaces for Discursive Contestation: 'Now Is Not the Time'	181
	Conclusion	187
7	Conclusion: Imagining Change – Determining the Parameters of Pluralism	191
	Expansions and Contractions: Tracking the Movement of National Priorities in Post-Uprising Tunisia	194
	Disruption, Change and Transformation: Situating Conflict	198

Appendix: List of Interviewees   204

Bibliography   210

Index   227

Preface

Since the Arab uprisings began in early 2011, a succession of dictatorships has fallen across the Middle East and North Africa, including in Egypt, Libya, Tunisia and Yemen. More recently, the broader world beyond the Arab Spring has witnessed a rise of nationalist movements that have used democratic systems and norms to amplify their voices, power and influence. From as early as 2015, populist parties and their accompanying discourses in Europe have increasingly benefited from perceptions of growing insecurity as a result of a combination of factors, including the recurrence of terrorist attacks, worsening economic security and opportunity in an increasingly globalised world and an unprecedented influx of refugees and migrants.[1] Consequently, populist parties and movements won significant inroads throughout 2016–2018 in France (the National Front, renamed in 2018 as the National Rally), Poland (Law and Justice Party), Germany (Alternative for Germany (AfD) Party), Austria (Freedom Party of Austria) and Italy (Five Star Movement and the Northern League). Elsewhere in Europe alone, politically influential populist parties with similar platforms, goals and ideas exist in countries from Denmark to Greece.

The rise of such parties has occurred at the same time as other political shifts that signal deep unease or distrust of longstanding political norms and orthodoxies, including the referendum on the United Kingdom's European Union membership (Brexit) and the presidential election in the United States in 2016, during which a wave of populism surged to destabilise the status quo. Many of these developments, from the Arab Spring to the Brexit, have been grounded in rhetoric and action as representing the will and needs of people who have been ignored, oppressed or delegitimised by unresponsive elites. But this does not mean that the uprisings and movements have opened

---

[1] J. Luengo-Cabrera, 'How Europe's Deteriorating Peace Is Facilitating the Rise of Populism', LSE-EUROPP Blog, 10 July 2018.

space for all citizens to achieve improved economic, social, legal and political rights and influence. Instead, drawing the line between democracy and authoritarianism today has become a precarious exercise. These movements, each of which shares degrees of xenophobia, racism, sexism, homophobia and anti-Islamic sentiments alongside a myriad of stigmatising attitudes and actions, have several critical impacts and outcomes in common, of which three are particularly noteworthy. The first has been a marked increase in inflammatory remarks and acts by individuals in the highest political offices against minorities and the most marginalised communities, thereby giving voice and licence to individuals to further discriminate with impunity. The second has been politicians' decisions to direct finite resources and international development aid away from the world's poorest and most vulnerable to priorities and initiatives that are more closely associated with building nation-states. And finally, the spaces for agonistic confrontation and debate have been increasingly squeezed, effectively constricting prospects for pluralism and objective analysis more broadly.

This book is about navigating the multiplicity of spaces that open following regime change and the numerous battles that ensue as actors at both social and political levels swiftly move to define a country's national identity and set its highest priorities. As the uprisings across the Middle East and North Africa unfolded in 2010 and 2011, this book originated with a question: What and who constitutes civil society in the region? And what does this mean both for the potential 'success' and 'failure' of nascent movements towards greater plurality and democratisation?

As a development practitioner working in the field of HIV/AIDS and sexual health, I perceived that civil society organisations working with vulnerable and marginalised groups would certainly face insurmountable challenges under authoritarian regimes, including repression and violence. Moreover, I often considered how they operated and under what incentive structures, given the great risks underlying this work. For example, across the Middle East and North Africa same-sex behaviour is criminalised through formal penal codes, sex work outside of legalised institutions is a criminal offense and drug use is illegal. Organisations that work with criminalised and marginalised populations choose to operate in the unlawful, the prohibited and the forbidden.

During the two-year period of critical sociopolitical disruption and transformation following the downfall of the Ben Ali regime in Tunisia from 2011 to 2013, I disentangle and engage with the concept of civil society theoretically and empirically in the Middle East and North Africa as it relates to marginalised groups and the organisations that choose to work with them in similar challenging settings. More importantly, I strongly advocate the importance of researching marginalised communities who experience the brunt of sociopolitical turmoil and who often struggle to participate in mainstream discursive arenas. What happens at the periphery sheds light on populations who are routinely stigmatised and criminalised, and more worryingly, who often find their human rights eroded as a result of populist decisions and moral panics associated with political transitions.

Overall, the aim of the book is to encourage academics, policymakers and donors who regularly engage with the often overused concept of civil society to do so in a critical manner, one in which the tremendous dynamism and volatility of the interactions and relationships between these groups and actors can be appreciated. The events that transpire following the downfall of an authoritarian regime can provide a snapshot for instructive analysis during a finite but unpredictable period. Ultimately, the aim is to capture, albeit momentarily, these diverse narratives and dynamic struggles as a nation pursues democratisation.

There are many individuals who I would like to acknowledge for their support during the insightful and transformative process to develop this book. First, I want to acknowledge the careful and motivational direction given to me by my PhD supervisor, Dr Michael Jennings, in the Development Studies Department with the School of Oriental and African Studies (SOAS). I would also like to thank the additional members of my Supervisory Committee: Professor Gilbert Achcar in the Development Studies Department and Professor Charles Tripp in the Department of Politics at SOAS. The time and insight each member of my Supervisory Committee gave to me during this process contributed greatly to my efforts and ability to complete this project.

I am also grateful to my doctoral examiners, Dr Maha Abdelrahman with the University of Cambridge and Dr Michael Willis with the University of Oxford, as well as my anonymous peer reviewers, for their guidance to ensure that I showcased the critical findings of the research in Tunisia. I also want to thank my colleagues Dr Subir Sinha and Dr Rahul Rao of the Development Studies and the International Relations Departments at SOAS, both of whom put me in touch with transformative literature and materials on civil society, social movements and sexual minorities that were ultimately vital to my research.

I want to acknowledge the support and inspiration I have received from many of my colleagues working in HIV/AIDS and in global health more broadly, many of whom helped me to conceive of this work and to see it through its various manifestations. I owe extreme gratitude to the United Nations Joint Programme on HIV/AIDS (UNAIDS) Middle East and North Africa Regional Support Team, in particular to Hind Khatib, Dr Hamidresa Setayesh and Simone Salem. Special thanks also are due to my colleagues at the International HIV/AIDS Alliance, Dr Abdelkader Bacha, Anton Kerr, Manuel Couffignal, Kevin Orr and Tania Kisserli. I owe a special appreciation to Dr Shereen El Feki, who on a warm evening in Yemen in 2007 motivated me to research civil societies in the Middle East and North Africa. I am grateful for her critical insight and beautiful sense of humour.

I would like to also acknowledge my friends and colleagues from my various life paths who have offered their editing skills to different chapters of this book, including Rachel Guisselquist, Judy Levinson, Susan Rosenfeld, Todd Summers and in particular Jeff Hoover. In addition, I want to thank my departmental colleagues from SOAS, Dr Marion Pechayre and Dr Sharri Plonski, for offering both motivational and technical support to this manuscript. I also owe special thanks to the Barclay's BRISMES Scholarship Fund and the Fund for Women Graduates (FfWG), both of which supported me in the final stages of the development and writing of the research.

Most importantly, given the personal and professional challenges they have experienced and their courage in the face of recurring obstacles and threats, I also want to personally thank each individual who kindly allowed me to interview them in Egypt and Tunisia. To protect their voices and to underscore the uncertainty following any sociopolitical transition from authoritarian rule, I have chosen not to name them. In particular, I am grateful to my colleagues who continue to push boundaries and remind decision makers of the need to prioritise the voices of marginalised populations in the Middle East and North Africa. I also owe immeasurable gratitude to the host family with whom I stayed in Tunisia for bringing me into their home and showing me a level of generosity and kindness that I will always cherish. They have given me an enduring friendship through our walks, discussions, meals and laughter. I also would like to acknowledge my friend and mentor from the very first day of this journey, Dr Katherine Natanel with the University of Exeter Institute of Arab and Islamic Studies. She has demonstrated a remarkable sense of grace and grit in her own work that has inspired and motivated me over the years. Not least, I would like to thank my family, including my mother, Loretta Fortier and especially my partner, Peter Hayward, for the many sacrifices he has made to ensure I complete this personal aspiration. Finally, I would like to thank my editor and constant motivator over the years, Maria Marsh with Cambridge University Press.

1 | Introduction
In the Pursuit of Dignity and Freedom

Here AIDS is no longer a priority. Instead there are discussions around single mothers and even the introduction of temporary marriage. How can we even begin to explain what we want to do in this environment? We therefore have to look at our strategy and think again. We could address some of these issues before the revolution but not now – we have to work with a view to protecting these populations, what we do and say could affect them negatively.

– Human rights lawyer, Tunis[1]

In February 2011 during what was described as a 'wave of violence', it was estimated that 2,000 individuals attacked a *maison close* in the old town of Tunis, the Tunisian capital, followed by similar attacks on *maisons closes* in Medenine, Sfax, Kairouan and Sousse, with sex workers chased out and some of the establishments firmly boarded and bricked over.[2] *Les maisons de tolerance* or *les maisons closes* are a remnant from the French colonial period in Tunisia.[3] In 1942 the French authorities in Tunisia introduced the *maisons closes*, or institutional brothels, with a decree outlining the regulations for legal prostitution.[4] Before 2011, some 300 legal sex workers were working across the urban areas of Tunisia, such as in Tunis, Sousse, Sfax, Gabes

---

[1] Interview in Tunis (36), 16 February 2012.
[2] I. Bensaied, 'Les Islamistes s'Attaquent aux Maisons Closes', France24.com (18 March 2011).
[3] It is also argued that 'tolerated prostitution' in North Africa stretches back to the beginning of the Ottoman period in the seventeenth century. See: A. Largueche and D. Largueche, *Marginales en Terre d'Islam* (Tunis: Cérès Editions, 1992), pp. 19–22.
[4] S. El Feki, *Sex and the Citadel: Intimate Life in a Changing Arab World* (London: Random House, 2013), p. 202; for additional information on the history of prostitution, see M. Snoussi 'La Prostitution en Tunisie au Temps de la Colonisation' in J. Alexandropoulos and P. Cabanel (eds.), *Mosaique: Diasporas, Cosmopolitisme, Archeologies de l'Identite* (Toulouse: Presses Universitaires du Mirail, 2000), pp. 389–413.

and Kairouan; more than 100 women were working in Tunis alone, while the *maison close* in Sfax was the third-largest legal establishment for sex work in Tunisia.[5] Prior to the Tunisia uprising in 2010–2011, both the Ministry of the Interior and the Ministry of Health had supervisory responsibilities over the *maisons closes*: sex workers would submit a formal application to the former for permission to work, and the latter was responsible for ensuring that public health was protected.

The individuals who participated in the attacks on the *maisons closes* in 2011 openly regarded the establishments as symbols of the debauchery and impiety of the former secular authoritarian regimes of Habib Bourguiba and Zine El Abidine Ben Ali. This movement from the street to shut down the *maisons closes* was diffused through local mosques and via the internet in an effort to reclaim Tunisia's moral identity.[6] These targeted acts, led by members of communities rather than a formal government authority, sharply reverberated among marginalised communities and organisations working with them. Organisations working in human rights and with vulnerable groups such as those affected by HIV/AIDS in Tunisia became anxious about the attacks on the *maisons closes* so soon after the uprising began in December 2010. A woman supporting HIV/AIDS outreach work with sex workers explained, 'These invisible forces appeared suddenly ... They closed up the doors to the *maisons closes* with bricks. This caused quite a disruption ... Quite a few sex workers left the centre and moved underground to do clandestine sex work feeling it was safer.'[7]

The downfall of a dictator opened a space in which numerous actors rushed in to seize the opportunity to genuinely and actively participate in the sociopolitical transformations of post-revolution Tunisia. New actors and groups immediately emerged at the forefront to claim new spaces and set fresh priorities for the Tunisian state. For some actors manoeuvring in Tunisia's public spaces, the 2010–2011 uprising allowed them to have a strong voice that was previously muted under the former regimes. For others, the conflicts and contestations that emerged between the different groups brought new repressions and

[5] F. Abid and C. Ghorbel, 'Enquête sur l'Utilisation de Préservatif Auprès des Jeunes Clients des Professionnelles du Sexe Declarées', Ministère de la Santé Publique, 2009, p. 11, cited in El Feki, *Sex and the Citadel*, p. 202.
[6] Bensaied, 'Les Islamistes s'Attaquent aux Maisons Closes'.
[7] Interview in Tunis (20), 16 January 2012 and 13 March 2013.

exclusions – this time not from the regime, but from among the actors engaging in collective action and the various other groups that considered themselves part of 'civil society'. More controversial or divisive issues such as the status of women, legalised prostitution, homosexuality and human rights became highly contested as a multitude of disparate visions filled these new spaces. Vulnerable populations and the organisations working with them soon found themselves operating on uncertain terrain where providing support to marginalised and routinely criminalised communities brought new challenges. Following the 2010–2011 Tunisia uprising, some of these actors eventually developed nostalgia for a dictator where the rules of the game were clearly defined and they could find a means to manoeuvre within the parameters set by the authoritarian regime. The unsettled social, political and cultural situation made the future difficult to predict. Would the various conflicts between civil society groups serve as vital tools for widening previously constrained discursive spaces? Or ultimately, would the volatility and uncertainty of democratisation impede peripheral actors and consequently limit the likelihood of contentious issues from fully entering Tunisia's national deliberations?

The Downfall of a Dictator and the Resurgence of Civil Society

Mohamed Bouazizi's self-immolation in the town of Sidi Bouzid, on 17 December 2010, ignited a succession of uprisings across the Middle East and North Africa. Over the next several months, one revolution inspired another 'in a domino effect of sympathy and solidarity',[8] with Tunisia, Egypt, Yemen, Libya, Syria and Bahrain all affected to varying degrees. Individuals across the region relinquished their fear of repressive regimes, thereby revealing the true vulnerability of the ruling elites. Only two days after the 26-year-old Bouazizi's death on 4 January 2011, wider protests across Tunisia began, and soon after, the government declared a state of emergency. Within weeks, cries of 'Ash-sh'ab yurid isqat al-nizam' ('The people want the overthrow of the regime') and 'khobz wa maa, Ben Ali leh' ('Bread and water, no to Ben Ali') eventually led to Zine El Abidine Ben Ali's televised public acknowledgement of 'Ana fahmt' ('I have understood'). On 14 January, he and

---

[8] T. Manhire, *The Arab Spring: Rebellion, Revolution and a New World Order* (London: Guardian Books, 2002), p. xi.

his family fled for Saudi Arabia. Hamit Bozarslan poignantly writes that 'the system appeared as "unbelievable" in its own being than in its demand for obedience'.[9]

Those spearheading and participating in the Tunisian revolution from December 2010 to January 2011 called not only for bread and water but more broadly for employment, freedom and dignity as the immolation of Bouazizi managed to encapsulate and direct attention towards the issues of inequality and humiliation.[10] The more than 300 deaths in the days during and after 14 January strengthened the will of the protesters who united together in the face of their own apprehensions against a repressive regime.[11] Protesters held night-time candlelight vigils for those killed in the violence and brought blankets, food and tea to fellow demonstrators. Many report a time of unprecedented national solidarity and some today are still unable to believe they took part in the downfall of the Ben Ali regime. Kmar Bendana in *Chronique d'une Transition* observed, 'The horizontal unfolding, which surprised journalists, diplomats, bloggers and spectators with its rhythm and efficiency ... where Tunisians were perceived as positive heroes as well as protagonists involved in an unexpected democratic process.'[12]

Following the 2010–2011 uprising in Tunisia, measures to initiate greater political liberalism were instigated almost immediately. In October 2011, Tunisia was the first post-revolution country in the Arab world to hold democratic elections. Tunisia's perceived departure from authoritarian rule soon nourished expectations among a range of stakeholders, from individuals to the international community, for an expansion of space for political liberalisation, pluralism, redistribution and – perhaps most importantly – recognition. For example, scholars on the concept of 'global civil society' – Helmut Anheier, Mary Kaldor and Marlies Glasius – questioned whether or not the uprisings in the region were the signal of a new beginning, the start of 'a new political

---

[9] H. Bozarslan, 'Réflexions sur les Configurations Révolutionnaires Tunisienne et Égyptienne', *Mouvements des Idées et des Luttes*, no. 66 (Summer 2011), p. 18.
[10] A. Deboulet and D. Nicolaidis, 'Les Hirondelles Font-Elles le Printemps?', *Mouvements des Idées et des Luttes*, no. 66 (Summer 2011), p. 9.
[11] K. Bendana, *Chronique d'une Transition* (Tunis: Les Editions Script, 2011), p. 66.
[12] Ibid., pp. 61–62.

movement'. They advocated that the events of 2011 gave new meaning to the concept of global civil society as the emerging emancipatory agenda fused with post-1968 issues of social justice.[13] International optimism following the uprisings in the region reinvigorated interest in the links between democracy, development and good governance – as did similar events in Eastern Europe and Latin America in the 1980s – the concept of civil society was once again resurrected to serve as the antonym of authoritarianism.

From 2011 to 2013, the landscape for collective action and grassroots movements in Tunisia widened with the establishment of several thousand new civil society organisations. The deregulation of the former and more rigid laws of association allowed organisations operating in Tunisia's physical and symbolic public spaces to engage more openly in a broad range of activities including civic activism, human rights, social welfare initiatives and direct outreach work with deprived communities across the country.[14] It is estimated that 1,700 new associations were formally created from January to October 2011, with a further 600 civil society organisations registering between October 2011 and March 2012.[15] Individuals acting inside Tunisia's public spaces also re-appropriated the concept of *muwatana* or *citoyenneté*, which refers to citizens feeling engaged and mobilised as equal partners in the future of the country, with or without the state to accompany them along the way. This took the form of popular protest, mass mobilisation and demonstrations alongside collective action. The concept equally manifested in growing notions of voluntarism

---

[13] H. Anheier, M. Kaldor and M. Glasius, 'The Global Civil Society Yearbook: Lessons and Insights 2001–2011' in M. Kaldor, H. Moore and S. Selchow (eds.), *Global Civil Society 2012: Ten Years of Critical Reflection* (Hampshire: Palgrave Macmillan, 2012).

[14] During the first phase of Tunisia's transition, the 'High Authority for the Realisation of the Objectives of the Revolution, Political Reform and Democratic Transition' was established to oversee the transition from revolution to elections. Among its many remits, it was tasked with modifying the text on the laws of association. For additional information, see S. Zemni, 'The Extraordinary Politics of the Tunisian Revolution: The Process of Constitution Making', *Mediterranean Politics* (2014), pp. 1–19; A. Guellali, 'Pathways and Pitfalls for Tunisia's New Constituent Assembly', ThinkAfricaPress.com, 14 October 2011; and decree laws no. 14 of 23 March 2011 and no. 27 of 18 April 2011.

[15] Union Européenne, 'Rapport de Diagnostic sur la Société Civile Tunisienne', Mission de Formulation Programme d'Appui à la Société Civile en Tunisie, March 2012, p. 5.

among Tunisians, resulting in local collections for vulnerable communities, Tunisian diaspora raising money to purchase emergency transportation for their local towns and even neighbourhood members meeting in a family's garage to plan support to marginalised women. Immediately following the downfall of the Ben Ali regime, one could observe a return to the self-organisation of the grassroots, agency, self-determination and self-management agendas set in community mobilisation unmistakable in the popular social movements of Eastern Europe and Latin America only three decades earlier. Larbi Sadiki's conceptualisation of the *faragh* succinctly captures how it is precisely within such a power void that a multiplicity of deliberations flourish, sparking both 'contests and counter-contests' within these spaces.[16] As such, by looking more closely to this period, it is not only possible to discern the multiple conflicts and contestations among civil society actors and organisations but also to perceive the combined sociopolitical divisions that have a remarkable effect on the various issues that materialise following the collapse of a dictatorship. With the numerous inclusions and exclusions that take place among civil society actors embodying disparate ideologies during a period of simultaneous disruption and transformation, various groups consequently emerge either as publics or are eventually sidelined as peripheral counterpublics. The aim of this book is to determine the function of conflict within civil society – the consequences of these splits, shifts and divergences – in order to probe further what can be discerned from the sites and areas of contestation during a transition from authoritarian rule.

This book is situated within the tumultuous and uncertain period from the downfall of the Ben Ali regime in 2011 to the two years of social, political and economic transformation following this critical event in the history of Tunisia. Ultimately, it observes what happens when a space opens up and who rushes in to fill that ephemeral space. To do this, the book looks to the myriad actors and organisations that consider themselves 'civil society', including those organisations legally established during the period of authoritarian rule prior to December 2010 as well as the nascent organisations created through the revised and expanded laws of association in 2011. Through the examination of these organisations, it can be of little surprise that while there are

---

[16] L. Sadiki, H. Wimmen and L. Al-Zubaidi, *Democratic Transition in the Middle East: Unmaking Power* (London: Routledge, 2012), p. 8.

areas of consensus and solidarity among these different actors, there are also areas in which there is intense disagreement and divergence. Just as there is harmony among these actors, there is also conflict. In particular, the book analyses the conflicts and contestations that emerged among the different elements of civil society during a period of remarkable sociopolitical transformation in which the stakes were arguably higher in regards to defining national priorities. Identifying the sites of conflicts during these periods can reveal the characteristics that contradict 'liberal' understandings of civil society as well as emphasise the volatile nature of democratisation itself. Critically, the purpose of this analysis is to also determine whether these conflicts and contestations are destructive or in fact productive forces to maintain deliberative spaces for discursive contestation – as agonistic forces capable of generating and sustaining pluralism more broadly during the tumultuous transition from authoritarian rule. I maintain here and throughout the book that during periods of sociopolitical turmoil such as seen through the lens of the Arab uprisings, contestations among civic actors are in fact productive as they enable disputation and counter contests; we should in fact be worried when there is an absence of conflict as this indicates that discursive spaces are contracting and pluralism is narrowing. I reason that conflict is in fact essential to pluralism and dialogism.

The book undertakes a conceptual and empirical analysis of 'civil society' to comprehensively establish what actually transpires among civil society actors and groups. By combining elements of both Chantal Mouffe's and Neera Chandhoke's understandings of civil society and discursive space, I define civil society here as a field of actors, groups and organisations, acting and manoeuvring within a multiplicity of physical and symbolic public spaces. These public spaces serve to harness a discursive arena in which these different actors can deliberate and contest critical matters of concern, both through their voices and their deliberate actions.[17] The analysis looks to how and where these conflicts are manifested among civil society actors – in the symbolic and physical occupation of the public space, within social divisions and in mapping national democratic priorities. The primary context is

---

[17] C. Mouffe, *Agonistics: Thinking the World Politically* (London: Verso, 2013) and N. Chandhoke, *State and Civil Society: Explorations in Political Theory* (New Delhi: Sage Publications, 2005).

grounded in events that took place during the two years subsequent to the downfall of the authoritarian regime in Tunisia in January 2011 and as such the book identifies and explores three principal themes: the 'illiberal' effects of the opening of the public space(s), the emerging sociocultural and socio-religious divisions (including the rise of associational or social Islam) and finally the exclusionary (and undemocratic) nature of consensus in 'liberal' democracies. Effectively, these three themes bring into sharp relief the different divergences and sites of contestation that can arise as a country embarks on the pursuit of democratisation. They illustrate simultaneously the dynamism of a host of actors and groups collectively mobilised to shape the priorities of Tunisia and also the genuine constraints for actors limited by the political residue they have inherited. As such, each core theme reveals across the two years a gradual narrowing down of contests and counter-contests in public spaces, demonstrating ultimately the enduring impact of decades of authoritarian rule on all actors at both the political and social levels. First, this has direct implications for the maintenance of donor-driven 'civil society strengthening', 'capacity building' and 'democracy promotion' initiatives in middle- and lower-income countries, in particular those transitioning from authoritarian rule. And second, perhaps more importantly, in underscoring the violent nature of democracy, this finding has implications for how the role and capacities of these actors is understood more broadly in democratisation narratives prior to and during transitions from authoritarian rule.

Situating the Research within Marginalised Communities

The analysis throughout the book is grounded in the discipline of international development studies, in particular in terms of how it considers and situates the concept of civil society in neoliberal discourses, and as such, within understandings of 'liberal' democracy. I frame the analysis within discourses on neoliberalism for two principal reasons. The first is because many would argue that the socioeconomic inequalities caused by neoliberal policies in the Middle East and North Africa are the root causes of the Arab uprisings.[18]

---

[18] P. Aarts and F. Cavatorta, *Civil Society in Syria and Iran: Activism in Authoritarian Contexts* (London: Lynne Rienner, 2013), p. 8; R. Hinnebusch,

Second, I argue, alongside writers such as Line Khatib, that political and economic liberalisation have ultimately legitimised civil society actors and groups that would have otherwise remained unempowered in many countries in the Middle East.[19] Neoliberalism (and its accompanying discourses) can be defined as a political project of economic, state and social transformation with its own structural adjustment programmes embodying a set of specific economic policies and conditionalities designed and, in some cases, imposed on countries by the World Bank and International Monetary Fund (IMF). Over the last few decades, neoliberal policies have entailed a total reconfiguration of the social contract between the state and its citizens, often provoking major socio-economic disruption. Consequently, with the development of the 'Washington Consensus' and the 'New Policy Agenda' in the 1990s, the role(s) of civil society became paramount in serving both as a cost-effective provider of services and as a torchbearer for democratic values and good governance. Moreover, the concept of civil society has since been rearticulated to contain a burden of virtues that even includes the instigation of the transition to and consolidation of democracy.[20] The normative weight of the concept alone often renders it a challenge to engage critically and thoughtfully with its various attributes and functions. Consequently, within neoliberal discourses the contests and counter-contests that manifest among these actors are often misunderstood, overlooked or de-emphasised. And perhaps an even graver consequence of the prominence of civil society within neoliberal discourses is that these actors can inadvertently serve to further legitimise the very regimes preventing genuine democratic outcomes.[21]

As such, I undertake a critical examination of the concept of civil society, looking to contemporary and neoliberal understandings of the concept in which the significance of conflict among these actors is both emphasised and de-emphasised throughout history. This approach

---

'Change and Continuity after the Arab Uprising: The Consequences of State Formation in Arab North African States', *British Journal of Middle Eastern Studies*, vol. 42, no. 1 (2015), pp. 12–30; V. Durac and F. Cavatorta, *Politics and Governance in the Middle East* (London: Palgrave, 2015).

[19] L. Khatib, 'Syria's Civil Society as a Tool for Regime Legitimacy' in Aarts and Cavatorta (eds.), *Civil Society in Syria and Iran*, p. 19.

[20] See L. Diamond, 'Toward Democratic Consolidation', *Journal of Democracy*, vol. 5, no. 3 (July 1994), pp. 4–17.

[21] A. Jamal, *Barriers to Democracy: The Other Side of Social Capital in Palestine and the Arab World* (Princeton: Princeton University Press, 2007).

allows for a further contribution into how civil society is understood conceptually and empirically in different contexts, specifically during transitions from authoritarian rule. And while Chapter 2 undertakes a theoretical analysis of the evolution of the concept of civil society with its end point situated within discourses on neoliberalism, civil society activism is also considered as I acknowledge the numerous indeterminate factors behind why these actors regularly choose to participate in public spaces despite an often high cost and risk associated with their engagement.

The book looks to a range of actors who emerged to fill the public space following the Tunisian uprising in 2010–2011. This includes not only nascent humanitarian development organisations but also organisations working with groups on the periphery, which may often be excluded from the mainstream public and its accompanying discourses. Specifically, this comprises human rights organisations established before and after the downfall of the regime in 2011, humanitarian development organisations (including Islamic associations) created after 2011, and organisations working with communities living with and affected by HIV/AIDS and sexual minorities established before and subsequent to the uprising in Tunisia.

I examine organisations working in HIV/AIDS because many of these organisations work with vulnerable populations, such as sex workers, gay, bisexual and transgender populations, people who use drugs and prisoners. Even though the work of these organisations often concentrates on close programmatic outreach interventions and service provision to affected communities, it also assumes an inherent political nature because many organisations advocate for the provision of costly HIV treatment by the government; highlight instances of institutional stigma and discrimination; and call for the eradication of controversial legal stipulations that criminalise sex work, homosexuality or same-sex relations and drug use. Therefore, one of the underlying aims of the book is to also emphasise, and at the same time advocate, that it is vital to research communities that are routinely marginalised. Through HIV/AIDS one encounters highly contentious and in fact illegal groups of people who feel the sizeable brunt of any sociopolitical turmoil. More importantly, these groups serve to remind us that what happens on the periphery is indeed highly relevant to understanding the broader sociopolitical and sociocultural landscape of a country.

To provide some context to understanding HIV/AIDS in the region, the Middle East and North Africa continues to have one of the fastest-growing epidemics compared with other regions, with concentrated epidemics in each of the sub-regions including the Maghreb, Shaam or Mashriq, and the Gulf Cooperation Council (GCC) countries. With a rise in new infections since 2001, the total number of adults and children living with HIV in the Middle East and North Africa region was estimated in 2016 to be 230,000 [160,000–380,000], with new infections among adults and children estimated to be 18,000.[22] The increase in new infections is attributed to a growing HIV prevalence among key populations at higher risk of acquiring HIV, who transmit the virus to individuals both at higher and lower risk of infection. In 2016, the estimated number of deaths due to HIV/AIDS was 11,000 [7,200–17,000], with only 24 per cent of people living with HIV on antiretroviral therapy treatment, or approximately 54,000 individuals.[23] These trends and figures are the result of an overall acceleration in the epidemic throughout the region, an increase in the total number of women living with HIV and the continued lack of adequate services to prevent new infections, particularly among children.[24] The HIV epidemic in the Middle East increasingly reflects the diversity of the region as different populations are more heavily affected in various geographical areas. This diversity is magnified by disparate attitudes, policies, political commitments and availability of and access to HIV/AIDS services.[25] Moreover, in some countries such as Libya, Syria and Yemen, chronic conflict and sociopolitical unrest across the region over the last several years have also exacerbated the epidemic by not only disrupting vital services, such as access to treatment and service delivery, but also by aggravating the conditions that intensify vulnerability to acquiring HIV/AIDS.[26]

In selecting this range of organisations (and the populations with whom they work) – and by including civil society organisations that operated both during the Ben Ali regime as well as organisations that were established after the regime's downfall – the book also brings into relief the multiple challenges and advances these organisations experienced. Moreover, it serves to remind us of the formidable role

[22] UNAIDS, 'Regional Factsheet', 2016.   [23] Ibid.
[24] UNAIDS, 'Middle East and North Africa Regional Report on AIDS', 2011.
[25] Ibid.
[26] UNAIDS, 'Regional Report for the Middle East and North Africa', 2013, p. 20.

of the state, which regularly opens and tightens the spaces within which these organisations function. Finally, it is often easy to overlook the groups and actors that find spaces contracting around them during periods of sociopolitical transformation as the priorities for democratisation are outlined and the hierarchy of concerns push certain issues and groups to the periphery; some are even negated entirely. Issues perceived as contentious are often sidelined in favour of those that are acceptable to the greater public and that equally feature the collective imaginings of a country's new national identity. This tightening of certain spaces for individuals and organisations underscores the complex and unstable nature of democratisation and, more importantly, the fundamental role of conflict among civil society actors. The contestations between these actors are perhaps the only genuine indication we have of the presence of pluralism.

Tunisia in Transition: A Critical Approach

Conducting research immediately following what was considered the height of the 'Arab Spring' brought challenges as well as opportunities to observe a period of remarkable sociopolitical transformation under the microscope. Following the downfall of the Ben Ali regime in Tunisia, the country was not only closely monitored by newly politicised Tunisian nationals but also by international governments, policymakers, donors and academics globally. After decades of authoritarian rule across the region, onlookers followed Tunisia in hopes that the power of *Al-Shaab* could triumph over corrupt and repressive regimes. This book looks closely to the transformations within civil society from January 2011 to July 2013, from the peak of the post-revolution euphoria to the moment enthusiasm for a smooth transition effectively waned, arguably following the targeted assassinations of opposition political actors Chokri Belaid and Mohamed Brahmi.

Contextualising the book in part within such a period of political transformation or 'transition' is not without contention, however, just as scholars are cautious in their use of concepts such as 'revolution' versus 'uprisings' when reflecting upon events in the region during this time. A critical amount of literature on the Middle East and North Africa has centred on the debates regarding democracy or rather the limits of democratisation paradigms in the region. More recently, this has created the delineation between the transitology literature, concerning transitions to democracy, and literature concerning paradigms on 'authoritarian resilience'.[27] The transitology literature in particular has afforded a significant role for civil society actors in the region.[28] The literature on transitions from authoritarian rule was initially grounded in the empirical evidence on transitions from totalitarian and military rule in Southern and Eastern Europe and Latin America.[29] This literature also concentrated on the 'transition to democracy' specifically, suggesting both a normative and linear consideration of the trajectory of the state to a final end point manifesting in both stable macroeconomic growth and democracy. Following the Arab uprisings this noted 'transitological bias'[30] was immediately evident and prevalent among multilateral institutions, governments, journalists and citizens of the region; and often, this bias among the various actors and entities was without critical scrutiny. Throughout the text, the comparisons to the social and political transitions in Latin America and Southern and Eastern Europe are acknowledged where they can be made, in particular relation to the rise of efforts towards liberalisation and/or the role of civil society actors within or outside these processes. Nevertheless, the book also urges caution when comparing the events across the Middle East and North Africa in 2011, in terms of how they relate to generalities between 'transitions to democracy'. There are some commonalities across the disparate time periods, countries and events; however, the specificities can also remind us that

---

[27] See Aarts and Cavatorta (eds.), *Civil Society in Syria and Iran*; Jamal, *Barriers to Democracy*; and P. Rivetti, 'Continuity and Change before and after the Uprisings in Tunisia, Egypt and Morocco: Regime Reconfiguration and Policymaking in North Africa', *British Journal of Middle Eastern Studies*, vol. 42, no. 1 (2015), pp. 1–11.

[28] Aarts and Cavatorta (eds.), *Civil Society in Syria and Iran*, pp. 5, 210.

[29] See S. Huntington, *The Third Wave: Democratization in the Late Twentieth Century* (Norman: University of Oklahoma Press, 1991); G. O'Donnell and P. Schmitter (eds.), *Transitions from Authoritarian Rule: Tentative Conclusions about Uncertain Democracies* (Baltimore: Johns Hopkins University Press, 1986); G. O'Donnell, P. Schmitter and L. Whitehead (eds.), *Transitions from Authoritarian Rule: Comparative Perspectives* (Baltimore: Johns Hopkins University Press, 1986); F. Miszlivetz, '"Lost in Transformation": The Crisis of Democracy and Civil Society' in Kaldor, Moore and Selchow (eds.), *Global Civil Society 2012*; Diamond, 'Toward Democratic Consolidation'; and G. Denoeux, 'Promoting Democracy and Governance in Arab Countries' in S. Ben Nefissa, N. Al-Fattah, S. Hanafi and C. Milani (eds.), *NGOs and Governance in the Arab World* (Cairo: American University in Cairo Press, 2005).

[30] Rivetti, 'Continuity and Change before and after the Uprisings in Tunisia', p. 2.

a transition concerns not only democratisation but also the critical socio-economic and sociocultural transitions that are playing out both internally and externally to the regimes themselves.[31] For this reason, and throughout the book, while a transition is acknowledged to have taken place, semantic and/or linear links to the 'transition to democracy' are avoided where possible. Rather, the book underscores Guillermo Schmitter and Philippe O'Donnell's most noteworthy contribution of the notion of the 'uncertain something else' allowing one to capture the 'extraordinary uncertainty of the transition, with its numerous surprises and difficult dilemmas'.[32] This also parallels with the more immediate literature following the Arab uprisings that acknowledges more of a consensus on the 'open-ended nature of the uprisings' and equally the necessity to analyse change both within and outside of paradigms of democracy.[33] Finally, rather than to understand transitions as both normative and linear considerations regarding the trajectory of the 'modern' state, the understanding and use of transition here emphasises sociopolitical and socio-economic disruption, change, and transformation at manifold levels. Fundamentally, a transition must be disruptive to be transformative.

Generalities and Specificities of Transitions

Schmitter and O'Donnell refer to the transition as 'the interval between one political regime and another'.[34] Their analysis ceases from the point at which a new regime is installed. They write, 'Transitions are delimited, on the one side, by the launching of the process of dissolution of an authoritarian regime and, on the other, by the installation of some form of democracy, the return to some form of authoritarian

---

[31] Al-Sayyid notes that historically a significant limitation of transitology literature is that it analysed changes *of* regimes rather than *in* the regimes themselves. See: M. Al-Sayyid, 'Civil Society Activism in Authoritarian Regimes' in Aarts and Cavatorta (eds.), *Civil Society in Syria and Iran*, p. 207.

[32] O'Donnell and Schmitter (eds.), *Transitions from Authoritarian Rule: Tentative Conclusions*, p. 3.

[33] Rivetti, 'Continuity and Change before and after the Uprisings in Tunisia', p. 5 and F. Cavatorta, 'No Democratic Change … and Yet No Authoritarian Continuity: The Inter-Paradigm Debate and North Africa after the Uprisings', *British Journal of Middle Eastern Studies*, vol. 42, no. 1 (2015), pp. 135–145.

[34] O'Donnell and Schmitter (eds.), *Transitions from Authoritarian Rule: Tentative Conclusions*, p. 6.

rule, or the emergence of a revolutionary alternative.'[35] Given the different attempts to set out some general parameters to define and understand the manifold sociopolitical transitions from authoritarian rule based upon the experiences of countries in Southern and Eastern Europe and Latin America, it is important to set out what can be understood as general overall to sociopolitical transitions. In looking to the works of O'Donnell and Schmitter, for example, it is possible to identify three core areas in which there are commonalities across, at least, the initial stages of the different transitions in Eastern Europe, Latin America and the Middle East. They are: (1) the mobilisation or a popular upsurge on behalf of the citizen population, (2) the processes for redefining or extending rights or 'liberalisation' measures and (3) the 'resurrection of civil society'. There are also areas that are specific to the transitions that occurred across the Middle East and North Africa following the uprisings in 2010–2011. They are: (1) severe macroeconomic instability/crises and (2) no identified leadership either from a specific individual, party or group.

During the sociopolitical transitions from authoritarian rule that took place in Eastern Europe, Latin America, and the Middle East and North Africa, one can point to similar captivating and vivid, oscillating images of masses of citizens participating in what O'Donnell and Schmitter refer to as the 'popular upsurge'. These images portray a very physical occupation of space by individuals in peaceful protest adhering to non-violent collective action, for example during the Velvet Revolution in Prague in 1989 as well as the protests on Avenue Bourguiba in Tunis in 2010 and 2011. O'Donnell and Schmitter write:

> The catalyst in this transformation comes first from gestures by exemplary individuals, who begin testing the boundaries of behavior initially imposed by the incumbent regime ... In the precarious public spaces of the first stages of the transition, these individual gestures are astonishingly successful in provoking or reviving collective identifications and actions; they, in turn, help forge broad identifications which embody the explosion of a highly repoliticised and angry society.[36]

The often non-violent and heterogeneous nature of the popular upsurge not only brings along with it the element of surprise but also a physical and symbolic representation of the 'people' united in

[35] Ibid.   [36] Ibid., p. 49.

solidarity against authoritarianism or totalitarianism. This popular upsurge can also involve mass unrest, non-compliance, multiple and often simultaneous demonstrations across urban and rural centres, tactics of disruption and popular activism. For example, following the self-immolation of Mohamed Bouazizi on 17 December 2010, national scale mass mobilisations had organised only 10 days later across Tunisia in Al-Miknassi, Kairouan, Sfax, Ben Guerdane and Tunis. What is important to acknowledge is that not only did these various popular upsurges eventually contribute to the momentum of the downfall of a host of authoritarian and totalitarian regimes across the three regions in the 1980s and again from 2010 to 2011, but these mass demonstrations were also maintained across several weeks and months in order that initial moves towards regime change and democratisation did not dissipate. Larbi Sadiki, for example, poignantly captures movements of democratic struggle in the Middle East and North Africa, stating, 'The name of the game here is populating all visible cracks in the hegemon's body politic.'[37]

Not long after the initial moments of mass popular mobilisations, political liberalisation and the 'resurrection of civil society' were also general features across the sociopolitical transitions in these different regions. The regimes that underwent sociopolitical transformations (and that pursued paths to some form of democratisation) in Eastern Europe (Czechoslovakia, Hungary, Poland and Yugoslavia); Latin America (Argentina, Bolivia, Brazil, Chile, Peru and Uruguay); and the Middle East and North Africa (Egypt and Tunisia)[38] all at one point or another introduced a range of procedures to redefine and extend rights to citizens. Such liberalisation measures often may have come after extensive periods of repression or strict restrictions against collective action, political opposition, free speech/press and the right to association; they were either immediately introduced prior to the downfall of the regime or within the first months of the transition. This, in some cases, almost immediate opening of public space(s) entailed the

---

[37] L. Sadiki, 'The Void of Power and the Power of the Void' in Sadiki, Wimmen and Al-Zubaidi (eds.), *Democratic Transition in the Middle East*, p. 16.

[38] Although a number of the countries in which citizens staged mass protests following the uprising in Tunisia in 2010 did result in the downfall of authoritarian regimes, such as in Libya and Yemen, as a result of ongoing conflict these countries have not been engaged in consistent processes to democratise their political systems.

registration of new (or resurgent) political parties, the liberalisation of the press and broader media and the drafting (or redrafting) of laws of association, allowing a multitude of different forms of collective activism and mobilisation to emerge. O'Donnell and Schmitter write, for example, that 'data sources, book manuscripts, essays, and pieces of research which were prepared during the years of severe repression but which authors could not (or dared not) make public now emerge ... Thus, once the first steps towards liberalisation are made and some dare to test their limits, the whole texture, density, and content of intellectually authoritative discourse changes.'[39]

Often as a result of these liberalisation measures during the initial stages of transitions from authoritarian or totalitarian rule, one begins to witness the 'resurrection of civil society'.[40] While it may not be unequivocal, it is highly likely that different forms of this kind of collective organisation of civil society existed before the downfall of the incumbent regime, for example either through a degree of sanctioned civil society permitted by the authoritarian regime or clandestine social movements/activism hidden under the radar to circumvent despotic predispositions on the part of the state. Nevertheless, this resurrection occurs when the cost of collective action and mobilisation are lowered, and more importantly, when fear is no longer a factor.[41] O'Donnell and Schmitter, referring to Latin American and Eastern European cases, observe, 'There are suddenly a multitude of popular forums ... in which the exercise and learning of citizenship can flourish in deliberations about everyday concern.'[42] Equally, Sadiki, writing of the political transformations following the Arab uprisings, notes the 'endeavour by these emerging voices and actors to inhabit the democratic void with the view to record presence (and thus roll back

---

[39] O'Donnell and Schmitter (eds.), *Transitions from Authoritarian Rule: Tentative Conclusions*, p. 51.

[40] Ibid., p. 48.

[41] See J. Gunning and I. Baron, *Why Occupy a Square: People, Protests and Movements in the Egyptian Revolution* (London: Hurst and Company, 2013); J. Beinin and F. Vairel, 'Afterword: Popular Uprisings in Tunisia and Egypt' in J. Beinin and F. Vairel (eds.), *Social Movements, Mobilization, and Contestation in the Middle East and North Africa* (Stanford: Stanford University Press, 2011); and O'Donnell and Schmitter (eds.), *Transitions from Authoritarian Rule: Tentative Conclusions*, p. 49.

[42] O'Donnell and Schmitter (eds.), *Transitions from Authoritarian Rule: Tentative Conclusions*, p. 53.

absence) and dynamically seek to create and maintain spaces of democratic struggle'.[43]

Furthermore, O'Donnell and Schmitter, detailing the risks taken by human rights activists during the transitions from military rule in Latin America, underscore the powerful and critical element of the 'recovery of personal dignity' inherent in the (re-)emergence of some of these organisations during this potent period of 'resurrection'.[44] The notion of 'dignity' featured prominently alongside 'employment' in the principle slogans of the Tunisian uprising, carrying with it a moral authority to give name to the violence and repression of the Ben Ali regime. And while the concept of civil society will be explored in greater detail in the next chapter, as well as in relation to mobilisations in Eastern Europe and Latin America, it is important to recognise the (re-)emergence of these actors and organisations immediately prior to or following transitions from authoritarian rule. In the transition countries considered as part of the 'third wave of democratisation' and in post-uprising Tunisia, thousands of civil society organisations were established to participate in the rebuilding of what would come after years and in some cases decades of authoritarian rule. And while I urge caution, in line with writers such as Vincent Durac and Francesco Cavatorta, in drawing a positive correlation between civil society and democratisation,[45] this 'resurrection' is certainly not without consequence.

Given some of the commonalities in these regions, it is also necessary to articulate what is specific to the various and multiple sociopolitical transformations following the downfall of the Ben Ali regime in Tunisia in 2011. The first area, which is particular to the Middle East and North Africa, and to Tunisia, lies in the macroeconomic specificities. The macroeconomic specificities are significant as they are situated in arguments advocating that once a country reaches a certain point of strong macroeconomic stability and growth, or socioeconomic status, its citizens will consequently demand more representative and accountable governance institutions.[46] However, all North

---

[43] L. Sadiki, 'The Void of Power and the Power of the Void', p. 16.
[44] O'Donnell and Schmitter (eds.), *Transitions from Authoritarian Rule: Tentative Conclusions*, p. 52.
[45] Durac and Cavatorta, *Politics and Governance in the Middle East*, p. 162.
[46] Based on the theories of Seymour Lipset; see J. Waterbury, 'Democracy without Democrats? The Potential for Political Liberalization in the Middle

African regimes in particular faced foreign exchange crises and severe debt across the late 1980s and 1990s due to the depression in oil prices across the region.[47] Moreover, despite the security that oil rents provided the region, the Middle East and North Africa until 2010 had some of the lowest growth and human development indicators across all middle- and lower-income countries.

From the 1970s, countries in the Middle East and North Africa adopted policies of *infitah* (opening), whereby the privatisation of the public sector was accompanied by a diminishing social contract between the state and its citizens.[48] From this period the gross domestic product (GDP) per capita average annual growth rate in the Middle East and North Africa from 1970 to 1990 and from 1990 to 2010 was −0.2 per cent and 2.4 per cent, respectively. From 1990 to 2010 this growth rate was lower than all other middle- and lower-income regions bar sub-Saharan Africa (2 per cent from 1990 to 2010).[49] Moreover, from 2000 to 2008 GDP average annual growth rate was 4.7 per cent for the Middle East and North Africa, representing the lowest across all regions during this period.[50] Despite some of the lowest growth figures overall for the region in comparison to other regions during the same period, what is particular to the region is the 'social situation', or what Gilbert Achcar refers to as three critical words that are specific to the Middle East: poverty, inequality and precarity. And while Achcar provides a much more in-depth analysis in *The People Want*, it is worth pointing out some of these social indicators here. The unemployment rate in 2010 for North Africa of 9.6 per cent, for example, was higher than that in sub-Saharan Africa (8.2 per cent) and higher for all other regions outside the Middle East. Moreover, the unemployment rate of youth in 2010 in North Africa of 23 per cent was also far greater than any other region outside the Middle East.[51] Specific to Tunisia, overall unemployment among youth undergraduates was critical at 44.4 per cent in 2009, as compared to 8.6 per cent in 1999.[52] In addition to figures that set out some

East' in G. Salame (ed.), *Democracy without Democrats: The Renewal of Politics in the Muslim World* (New York: I. B. Tauris, 1994).
[47] Hinnebusch, 'Change and Continuity after the Arab Uprising', p. 18.
[48] G. Achcar, *The People Want: A Radical Exploration of the Arab Uprising* (London: Saqi, 2013), p. 23.
[49] Ibid., p. 24.   [50] Ibid., p. 27.   [51] Ibid., pp. 38, 40.
[52] Durac and Cavatorta, *Politics and Governance in the Middle East*, p. 23.

of the highest levels of female unemployment and total youth in the population, the social development statistics for the region are critical and particular.

The second area that is specific to the uprisings in Tunisia was that there was no identified leadership, either from a specific individual, party or group, but rather splintered and fragmented mobilisations across class, rural, urban, income levels and religious affiliations in particular during the earlier stages of the uprisings. Specifically it has been noted that during the Arab uprisings there was an absence of hierarchy in conjunction with a 'high degree of decentralisation.'[53] And while many of these mobilisations appeared collective in nature, with the aim of bringing about the downfall of the Ben Ali regime, many autonomous actors and groups engaged in these spaces. Paul Aarts and Francesco Cavatorta emphasise that while formal civil society organisations and trade unions actively participated in the uprisings for example, this more formally organised activism was also accompanied by informal and non-traditional mobilisations.[54] As indicated earlier, the root causes of the uprisings across the region were against the socio-economic liberalisation of the economy over two decades. As such, Aarts and Cavatorata argue, 'This means that mass protests due to worsening economic conditions were the force behind the uprisings, with political demands entering the scene later on.'[55]

Despite viable democratic elections following the downfall of the authoritarian regime in Tunisia in 2011 and again in 2014, the country's sociopolitical environment is still very much in transition, with resurgent protests across the country in 2018 against economic austerity measures.[56] While it is possible to highlight elements that are more common to transitions, the specificities of each country's sociopolitical context prior to regime change and particular transition process will inevitably determine very different outcomes. As such, applying a concept that is likely to overlook national and local processes at the micro-level is problematic. Furthermore, to echo Francesco Cavatorta's sentiment in 'No Democratic Change ... and Yet No Authoritarian Continuity', the delineation between authoritarianism and democracy

---

[53] Ibid., p. 184.
[54] Aarts and Cavatorta (eds.), *Civil Society in Syria and Iran*, p. 8.   [55] Ibid.
[56] 'Tunisia Austerity Protests Go on Amid Wave of Arrests', *Al Jazeera* (26 January 2018).

is increasingly blurred, forcing those who continue to engage with these terms to further scrutinise their value.[57] Therefore, rather than disregarding the term completely, the book engages with the term 'transition' in its most stripped down and bare form – as a simultaneous process of disruption and transformation, as a tool to invite openness to uncertainty.

Limitations

There are two principal limitations to the research conducted in the writing of the book worth noting here. The first is that while renowned organisations such as LTDH (Tunisian Human Rights League) and UGTT (General Labour Union of Tunisia) have played a vital role in Tunisia's civil society and sociopolitical landscape, the book does not examine these organisations in detail. This is primarily because much has been written on these organisations by other scholars;[58] in addition, the two organisations are larger umbrella network organisations comprising several interests and groups, as for example UGTT represents all workers' interests in all sectors on labour laws and rights. The book concentrates on smaller organisations, some of which operate on the periphery with vulnerable groups and/or at the margins of mainstream sociopolitical priorities. The second limitation is that a range of Tunisian Francophone media is featured throughout the book. The purpose of this is to intentionally underscore the popular national sentiment during the research period. As such, much of the Tunisian media presented reflects a liberal-secular bias, highlighting many journalists' predilections for fear mongering, the generation of moral-panics and sensationalism – exacerbating perceived social divisions and post-uprising sentiments of chaos. Finally, it is important to also

---

[57] Cavatorta, 'No Democratic Change ... and Yet No Authoritarian Continuity', p. 145.
[58] See H. Yousfi, *L'UGTT: Une Passion Tunissienne: Enquête sur les Syndicalistes en Révolution (2011–2014)* (Tunis: IRMC-Med Ali, 2015); D. Cavallo, 'Trade Unions in Tunisia' in E. Lust-Okar and S. Zerhouni (eds.), *Political Participation in the Middle East* (Boulder: Lynne Rienner, 2008); R. King, 'Regime Type, Economic Reform, and Political Change in Tunisia' in Y. Zoubir (ed.), *North Africa in Transition: State, Society, and Economic Transformation in the 1990s* (Gainesville: University Press of Florida, 1999); and M. Ben Romdhane, *Tunisie: Etat, Economie et Société: Ressources Politiques Légitimation Regulations Sociales* (Tunis: Sud Editions, 2011).

emphasise that the book does not aim to determine whether civil society actors and organisations were instrumental in democratisation. Prior to the uprising in Tunisia, numerous actors participated in a gradual chipping away of the Ben Ali regime over several years, with acts of both overt and underground resistance. It is not possible to catalogue all of these diverse actors or the multiplicity of their actions. Some critical phenomena will not be captured and some questions will remain unanswered. Ultimately, the aim is to capture, albeit momentarily, these diverse narratives and dynamic struggles as a nation pursues democratisation.

Structure of the Book

The book is organised across seven chapters, with two principal chapters laying the foundations for the overall context – Chapters 2 and 3. Chapter 2 is a theoretical examination of the concept of civil society with an initial concentration on the theories of the writers who underscored the significance of the conflicts and contestations among civil society actors and groups, specifically Georg W. F. Hegel, Karl Marx and Antonio Gramsci. It also critically explores the moments during which the concept of civil society re-manifested both ideologically and in practice throughout the social movements and transitions from authoritarian rule in Eastern Europe and Latin America. More significantly, it traces the period from which the concept of civil society was ideologically re-appropriated and transplanted into neoliberal discourses. The chapter subsequently outlines the dual role with which civil society has been tasked in dominant international development policy, both as a provider of social welfare services and as a torchbearer for democratic values and good governance. In more fully understanding the incompatibility between the two ideologies, namely the Gramscian conception that originally emphasised the significance of conflict among and between civil society actors, and the neoliberal understanding that later comes to de-emphasise and overlook conflict, it is possible to better situate the intense divergences between these actors following a sharp transition from authoritarian rule.

Chapter 3 begins with an analysis of the origins, structure, and leadership of the pre- and post-independence state, through the consideration of some of the factors that influenced the nature of the Tunisian state seen today. The brief consideration of the origins and structure of the pre-independence Tunisian state looks specifically to the influences of Ottoman control from the sixteenth century and French colonial rule from 1881. It then examines the leadership of the post-independence state from 1956 to 1987 under Habib Bourguiba and from 1987 to 2010 under the regime of Zine El Abidine Ben Ali. These origins and initial structures of the Tunisian state provided the opportunity to not only consolidate the bureaucratic apparatus necessary to govern and maintain legitimacy but also to bring peripheral regions and tribal populations under greater state social control by the middle of the twentieth century. The chapter describes how from 1956, Bourguiba was able to steer the post-independence Tunisian state through periods of sociopolitical and economic turmoil and to govern a highly efficient and highly centralised state apparatus. It also underscores how the Tunisian state soon entered into an 'authoritarian spiral', the residue of which would carry over into the leadership of the Ben Ali regime from 1987. Despite initial signs to the contrary, not long after Ben Ali assumed the presidency tendencies for authoritarian rule re-materialised. Civil society organisations that chose to operate during this period accepted known risks of harassment and intimidation, particularly if their interventions were perceived to be political in nature. In addition to the targeting of secular organisations, the regime gradually closed down spaces for religious, namely Islamist, actors and groups to manoeuvre. Over time, this directly impacted the nature and structure of Tunisian society – with the vigorous targeting of the Islamists by the government, some secular organisations also began to distance themselves from Islamist associations. The conditions set by the two regimes, and the residue of authoritarian rule that would carry over into post-uprising Tunisia, would leave its mark on Tunisia's new and expanding symbolic and physical public spaces.

In Chapter 4, the first core theme of the book is analysed: the 'illiberal' effects of the opening of the public space(s). It observes the moments following the downfall of the Ben Ali regime in January 2011 when Tunisia's public spaces opened as a result of almost immediate political liberalisation measures implemented by the transition governments. The initial months following the Tunisia uprising are detailed, including the outcome of the elections to the National Constituent Assembly in October 2011 where the Islamist Ennahda party gained the majority through the formation of a coalition, known as the 'Troika', with two secular parties, Ettakol and the Congress for the

Republic. It illustrates the manifold expectations and contestations that emerged among the different actors in Tunisia's political as well as public spaces, through a narrative of the key events that transpired during the two years after the uprising. In particular, touchstone issues resurfaced such as the freedom of the press; the status of women; support for and recognition of vulnerable (and criminalised) populations such as people affected by HIV/AIDS, sex workers and homosexual communities; and a key symbol of national identity, the Tunisian flag; each became key areas of contestation as actors manoeuvring in Tunisia's public spaces expressed their priorities and visions for post-uprising Tunisia. As such, this chapter also analyses the 'resurrection of civil society' in which thousands of civil society organisations were legally established as a consequence of the amendments to the laws of association initially promulgated by Bourguiba in 1959 and redrafted by the High Authority in the months following the uprising. The thousands of new organisations created during this time acted alongside and shared the same symbolic as well as physical public spaces with Tunisia's historic civil society organisations, created in the decades prior to the 2010–2011 uprising. Each set of organisations encountered opportunities and challenges as they endeavoured to participate in Tunisia's expanding public spaces. Effectively, this chapter emphasises that there is a tumultuous but definitive period following the implementation of political liberalisation measures during which actors can take maximum advantage of these expanding spaces, and where the field for discursive contestation and pluralism is at its widest.

Chapter 5 analyses the second core theme of the book, namely the emerging sociocultural and socio-religious divisions, including the rise of associational or social Islam following the downfall of the Ben Ali regime in 2011. The chapter continues to map the areas where conflict materialises in Tunisia following the 2010–2011 uprising. It analyses in more depth the emerging conflicts and divisions between the secular and religious actors to further determine the function of conflict within civil society – the consequences of these divergences for understandings on civil society. The chapter describes the different 'Islamist' groups that emerged to participate in Tunisia's public spaces, including those that were denied the opportunity to engage in legalised/formal civil society organisations under Ben Ali but then, following the revolution, chose to participate with great determination in the shaping of post-uprising Tunisia. It also analyses the reactions from organisations, many of which were secular, operating on the periphery with marginalised and vulnerable groups to new actors inhabiting these spaces. This chapter demonstrates that civil society became more conflictual following the initial expansion of Tunisia's public spaces and during the two years following the downfall of the Ben Ali regime. As the stakes for shaping Tunisia's national identity intensified, the conflicts between civil society not only reinforced social divisions but also further legitimised exclusions in the name of democracy.

Chapter 6 examines the third and final theme of the book, specifically the exclusionary (and undemocratic) nature of consensus in 'liberal' democracies. From the point at which the discursive arena is at its widest following the political liberalisation measures put in place by the transition government(s), to when gradually these spaces are narrowed down through 'the hegemony of consensus', this chapter frames the touchtone issue of homosexuality in post-uprising Tunisia. It follows the experiences of the founding members of the organisation Damj ('reintegration'), established after the 2010–2011 uprising. The organisation was created to defend human rights and the rights of minorities, including lesbian, gay, bisexual and transgender (LGBT) populations. Through this case study, it is possible to examine the ways conflict manifests among civil society groups and actors by looking to the sites of these conflicts as well as the consequences for these actors. Members of these communities not only experienced simultaneous expansions in the public space to manoeuvre but also experienced constraints, such as increases in discrimination and violence. Gay, bisexual and transgender communities worked to put issues of human rights and freedom from violence on the national agenda; however, actors both internal and external to civil society acted to exclude marginal views in the name of consensus and democracy. Following a transition from authoritarian rule, consensus effectively becomes a key means to enforce hegemonies as the post-revolution hierarchy of priorities is redefined and 'other' is pushed to the periphery or negated entirely. Consequently, consensus becomes a critical mechanism through which conflicts are muted and discursive arenas are squeezed.

In the weeks before and after the ousting of the Ben Ali regime, individuals and communities came together in the streets across Tunisia in apparent solidarity, calling for freedom and dignity. Even two years after the 2010–2011 uprising, many spoke of nostalgia for the moments when the country rallied together in unison for a higher standard of democracy. Yet by 2013, Tunisia was characterised by an emerging 'secular-Islamist' stalemate at the political level as well as by conflict, and at times even hostility, among members of civil society. Touchstone issues such as the status of women, the freedom of the press and issues related to marginalised and stigmatised populations such as sex workers and homosexual communities often sparked contestation and occupied significant discursive space among civil society. As a result, rather than a continued expansion of opportunities for agonistic debate, relationships between actors were often antagonistic as the country was driven by the pursuit of consensus on national priorities and identity following the downfall of the Ben Ali regime. In effect, during this period there was a constant jostling of visions and ideologies for post-uprising Tunisia in the country's expanding public spaces. Did this multiplicity of discourses at the time yield consensus or subjugation, tolerance or repression, harmony or conflict in Tunisia's rapidly fluctuating post-revolution environment? Ultimately, did it provide fertile terrain for dignity and freedom following decades of authoritarian rule?

2 Situating Civil Society
Emancipation or Liberalisation

> Cited as a solution to social, economic, and political dilemmas by politicians and thinkers from the left, right, and all perspectives in between, civil society is claimed by every part of the ideological spectrum as its own. But what exactly is it?
>
> Neera Chandhoke, 'Civil Society'[1]

From December 2010, a number of countries across the Middle East and North Africa entered into periods of sociopolitical transition from authoritarian rule in the pursuit of the uncertain something else. Tunisia not only continues to map its own transition path(s) based largely on popular aspirations for change and a desire for a higher or greater standard of democracy,[2] but also on the residue of power it has inherited. During the two years following the Tunisia uprising, frequent mass demonstrations were mobilised to remind state power that the people as watchdog over creeping authoritarianism remained ubiquitous and ever vigilant.

The events of the 'Arab Spring' continue to spark a range of vibrant discussions and questions concerning the hegemony of the neoliberal architecture and at the same time underscore the normative frame implicit in concepts such as civil society, specifically in relation to democratisation. Inherent to these debates is divergence over the exact nature and functioning of civil society given the often unattainable expectations for these actors, and whether the manifold views and priorities among its members will eventually be able to deliver a greater standard of democracy or instead impede this process. At the core of

---

[1] N. Chandhoke, 'Civil Society', *Development in Practice*, vol. 17, no. 4–5 (2007), p. 608.
[2] In his lecture on 'Secularism, Human Rights and the Middle East: Challenges and Reflections' at the London School of Economics (LSE) on 23 October 2012, Gilbert Achcar articulated that what the demonstrations across the regions shared was aspirations for a higher or greater standard of democracy.

these deliberations on civil society are also questions regarding the role of conflict, the hegemony of consensus, the limitations of pluralism and whether civil society can effectively offer an alternative to dominant development and donor discourses. For example, in *State and Civil Society: Explorations in Political Theory,* Neera Chandhoke contends, 'Basically it (civil society) refers to an entire tradition of political thought which has dealt with issues of human emancipation.'[3] Ultimately, as others have done, I am seeking to understand whether the concept of civil society as it is currently understood has the potential to be politically transformative.[4]

The voices of civil society, or *al-mujtama al-madani* and *al-mujtama al-ahli,*[5] are traditionally thought to have had limited influence on the weighty authoritarian regimes of the Middle East and North Africa. Augustus Norton observes, 'There, civil society is said to be deficient, corrupt, aggressive, hostile, infiltrated, co-opted, insignificant or absent, depending on which observer one prefers to cite.'[6] The ongoing social movements in the Middle East and North Africa also continue to raise questions regarding the scope of civic activism and collective pursuits in public spaces, including the nature of civil society's relationship to the state, its ability to function independently within authoritarian regimes, the question of whether civil society has inherited the social contract from 'weaker' states in the region and perhaps most importantly, its role in the transition to and consolidation of democratic processes and in democratisation more broadly. The concept of civil society – specifically the more hegemonic 'liberal' understanding – is habitually utilised by scholars, international institutions, state entities and NGOs to such an extent that actively engaging with the concept remains essential. Therefore, it becomes even more imperative to routinely and critically scrutinise the implications of the concept as well as the different agents who gain and lose in its application.

---

[3] Chandhoke, *State and Civil Society,* p. 33.

[4] See M. Abdelrahman, *Civil Society Exposed: The Politics of NGOs in Egypt* (London: Tauris Academic Studies, 2004), p. 1 and Chandhoke, 'Civil Society'.

[5] *al-mujtama al-madani* invokes the sense of institutions organised along civil lines with the word *madani* derived from *medina* or 'city', or the more traditional reference to *al-mujtama al-ahli*, which refers to a wider variety of communal and religious institutions. See A. Sajoo, *Civil Society in the Muslim World: Contemporary Perspectives* (London: I. B. Tauris, 2002), p. 15.

[6] A. Norton, 'The Future of Civil Society in the Middle East', *Middle East Journal,* vol. 47, no. 2 (Spring 1993), p. 212.

To do this, this chapter first analyses how the writers who emphasise the conflictual nature of the interactions between civil society actors and groups understood the concept. Second, it explores how civil society is framed within neoliberal policies, looking to how neoliberalism in fact de-emphasises the conflicts and contentions between these organisations while simultaneously providing these actors with an unprecedented authority and legitimacy in national and international arenas. By further understanding the points at which these conflicts are emphasised and de-emphasised across history, it becomes possible to appreciate more holistically the civil society that emerged in Tunisia prior to and following the downfall of the Ben Ali regime in 2011.

To maintain conceptual clarity in terms of how the concept of civil society is used across the book, it is necessary to establish here that civil society is a field of actors, groups and organisations, acting and manoeuvring within a multiplicity of physical and symbolic public spaces. These public spaces serve to harness a discursive arena in which these different actors can deliberate and contest critical matters of concern, both through their voices and their deliberate actions. While some writers, such as Chandhoke in *State and Society*, use the concept of the public sphere and civil society interchangeably, doing so can create slippages between the two concepts.[7] Moreover, Jurgen Habermas attributes both a horizontal as well as vertical relationship between civil society and the public sphere.[8] For example, Habermas describes an idealised public sphere in which equal individuals participate alongside each other to occupy a central position within the public through rational-critical debate – eventually through the 'coffee houses, salons, and table societies'.[9] He writes, 'Transcending the barriers of social hierarchy, the bourgeois met here with the socially prestigious but politically uninfluential nobles as "common" human beings ... Social equality

---

[7] Chandhoke, *State and Civil Society*, p. 9.
[8] J. Habermas, *The Structural Transformation of the Public Sphere: An Inquiry into a Category of Bourgeois Society*, trans. by T. Burger and F. Lawrence (Cambridge: Polity Press, 1989). Habermas suggests that the public sphere sits *within* civil society (p. 34) and simultaneously he articulates that the public sphere *regulates* civil society – suggesting a vertical relationship (p. 52).
[9] Habermas, *The Structural Transformation of the Public Sphere*, p. 30.

was possible at first only as an equality outside the state.'[10] He articulates a public that was in principle inclusive and whereby everyone, through their own consciousness of being part of a larger public, had to be able to participate.[11] However, Habermas is criticised by writers such as Nancy Fraser for not fully emphasising unequal status relations, the lack of participatory parity and the normative preference for a singularity of publics.[12] She attributes this to Habermas' emphasis on the nature of the public sphere as an idealised entity based on the principles of inclusion and accessibility. Her premise rests on her understanding of Habermas' unexplored consideration of the 'social question' in which society was increasingly marked by class struggle and eventually splintered off into a host of 'competing interest groups'.[13] Fraser acknowledges that for Habermas the full potential of the bourgeois conception of the public sphere never developed in practice[14] because Habermas himself admits that the one public sphere was always a fiction, presented as an institutionalised idea rather than true state of interaction.[15]

Given Habermas' own inconsistencies in his distinction between the public sphere and civil society, and the idealised nature in which the concept of the public sphere was theorised, the concept of the public sphere is not used here. Instead the book describes the symbolic and physical public spaces both afforded to civil society actors by the different governance mechanisms, such as through the institutions of the state and from within the neoliberal architecture, as well as the spaces these actors carve out for themselves when room to manoeuvre is detected. In this sense and alongside writers such as Chantal Mouffe, rather than to refer to a single space, 'a multiplicity of discursive surfaces and public spaces' are emphasised across the text.[16]

Locating Civil Society Following the Emergence of Capitalism

Throughout the last century the concept of civil society has taken on many different forms and has often been related to or polarised

---

[10] Ibid., pp. 34–35.   [11] Ibid., p. 37.
[12] See: N. Fraser, 'Rethinking the Public Sphere: A Contribution to the Critique of Actually Existing Democracy', *Social Text*, no. 25/26 (1990).
[13] Fraser, 'Rethinking the Public Sphere', p. 59.   [14] Ibid.
[15] Habermas, *The Structural Transformation of the Public Sphere*, pp. 36, 56.
[16] Mouffe, *Agonistics*, p. 91.

against institutions such as the state, the economic market, the private sphere or the family-household domain. The concept has also been intrinsically linked to a modernisation trajectory in which the density of civil society is associated with progress and a lack of civil society with those of traditionalist or primordial institutions. Some scholars, such as Alan Kidd, argue the collapse of the Communist states was responsible for stimulating an increased interest in the concept of civil society during the 1990s, notably the emphasis upon its importance to democracy;[17] others, meanwhile, would point to the emergence of the good governance discourse supported by proponents of neoliberal paradigms from the mid-1980s as responsible for its popularity. The concept remains highly contested territory[18] and retains a high degree of complexity.[19] Jean Roca contends that the identities of civil society actors are 'increasingly multiple and mobile, and allegiances are fluid. It would therefore be wise ... to speak of "civil societies"'.[20]

For example, John Keane, relying on its more classical usage, argues, 'Civil society is an ideal-typical category ... that both describes and envisages a complex and dynamic ensemble of legally-protected non-governmental institutions that tend to be non-violent, self-organising, self-reflexive and permanently in tension with each other and with the state institutions that frame, construct and enable their activities.'[21] Amyn Sajoo, adopting a more hybrid understanding, contends civil society comprises 'not only the more formal webs of associations of civil society, but also its more fluid communicative actions – outside the direct mediation of the political (that is, formal state) sphere'.[22] While in *Global Civil Society 2012: Ten Years of Critical Reflection*, in consideration of the recent social movements in the Middle East

---

[17] A. Kidd, 'Civil Society or the State: Recent Approaches to the History of Voluntary Welfare', *Journal of Historical Sociology*, vol. 15, no. 3 (September 2002), p. 334.
[18] M. Edwards, *Civil Society* (Oxford: Polity Press, 2004), p. vii.
[19] S. Giner, 'Civil Society and Its Future' in J. Hall (ed.), *Civil Society: Theory, History, Comparison* (Cambridge: Polity Press, 1995), p. 302.
[20] J. Roca, 'Insiders and Outsiders: NGOs in International Relations' in Nefissa, Al-Fattah, Hanafi and Milani (eds.), *NGOs and Governance in the Arab World*, p. 43.
[21] Edwards, *Civil Society*, p. 20, citing J. Keane, *Civil Society and the State: New European Perspectives* (London: Verso, 1988), p. 6.
[22] Sajoo, *Civil Society in the Muslim World*, p. 5.

and North Africa, Anheier, Kaldor and Glasius describe civil society as 'the medium through which individuals participate in public affairs, through which they endorse or challenge the dominant discourse'.[23] Moreover, Vincent Durac and Francesco Cavatorta differentiate between the more common dichotomy between the 'civil' and the 'uncivil' versus the alternative understanding that emphasises the engagement of the '*civis*' in a multitude of different issues to influence decision-making.[24] There is ongoing debate about which groups civil society does and does not include (and often based on the origins of the concept) as well as the notion that certain institutions can gain from how the parameters of the concept are defined. Mary Kaldor argues that in fact, the literature on civil society is so diverse it permits varying degrees of 'selectivity' in terms of which texts and meanings to study.[25] As such, by interpreting and also integrating the various meanings of the concept across disparate contexts, it is possible to construct a space for a broader discussion of the implications for this concept following the events of 2010–2011. The next section begins with an examination of the theories of Hegel, Marx and Gramsci on civil society as these theorists were not only concerned with how civil society could be organised and transformed but also underscored the conflictual nature of this domain.

Emphasising Conflict: A Critical Exploration of Hegel, Marx and Gramsci

Hegel, Marx and Gramsci each understood that civil society was linked with the emergence of capitalism, and together they were able to demonstrate how civil society routinely oppressed its different inhabitants. They were equally concerned with the composition of civil society and its organisation, leadership and direction. Georg W. F. Hegel was one of the first to clearly distinguish the state from civil society and hence the political from the civil.[26] Hegel, according to Keane, believed, 'Civil society cannot remain "civil" unless it is ordered

---

[23] Anheier, Kaldor and Glasius, 'The Global Civil Society Yearbook', p. 15.
[24] Durac and Cavatorta, *Politics and Governance in the Middle East*, p. 168.
[25] M. Kaldor, *Global Civil Society: An Answer to War* (Cambridge: Polity Press, 2003), p. 3.
[26] Chandhoke, *State and Civil Society*, p. 116.

politically, subjected to the "higher surveillance of the state".'[27] Furthermore, Hegel conceived of the state as a positive entity that safeguarded the conflicting elements of civil society because 'the state represents society in its unity'.[28] With Hegel's deep trust in state regulation, he understood civil society as a sphere of contradictions that could be resolved from above through the higher institutions of the state. Boaventura de Sousa Santos writes of Hegel, 'In his most Hegelian moment, civil society – rather than being the opposite of the state – is a transitional stage in the development of the idea, the final stage being the state. The family is the thesis, civil society is the antithesis, and the state is the synthesis.'[29] As such, Hegel conceived a distinct but also hierarchical relationship between the state and civil society. He described the modern individual as 'rootless', with limited protection against the state; civil society could therefore provide this grounding despite being an entity that was unable to organise itself or sustain an alternative public discourse from the state.[30] Hegel's understanding of civil society was effectively truncated as he described a restricted public space in which the emphasis was on the propertied classes and where marginalised groups and working classes were excluded from critical rational discourse(s).[31]

In response to the exclusion of the working classes from Hegel's understanding of the relationship between civil society and the state, Marx's emerging conception of this domain shifted the emphasis back to the power of the working classes. Marx also envisaged the space in which civil society operated and manoeuvred as conflictual, yet within this space civil society could overcome its own internal struggles and contentions. And although Marx aligned with Hegel on the notion that the state should in principle regulate civil society, he did not actually believe the state had the power to effectively do this. Furthermore, Marx perceived the negative role of the state that effectively encouraged political and social divisions, whereas for Hegel the state was a positive regulating entity. With the Marxian notion that the social in effect encompassed the political, the state would eventually mirror the

---

[27] Keane, *Civil Society and the State*, p. 52, citing G. Hegel, *Elements of the Philosophy of Right* (Cambridge: Cambridge University Press, 1991).
[28] Ibid., p. 53.
[29] B. Santos, *Toward a New Legal Common Sense: Law, Globalization and Emancipation* (London: Butterworths, LexisNexis, 2002), p. 365.
[30] Chandhoke, *State and Civil Society*, p. 119.   [31] Ibid., p. 142.

class configuration and divisions within society. These social divisions and struggles would also serve to eventually overthrow the state as Marx depicted a state that was subordinate to civil society. Chandhoke writes, 'The power of the organised working class within civil society creates the possibilities that the class will be able to liberate both itself and the civil sphere.'[32]

Both Hegel and Marx developed their conceptualisations on civil society and the state during a similar historical period following the emergence of capitalism.[33] Gramsci's understanding of civil society, however, emerged several decades later during which the impacts of the consolidation of capitalism were being exposed, and in which working class movements were failing. For Gramsci, civil society became the site where the state could reinforce its legitimacy through the educational, cultural and religious institutions.[34] Civil society could also become a space through which marginalised or subaltern groups/classes could challenge and eventually subvert the power of the state.[35] For Gramsci, this could be achieved through a more subversive process of 'normative consent', or what Gramsci eventually refers to as hegemony, in which consensus upon the fundamental principles of a sociopolitical discourse could materialise into a form of social control.[36] More importantly, Gramsci's understanding depicted civil society as a buffer to the state, as a sphere of actors that could effectively safeguard the state. On Gramsci Chandhoke writes, 'The life of the state is a "continuous process of formation and superseding of unstable equilibria" in civil society.'[37]

Gramsci articulated volatile and reversible hegemonies between civil society and the state, with the superstructures of civil society being imagined through the 'trench systems of modern warfare'. With each 'fierce artillery attack' the outer perimeter would be destroyed, but new layers would reveal 'a line of defence which was still effective'.[38] For Gramsci hegemony was never stable and was in fact always a contested and dynamic process activated through both practices of coercion and consent. Maha Abdelrahman states, 'In no other theory does the concept of civil society assume a more active and dynamic

---

[32] Ibid., p. 145.   [33] Ibid., p. 147.   [34] Ibid., p. 149.
[35] Abdelrahman, *Civil Society Exposed*, p. 22.   [36] Ibid., p. 23.
[37] Chandhoke, *State and Civil Society*, p. 151.
[38] A. Gramsci, *Selections from the Prison Notebooks*, ed. and trans. by Q. Hoare and G. Smith (London: Lawrence and Wishart, 1971), p. 235.

dimension than in Gramsci's analysis.'[39] Gramsci's analysis also situates power among state and non-state actors or between the state and the political/integral society. Ultimately for Gramsci, hegemony was not simply wielded by state institutions, but across and through civil society. Gramsci's conception of civil society has its most profound implication in the notion that rather than being a set of institutions, the state is effectively a complex web of social relations with, according to Chandhoke, the 'continuous and constant reference point for the state' being civil society.[40] Adam Morton, in fact, considers Gramsci to be one of the paramount theorists of capillary power given his emphasis on hegemony within forms of social relations. He argues, 'Hegemony within the realm of civil society is then grasped when the citizenry come to believe that authority over their lives emanates from the self. Hegemony is therefore articulated through capillary power ... when it is transmitted organically through various "social infusoria".'[41]

Hegel, Marx and Gramsci each underscored the conflictual nature of civil society; nevertheless, how they conceptualise these actors and the symbolic spaces in which they operate was different in terms of the agency and capacity for self-organisation they understand civil society could possess. Hegel depicts a civil society that is organised and regulated by the state with little or no capacity for agency or the ability to fully sustain an alternative public discourse. For Marx, however, the departure is first in the way he shifts the focus of the discourse and restores agency onto the marginalised and working classes, who for Hegel represent a sphere of instability. And second, the working class or proletariat in this sense act inside and as a part of civil society to self-organise to eventually participate in political action to disrupt capitalist systems of production. For Marx, civil society is able to resolve its own disharmonies through taking responsibility for its own agency.

Finally, Gramsci incorporates the dynamic influences of both thinkers on civil society and the state into his own understanding of civil society at a later stage in capitalist development. Gramsci and Marx both acknowledge the relationships of domination and hegemony within civil society, in particular how civil society could be the terrain not only for the reproduction of these relationships but also

---

[39] Abdelrahman, *Civil Society Exposed*, p. 22.
[40] Chandhoke, *State and Civil Society*, p. 153.
[41] A. Morton, *Unravelling Gramsci: Hegemony and Passive Revolution in the Global Political Economy* (London: Pluto Press, 2007), pp. 92–93.

the terrain in which this domination could be subverted. And while Marx places the emphasis on the working classes and class divisions, Gramsci broadens the scope of these actors to include educational, cultural and religious systems and institutions where not only class but also ideological battles are constructed and deconstructed. For both writers, civil society is a field of actors that can legitimise and delegitimise the power of the state, where power is unstable and hegemonies are reversible. Gramsci and Marx both depart from Hegel in that they denote agency to marginalised and subaltern groups and underscore the capacity for these actors to self-organise to the extent of being able to overthrow the state through revolution. However, for Hegel civil society would be eventually transcended by the state whereas Gramsci articulated the reverse as the state would be superseded by civil society. Furthermore, for Hegel, the formation and consolidation of the state with the 'universality' of the state being realised through the 'particularity' of civil society represents a final moment. For Gramsci, though, hegemony has to be constantly rearticulated – with the formation of the state and civil society as a continuous and relational process. Chandhoke writes, 'Thus hegemony is not something that can be established once and for all and then left to fend for itself. It has to be constantly reformulated and expressed. It is a process that brings the state into a continual relationship with society and enables it to vitalize itself.'[42]

A Re-Articulation of Civil Society in Eastern Europe and Latin America

The concept of civil society as articulated by Marx and Gramsci experienced a revival during the various sociopolitical movements of the twentieth century, in particular during the social movements and protests of the 1960s, 1970s and 1980s. During this period the world witnessed movements that effectively drew support from across class boundaries, such as the civil rights campaigns, feminist movements, student and youth movements and peace and anti-war protests. In particular, the theories of Marx and Gramsci played a central role in the resistance to authoritarian, autocratic and military regimes in Eastern Europe and Latin America in the 1970s and 1980s. Here the

---

[42] Chandhoke, *State and Civil Society*, p. 153.

concept of civil society became a vital tool for intellectuals in reframing the various resistance movements in these different regions. The emphasis during these movements shifted to more grassroots and informal forms of organisation, with political and non-political objectives stretching beyond the state as a primary focus. Perhaps more important was the manner in which the concept was reborn and rearticulated during this period as both an antonym to authoritarian rule but also later as a critical tool in the neoliberal arsenal to promote democratic movements and to curtail the role of the state in low- and middle-income countries. The manner in which the concept was utilised during the different resistance movements across these two regions sets the stage for how the concept of civil society is understood and used present day.

During the 1970s and 1980s in Eastern Europe, the failure of Communist reform was becoming more evident in one-party systems such as those in place in Poland, Yugoslavia, Czechoslovakia and Hungary. The heavy weight of the state bureaucratic apparatus increasingly used methods of surveillance and co-optation to manage citizen opposition. The ubiquitous repression found in the totalitarian regimes in the region manifested in either more overt, brutal and violent forms of oppression against public opposition or through concessions to sanctioned forms of political action to avoid open forms of political confrontation and antagonism.[43] Referring specifically to the Soviet-type regimes of the region, Keane writes, 'Their former brutality and monstrous delirium have given way to modes of control which are less brutal and more anonymous, selective and calculated.'[44] Hence during the 1980s, cognisant that neither reforming state power from above nor revolution from below was an effective strategy for emancipation from totalitarian regimes, intellectuals in Eastern Europe sought out alternatives to create civil and political channels for expression.[45] Civil and political actors perceived the necessity for a 'free zone' that would enable them to establish spaces for protection from the state as well as for solidarity and collective action.[46] Chandhoke writes, 'The Eastern Europeans called this free zone, peopled by social associations, self-help and self-management organisations, and characterised by mutual solidarity, "civil society".'[47] However, what would

---

[43] Keane, *Civil Society and the State*, p. 3.   [44] Ibid.
[45] Chandhoke, 'Civil Society', p. 609.   [46] Ibid., p. 610.   [47] Ibid.

begin as a space to foster agency as a counterpoint to oppressive states effectively transformed into social and political movements across the region in direct opposition to dictatorial state power. And although Gramsci may have not been directly credited in the sociopolitical movements in Eastern Europe, this notion of the reversal of hegemonies to overthrow state power was indeed relevant. Chandhoke contends, 'Gramsci's dictum that states that do not possess civil societies are more vulnerable than those that do possess them was to prove more than prescient in this case.'[48] The way intellectuals appropriated the concept of civil society served to not only severely disrupt, but to also bring down, a number of powerful states in the region. On the one hand it served as a tool to create a space for marginalised and disempowered groups to forge solidarities and remedy the suffering caused by years of state oppression. On the other, the formation of these alliances ultimately led to wider movements for emancipation through greater participation in discourses shaping the conditions of political and civil rights and in some cases even leading to political revolution. In the case of Latin America during a similar time period, it is also possible to observe the appropriation of the concept of civil society by intellectuals in the face of repressive regimes.

For the new Latin American left, the perceived importance of the self-organisation of the grassroots began to take hold during the 1980s. Civil society became a critical concept in leftist thinking, with civil society assuming an essential place in new radical democratic theory.[49] During the 1960s and 1970s, Marxist theory – in which the concept of civil society played only a marginal role – was dominant in Latin America. Faced with the incompatibility between formal political equality and the inequalities of global capitalism, Gideon Baker argues the Latin American left soon began to question the merits of democratic governments.[50] During this time, the concept of civil society that had initially been equated with resistance to authoritarian regimes in Latin America evolved into a distinct self-management agenda, or rather the notion of 'defence of freedom outside the state'.[51] As a result of repressive military rule across several countries in the region, members of opposition movements questioned whether or not the state

[48] Ibid., p. 611.
[49] G. Baker, *Civil Society and Democratic Theory: Alternative Voices* (London: Routledge, 2002), p. 53.
[50] Ibid., pp. 53–54.   [51] Ibid., p. 57.

was the most effective target for resistance.[52] Eventually this brought about a more positive and Gramscian understanding of the concept of civil society in which there was a conceptual and spatial relocation for opposition within the context of oppressive environments.

Gramsci's influence on the necessity to create spaces for civil society to manoeuvre within the context of pervasive state repression became increasingly relevant. Francisco Weffort, an influential Brazilian social scientist and former Marxist, writes, 'The discovery that there was something more to politics than the state began with the simplest facts of the life of the persecuted. In the most difficult moments, they had to make use of what they found around them.'[53] This resulted in a rethink of the ethos and tactics employed by these different actors, with a focus on the self-organisation of the grassroots and deprived communities as well as upon voluntarism, self-determination, self-management and community mobilisation over the notion of the seizure of power. More importantly, political transitions in Southern Europe during the mid-1970s pointed to the notion of a 'bloodless revolution' to effectively overthrow military dictatorships.[54] During this period, Gramsci's understanding of civil society opened the door for transformative political action emphasising the ability to manoeuvre outside and separate from the state. It is also important to point out the structural consequences of uneven development taking place globally during this time as well as the impact of peripheral capitalism on the popular classes. Baker contends that these structural features contributed to creating the (need for) spaces and the will towards more urgent and innovative forms for collective action.[55] In effect, from the 1970s a response by the popular classes to underdevelopment also emerged, thereby underscoring the exclusion of these actors from political and economic spheres. According to Baker, this effectively resulted in the creation of a multitude of different organisations cutting across the poor and marginalised in Latin America; the focus of these actors was on autonomy and self-constitution with manifold interests, extending beyond the notion of class reductionism.[56] Weffort, writing during this

---

[52] Ibid., p. 56.
[53] F. Weffort, 'Why Democracy?' in A. Stephan (ed.), *Democratising Brazil* (Oxford: Oxford University Press, 1989), pp. 347–348 as cited in Baker, *Civil Society and Democratic Theory*, p. 57.
[54] Baker, *Civil Society and Democratic Theory,* p. 56.   [55] Ibid., p. 74.
[56] Ibid., pp. 64–65.

period, states, 'We want a civil society, we need to defend ourselves from the monstrous state in front of us ... In a word, we need to build civil society because we want freedom.' From this time, according to Weffort, the concept of civil society became the 'new politics of the region' with an almost complete paradigm shift in which 'civil society' and 'democracy' replaced 'revolution' as the new discourse for Latin America. And eventually by the mid-1980s the region experienced transitions from military or authoritarian rule to democratic governments in Argentina, Bolivia, Brazil, Chile, Peru and Uruguay.

The concept of civil society as understood by Gramsci was arguably co-opted and transformed during the 1970s and 1980s social movements in Eastern Europe and Latin America. The concept was reborn as a remedy to the growing penetrations of the bureaucratic state, and in the case of the two regions, totalitarian and military regimes. In both regions the notion of civil society was primarily resurrected to restore agency and a sense of self-management onto marginalised populations, with an emphasis on the defence of freedom outside the state and 'free zones'. In both regions the social transformed into the political as citizens advocated for more representative and accountable forms of government, effectively calling for liberal democracy. Civil society emerged during this period as the 'antonym of authoritarianism'.[57] However, at the end of the 1980s development scholars note the emergence of what is considered the 'boom' of NGOs across low- and middle-income countries whereby the density of civil society organisations was invariably and often directly (and positively) linked with 'liberal' democratic governments and societies. The concept, in part through its ideological association with the end of socialist societies, eventually emerged as a critical instrument in the neoliberal arsenal for the promotion of democracy and for the minimalist state.[58]

Bringing Civil Society Back in: Neoliberal Policy and 'Liberal' Democracy

Transitions from totalitarian and authoritarian regimes in Eastern Europe and Latin America carried with them the often un-scrutinised ideological emphasis on the concept and capacity of civil society for emancipation and liberation. Scholars tracing the history and

---

[57] Chandhoke, 'Civil Society', p. 608.   [58] Ibid., p. 611.

emergence of civil society organisations, for example, note the period of the 1970s–1980s as the stage of 'institutionalisation' of NGOs, where a multitude of associations emerged in response to various and simultaneous global trends.[59] These trends included the oil crisis of the 1970s, the centrality of debt and macro-instability in low- and middle-income countries, the increased severity and duration of conflict, the emergence of international development discourses, the focus on poverty initiatives and the rise of social movements across different regions.[60] Alongside these trends neoliberalism began to materialise as the dominant political ideology with the notion of the 'minimalist' or limited state.

To give weight to this critique, it is essential that the fundamental policies and tenets of neoliberalism are considered; from here one is able to further discern where the concept of civil society and civil society organisations themselves fit within this political project. Moreover, it is in understanding these fundamental policies that it is possible to observe the evolving relationship of the state in relation to this concept. Neoliberalism can be defined as a political project of economic, state and social transformation with structural adjustment programmes embodying a set of specific economic policies and conditionalities designed by the World Bank and International Monetary Fund (IMF). The 'New Policy Agenda' (1990s), for example, combines neoliberal policy prescriptions with a focus on civil society organisations as the preferred channel for social welfare initiatives in addition to an emerging correlation between a healthy economy and democratic good governance. Michael Edwards and David Hulme consider this

---

[59] S. Charnovitz, 'Two Centuries of Participation: NGOs and International Governance', *Michigan Journal of International Law*, vol. 18, no. 183 (1996–1997), pp. 183–286.

[60] See: A. Bebbington, S. Hickey and D. Mitlin, *Can NGOs Make a Difference? The Challenge of Development Alternatives* (London: Zed Books, 2008); L. Gordenker and T. Weiss, 'Pluralising Global Governance: Analytical Approaches and Dimensions' in *NGOs, the UN and Global Governance* (Boulder: Lynne Rienner, 1996); M. Barnett and T. Weiss, 'Humanitarianism: A Brief History of the Present' in M. Barnett and T. Weiss (eds.), *Humanitarianism in Question: Politics, Power, Ethics* (Ithaca: Cornell University Press, 2008); and F. Manji and C. O'Coill, 'The Missionary Position: NGOs and Development in Africa', *International Affairs*, vol. 78, no. 3 (2002), pp. 567–583.

foremost role for these organisations as a fundamental and noteworthy change.[61] In order to comprehend the particular aspects of social transformation in neoliberal policies, it is first important to understand the economic and state aspects of these transformations as outlined within neoliberal policies.

A Project of Economic, State and Social Transformation

During the 1980s, emerging neoliberal policies, outlined in what came to be known as the 'Washington Consensus', underscored the notion that market failures and imperfections were widespread in lower-income countries. The growing perception within these institutions was that state intervention was the principal problem rather than the solution. In *Profit and Pleasure: Sexual Identities in Late Capitalism*, Rosemary Hennessey writes that neoliberalism therefore 'seeks to free up the operation of the capitalist market from public (state) controls and regulations; at the same time it tries to extend the rationality of the market ... to areas of social life that have not been primarily economic'.[62] Therefore, neoliberal policies emphasise that state expenditure would be better directed towards creating an enabling environment for growth, such as through tax concessions on profits, the liberalisation of price controls and the dismantling of state-owned enterprises. This entails a de-emphasis on public healthcare provision, education and social welfare programmes/measures. As fallout from the oil crisis in the 1970s, debt effectively created the leverage to allow the World Bank and IMF to impose structural adjustment packages modelling this philosophy. This included policies of market deregulation and privatisation, market stabilisation, market liberalisation (open markets, the lowering of trade barriers and deregulation), the removal of state subsidies and trade liberalisation alongside theories that stipulated a 'trickle-down' effect of wealth.[63] Neoliberalism aimed to establish that all needs could be met through the market and not

---

[61] M. Edwards and D. Hulme, 'Too Close for Comfort? The Impact of Official Aid on Nongovernmental Organisations', *World Development*, vol. 24, no. 6 (1996), p. 961.

[62] R. Hennessey, *Profit and Pleasure: Sexual Identities in Late Capitalism* (New York: Routledge, 2000), p. 75.

[63] See J. Stiglitz, 'The Post-Washington Consensus Consensus' (New York: The Initiative for Policy Dialogue, 2004), p. 7.

through the state, from which emerged the notion of the 'minimalist' state and the 'rolling back' of the state.

The depiction of the state as part of the problem rather than the solution had the knock-on effect of substantially reconfiguring the social contract between states and their citizens. Structural adjustment programmes articulated state withdrawal from the provision of public services alongside the reduction in size of state apparatuses and institutions. The austere nature of these policies, as well as the manner in which they could be imposed by international financial institutions, provoked significant socio-economic disruption. The consequences of these reforms in lower- and middle-income countries during the 1980s and early 1990s were severe. The impact of IMF and World Bank economic reform programmes led to significant levels of unemployment, poverty and social marginalisation in many countries, with increases in income disparity leading to significant changes in labour markets. It is estimated that by the late 1990s, one billion workers in lower-income countries were either unemployed or underemployed.[64] The earlier emphasis in regions such as Eastern Europe and Latin America on protecting civil society from the intrusions of the state or even the notion of preserving radical democratic practice was eventually replaced by the notion of the deep erosion of the social contract between the state and its citizens. In this context, millions of middle-class and public sector workers were 'pushed into the ranks of the urban poor in labour and housing markets' and consequently forced to provide for their own welfare.[65] Assef Bayat contends, 'One major consequence of the new global restructuring in the developing countries has been a double process of, on the one hand, integration and, on the other, social exclusion and informalisation.'[66] In addition, sizeable reductions in free access to public services such as health and education through the introduction of user fees opened the door to a new wave of marginalisation and vulnerability across class divides. Writers such as Hennessey consider the growing gap between the rich and poor to be 'neoliberalism's most glaring legacy'.[67]

Popular dissatisfaction with structural adjustment programmes and policies led to a multitude of political demonstrations, strikes

---

[64] A. Bayat, *Life as Politics: How Ordinary People Change the Middle East* (Stanford: Stanford University Press, 2010), p. 34.
[65] Ibid. [66] Ibid., pp. 33–34. [67] Hennessey, *Profit and Pleasure*, p. 75.

and riots globally. Between 1976 and 1992 there were 146 documented protests against austerity measures in 39 countries, mostly in urban areas.[68] In 1983, there were riots in Morocco in response to the government reducing consumer subsidies by 20 per cent; in 1984, Tunisian riots against austerity measures led to 84 deaths; in 1988, strikes in Algeria took place in response to the cost of living; and in 1998, there were approximately 70 strikes in Egypt against new labour laws governing larger companies, which stripped workers of job security.[69] In many cases national governments responded to the demonstrations with repressive measures and often violence, with civil society and political opposition parties becoming the target of oppressive tactics to manage insecurity. Eventually this led to two major consequences for both states and the international financial institutions. First, neoliberal policies framed within the Washington Consensus required an urgent rethink as a result of the severe socio-economic impact of these policies and continuing social unrest. Second, states were losing grip on their own legitimacy because of the implementation of harsh fiscal measures affecting middle and lower classes; faced with the risk of waning popularity, some governments delayed the implementation of unpopular policies or inevitably cherry-picked the structural adjustment policies they would implement. This phenomenon saw the emergence of Steven Heydemann's (2007) concept of 'authoritarian upgrading' in which regimes across lower- and middle-income countries were able to maintain control through the reconfiguration of authoritarian governance whilst simultaneously giving the outward impression of liberalising their political and economic systems.[70] And while many governments would tighten their grip on collective association, community mobilisation and social movements in response to the erosion of state legitimacy, they would also use the opportunity to transfer a significant proportion of the social welfare provision role onto civil society organisations. Maha Abdelrahman notes that central to the neoliberal paradigm is that, 'Rolling back of the state from areas of social services is expected to be balanced by NGOs filling the gaps created

[68] Manji and O'Coill, 'The Missionary Position', p. 578.
[69] Bayat, *Life as Politics*, pp. 69–70.
[70] S. Heydemann, 'Upgrading Authoritarianism in the Arab World', Brookings Institution, Analysis Paper no. 13 (October 2007) in Durac and Cavatorta, *Politics and Governance in the Middle East*, p. 13.

by the state's retreat.'[71] She argues further that neoliberal preferences for civil society promotion were based less on a given ideology and more on the notion that civil society organisations could serve as 'band-aids' to cover the wounds of austere structural adjustment programmes.[72] This parallels with James Ferguson and Akhil Gupta's perception of civil society organisations that have helped Western development agencies to circumvent uncooperative national governments, highlighting a 'disdain for the state' while simultaneously underscoring a 'celebration of civil society'.[73]

In the 1990s, Western governments and the World Bank began to criticise the merits of the market fundamentalism of the Washington Consensus, acknowledging that the strong market-based approach had not only profound negative socio-economic and political consequences but also that it was not resulting in strong economic growth. The reduction in the role of the state in these policies was questioned, for example, in the 'Post-Washington Consensus Consensus'. Joseph Stiglitz writes, 'The consensus (Washington Consensus) policies often assumed the worst about the nature and capability of governments and made that one size fit all.'[74] A 'Post-Washington Consensus' emerged whereby the role of the state was effectively brought back in, alongside an emphasis on good governance and poverty-reduction strategies. Stiglitz states, 'The Post Washington Consensus recognizes that there is a role for a market; the question is to what extent do the neo-liberals recognize that there is a role for the state, beyond the minimal role of enforcing contracts and property rights.'[75] From this period, civil society organisations were framed as partners of the state rather than as alternatives to the state.

Providers of Services or Agents of Democratisation?

From this period, civil society re-materialised to fill two primary roles. The first would be as cost-effective providers of social welfare services and poverty reduction agents in lower- and middle-income countries, effectively assisting the declining public sector. The second would be as

---

[71] Abdelrahman, *Civil Society Exposed*, p. 25.   [72] Ibid., pp. 25, 58.
[73] J. Ferguson and A. Gupta, 'Spatializing States: Toward an Ethnography of Neoliberal Governmentality' in J. Inda (ed.), *Anthropologies of Modernity: Foucault, Governmentality and Life Politics* (Oxford: Blackwell, 2005), p. 120.
[74] Stiglitz, 'The Post-Washington Consensus Consensus', p. 3.   [75] Ibid.

torchbearers for democratic values and good governance, thus becoming key agents in democratisation as well as for enhanced social justice.[76] Civil society understood as a 'cost-effective provider of services' has arguably resulted in a series of outcomes. First, civil society organisations were becoming increasingly associated with service provision within time-limited projects and financial sustainability. Growing concerns for risk aversion and burdensome transaction costs in low-income settings also led to a concentration of international donor aid to the larger civil society organisations.[77] Furthermore, donor decisions focused increasingly on technical criteria such as 'efficiency, value-added, cost effectiveness, and output-performance orientations'.[78] This led some to point out the increasing homogenisation of the civil society sector. Chandhoke argues that the concept of civil society that was once characterised by its 'subversive edge' has now been essentially 'flattened out'.[79]

Moreover, the overall preference for good governance discourses among neoliberals and international donors eventually took hold. Naila Kabeer explains, 'The good governance agenda which became popular within the donor community around this time highlighted the role of civil society in holding governments to account, suggesting a "virtuous circle" could be built between state, economy and civil society that would balance growth, equity and social stability.'[80] Notions of good governance coincided with increased donor pressure to meet international development goals in conjunction with the ineffective use by governments (in both low- and middle-income countries) of donor resources in primarily non-democratic settings. It is here where Robert Putnam's theories on civil society and 'social capital' were adopted to support the necessity to strengthen civil society. Putnam, under the influence of Alexis de Tocqueville, argued that the concentration of social capital could contribute directly to political

---

[76] See Edwards and Hulme, 'Too Close for Comfort'.
[77] N. Kabeer and H. Kabir, 'Quantifying the Impact of Social Mobilisation in Rural Bangladesh: Donors, Civil Society and "The Road Not Taken"', *Institute for Development Studies Working Paper*, no. 333 (2009).
[78] N. Kabeer, S. Mahmud and J. Castro, 'NGOs Strategies and the Challenge of Development and Democracy in Bangladesh', *Institute for Development Studies Working Paper*, no. 343 (2010).
[79] Chandhoke, 'Civil Society', p. 608.
[80] Kabeer, 'Quantifying the Impact of Social Mobilisation in Rural Bangladesh', p. 9.

stability and good governance.[81] Kabeer emphasises that according to Putnam, 'It was the density of associational life rather than the character of different associations that mattered for the development of generalised trust in a society, providing the basis on which its citizens were able to participate in democratic life and hold their governments accountable.'[82] In addition, Jonathan Fox explains that for Putnam, the nature of the unit of social capital is irrelevant, but rather 'that social capital is continuously distributed both horizontally and vertically'.[83]

Putnam's influence on neoliberal reforms in development and democratisation initiatives has been noteworthy, in particular for donor preferences to support the establishment and 'strengthening' of civil society organisations in authoritarian environments. For example, Guilain Denoeux describes the US government's predilection under former President Bill Clinton for demand- over supply-side civil society assistance strategies. 'Supply-side' strategies concentrated on increasing the 'quality of governance' or the 'quantity of democracy' provided through the state, whereas 'demand-side' approaches focused on strengthening civil society 'in relation to the state' to augment its own capacity to communicate demands for democracy and good governance. According to Denoeux, 'demand-side' approaches tended to reserve a privileged position to increase support to NGOs.[84] Denoeux contends that demand-side strategies rested on paradigms that explicitly supported both the notion that 'participation in voluntary associations fosters habits, values, attitudes, and skills conducive to democratic governance' and 'the denser and the more active the network of voluntary associations in which individuals take part, the greater this network can act as a counter-weight to the state'.[85] Evidence of demand-side strategies could soon be observed in the Middle East; for example, by the end of the 1990s it is estimated that

---

[81] R. Putnam, *Making Democracy Work: Civic Traditions in Modern Italy* (Princeton: Princeton University Press, 1993).

[82] Kabeer, 'Quantifying the Impact of Social Mobilisation in Rural Bangladesh', p. 8.

[83] J. Fox, 'How Does Civil Society Thicken? The Political Construction of Social Capital in Rural Mexico', *World Development*, vol. 24, no. 6 (1996), p. 1091.

[84] G. Denoeux, 'Promoting Democracy and Governance in the Arab World' in Nefissa, Al-Fattah, Hanafi and Milani (eds.), *NGOs and Governance in the Arab World*, p. 70.

[85] Ibid.

there were 15,000 registered civil society organisations in Egypt (double the amount existing in 1977), while the number of registered civil society organisations in Tunisia and Lebanon totalled around 5,000 and 3,500, respectively, towards the end of that same decade.[86] This more quantitative focus on the density of civil society organisations and more demand-oriented strategies overshadowed, however, the social function and nature of civil society manifesting during this period. This social function effectively served to provide safe spaces for marginalised groups and for community actors to meet. Within this context one observes a conglomeration of classical welfare associations, professional NGOs, state-sponsored NGOs, religiously oriented associations and grassroots movements providing new spaces to assemble – such as in civil society organisation headquarters – to gather and learn new skills, such as advocacy training and civic education, to network and forge solidarities.[87]

The next section further traces the rise of civil society organisations from the period of 'institutionalisation' or 'intensification' to the period of today known as 'empowerment' to underscore the prominence these different organisations began to assume within neoliberal reforms, in particular from the period of the Washington Consensus.[88] And while a significant proportion of the literature on these entities refers to NGOs, I use the term 'civil society' to refer to not only a broader set of organisations that includes activist organisations but also to emphasise the ideological association and appropriation of the concept that serves a range of disparate agendas present day.

The Institutionalisation of Civil Society and the Spaces in between

As a point of departure, in the article 'Is Social Change Fundable?' Jenny Pearce critically examines civil society organisations that emphasise their own commitment to progressive social change in Latin America. She looks back to some of the organisations that were established during the 1970s and 1980s in the region to advocate for radical social change. She concentrates on these organisations to bring into relief the notion that many of these same organisations are now members of the

---

[86] Bayat, *Life as Politics*, p. 84.   [87] Ibid., p. 86.
[88] Charnovitz, 'Two Centuries of Participation'.

more professionalised aid sector and are heavily dependent on both national and international donor funding. She asks, 'Should we be arguing for an end to external funding, and should we challenge any claim that its purpose is to further pro-poor social change in Latin America? Is it not only dangerous in practice to fund social change, but also misguided in principle?'[89] Highlighting some of the debates regarding civil society organisations from this period, Pearce underscores a fundamental shift in the nature of these organisations, i.e., from agents formerly organised to contest hegemony, to actors who are also capable of consolidating and maintaining hegemonies.

During the 1970s, two per cent of civil society organisation income globally came from official donors; from the mid-1990s income from official donors rose to 30 per cent. Moreover, from 1984 to 1994 the British government increased it's funding of civil society organisations by almost 400 per cent to £68.7 million.[90] In 2001, just six of the larger international NGOs controlled between US$2.5 billion and US$3 billion or between 45 and 55 per cent of all global humanitarian aid and assistance.[91] Finally, in 2011, US$19.3 billion was allocated to and through civil society organisations by the 24 Development Assistance Committee (DAC) country members.[92] This represents 14.4 per cent of total overseas development aid for 2011.[93] These figures point to several trends, among them the significant amount of funding made available in just more than two decades for civil society organisations from governments and, moreover, the increasing likelihood that these organisations could become reliant on these funding streams. Anthony Bebbington, Samuel Hickey and Diana Mitlin in *Can NGOs Make a Difference: The Challenge of Development Alternatives* and Steve Charnovitz in 'Two Centuries of Participation: NGOs and International Governance' chronicle the rise of these organisations, from several decades (Bebbington, Hickey and Mitlin) to more than two centuries (Charnovitz), aligning their increasing prominence with

---

[89] J. Pearce, 'Is Social Change Fundable? NGOs and Theories and Practices of Social Change', *Development in Practice*, vol. 20, no. 6 (2010), p. 622.
[90] Manji and O'Coill, 'The Missionary Position', p. 580.
[91] Barnett and Weiss, *Humanitarianism in Question*, p. 31.
[92] Organisation for Economic Co-operation and Development (OECD), 'Aid for CSOs: Flows of Official Development Assistance to and through Civil Society Organisations in 2011', October 2013.
[93] Ibid.

global trends and development discourses. Although this history can be traced back 200 years, I concentrate mainly on the period following the Cold War where the concept of civil society re-emerged alongside the pro-democracy social movements in Eastern Europe and Latin America. It is from this period where a significant qualitative and quantitative transformation of civil society organisations takes place.

Chronicling the Proliferation of Civil Society Organisations

Charnovitz and Bebbington, Hickey and Mitlin refer respectively to the periods of 'intensification' (1972–1991), 'institutionalisation' and the 'NGO boom' (1970s–1980s) of civil society organisations in broader discourses on development and poverty alleviation.[94] During these different periods these organisations were more formally integrated into official aid portfolios, with the growth of the civil society sector occurring in high income as well as in low-income countries. Here a shift occurred where civil society participation in social movements for emancipation from repressive structures and the denial of rights altered its course to focus more on poverty alleviation and basic needs.[95] It is also during this period when neoliberalism emerged as a prevailing paradigm alongside the design of structural adjustment packages for lower- and middle-income countries. As aforementioned, neoliberal policies during this time emphasised that, as an outcome of growing macroeconomic instability, state expenditure should be directed towards the creation of an enabling environment for growth rather than on the provision of public services. This left an opening for non-state actors such as civil society organisations to provide such services, namely the provision of social welfare interventions to poorer and marginalised communities.

Bebbington, Hickey and Mitlin describe the 'NGO boom' as a period marked by the increasing willingness of state and development agencies to fund a range of social welfare interventions.[96] Moreover, they note a strong correlation between the rise in foreign aid and the diminishing capacity for civil society to offer solutions or alternatives to the scale of suffering caused by the impact of unyielding structural

---

[94] Bebbington, Hickey and Mitlin, *Can NGOs Make a Difference?*, pp. 12–13 and Charnovitz, 'Two Centuries of Participation', p. 190.
[95] Manji and O'Coill, 'The Missionary Position', p. 575.
[96] Bebbington, Hickey and Mitlin, *Can NGOs Make a Difference?*, p. 13.

adjustment programmes. They write, 'Much was expected of NGOs in this period but there was little to no space to pursue large-scale or system-questioning alternative projects.'[97] Throughout this period, civil society organisations also assumed a greater role in United Nations fora, for example through their participation in the UN Convention on the Rights of the Child and the UN Conferences on Women (1975–1995). This more public role and participation in international deliberations eventually conferred more power and legitimacy unto civil society to contribute to development discourses; arguably, it is also with this increased participation from 'above' that civil society relationships and hence accountability to their counterparts 'below' came under greater scrutiny.[98]

From the 1990s the prominence of civil society organisations in neoliberal reforms could largely be discernible through overseas development assistance/aid budgets from the DAC countries. The amount of official funding for civil society organisations during this period more than tripled from US$2.1 billion to US$5.9 billion (1990–2000), with aid conditionalities from states and donors becoming significantly more rigid.[99] Bilateral and multilateral organisations allocated significant volumes of funding to mitigate the impact of structural adjustment programmes in lower-income countries, with civil society organisations becoming the preferred safety net for the vulnerable in these contexts. Bebbington, Hickey and Mitlin argue that these organisations were effectively integrated into mainstream neoliberal policies and as such distanced from their ability to provide alternatives to these programmes. They observe three primary trends during this period: the deepening of the democratisation and neoliberal agenda, the hegemony of the poverty agenda in international aid and the more recent emergence of the security agenda whereby international peace and security became integral to the development discourse.[100]

During what Bebbington, Hickey and Mitlin refer to as the 'fourth phase' of the history of civil society organisations, they document a growing concern over the practice, direction and focus of these

---

[97] Ibid.
[98] See Edwards and Hulme, 'Too Close for Comfort' and F. Manji, 'Collaboration with the South: Agents of Aid or Solidarity?', *Development in Practice*, vol. 7, no. 2 (May 1997), pp. 175–178.
[99] Barnett and Weiss, *Humanitarianism in Question*, p. 33.
[100] Bebbington, Hickey and Mitlin, *Can NGOs Make a Difference?*, p. 15.

organisations, their role in the overall reform agenda and their ability to be accountable to the communities where they work.[101] The aforementioned figures serve to illustrate an increasing depoliticisation of the civil society sector as it arguably moved further away from relationships with social movements and towards a more restricted role as public service contractors and instruments of democracy promotion. In 'Reflections on NGOs and Development', David Hulme considers whether civil society is genuinely capable of maintaining a dual strategy of engagement and advocacy in global development initiatives – an engagement that often requires cooperation and coordination with international donors, the state and with social welfare provision to deprived communities – and also the advocacy that is required to critique these very same actors and the broader Washington Consensus agenda.[102]

Today the concept of civil society features across multilateral institutional policy documents and guidelines and encourages multistakeholder partnerships in the design and implementation of anti-poverty and global health initiatives. Some donors through the disparate multilateral financing mechanisms even require a percentage of civil society organisation participation in national proposal consultation and development.[103] The concept of civil society and the role of these immeasurably different organisations have increasingly gained greater prominence in neoliberal discourses. This has resulted in careful consideration among some as to whether these organisations can effectively put forward alternatives to social change or realistically contest what are often more hegemonic international development discourses. And, arguably, as these organisations are expected to fill both a role of public service contractor for the provision of social welfare services and as agents to uphold democratic values and good governance, has civil society in some contexts instead become an instrument to maintain and consolidate these hegemonies? Therefore, it is worth considering how civil society engages in a particular context as well as the overall political environment in which they operate as either may or may not yield improved social or democratic outcomes.[104]

---

[101] Ibid.   [102] Ibid., p. 31.
[103] For more information, see the Global Fund Country Coordinating Mechanism Eligibility Requirements, Minimum Standards and Updated Guidelines: www.theglobalfund.org/en/ccm/guidelines.
[104] Jamal, *Barriers to Democracy*, p. 9.

The Spaces in between

Amaney Jamal argues that civic associations reproduce elements of the political context in which they exist and organise themselves. As such, she calls into question Putnam's theory on social capital and its links to democratic governance, in particular with regard to its applicability in authoritarian contexts.[105] Through her analysis of the West Bank and Morocco, she reasons that, 'Where associational contexts are dominated by state-centralized, patron-client tendencies, then associations, too, become sites for the potential replication of those vertical ties.'[106] This analysis, not unlike the analysis here on civil society's relationship to neoliberalism, situates the constraints for these actors within exogenous factors such as liberalisation and authoritarianism. These respective considerations of civil society fall into three of the five approaches on civil society activism in MENA, identified by Durac and Cavatorta in *Politics and Governance in the Middle East*, as they each concern the approaches 'civil society as liberal', 'civil society as regime tool' as well as 'civil society and authoritarian constraints'.[107] It can be argued that these approaches are closely inter-related in terms of how neoliberal policies have instrumentalised civil society actors within regimes while at the same time allowing for further authoritarian upgrading, depending on how the various policies are adopted and implemented. Moreover, it can be argued that the three aforementioned approaches do not allow for the possibility of political change and present a somewhat functionalist outlook for a group of actors that are vastly heterogeneous.

Across the text of the book I both acknowledge and explore the numerous indeterminate factors behind why these actors often choose to participate in public spaces despite an often high cost and risk associated with their engagement; however, I do not examine civil society activism per se. Durac and Cavatorta, for example, underscore the approach of 'civil society as activated citizenship' that emphasises the possibility for change and simultaneously considers a wider group of actors outside the associational or formal organisational realm.[108] I value the analysis of these authors and the implicit advocacy to look

---

[105] Ibid., p. 3. [106] Ibid., p. 20.
[107] Durac and Cavatorta, *Politics and Governance in the Middle East*, pp. 166–180.
[108] Ibid., p. 178.

at 'how society expresses itself' as well as depictions by writers such as Bayat on social non-movements as the collective actions of noncollective actors and the significance of passive networks.[109] Nevertheless, it is also through the examination of the actors and groups that choose with great intention to formally legalise their organisation and engage directly with the state through its laws of association that is it possible to observe the breadth of determinants for this engagement – to further civic engagement, to enact dissent, to increase influence, to both oppose and support the political, for social justice, for redress, to subvert, to enact change and also to enable continuity. More broadly, by choosing to examine civil society through the lens of neoliberalism, the impact of these policies and doctrines on these actors underscores how it has limited activism on the one hand and has eventually created the necessity and spaces for a different kind of civil society on the other. Raymond Hinnebusch subtly captures the constraints of this dichotomy, stating, 'While the uprising was spectacularly the product of agency – reaction against the previous features of the regional states, the structure – the durable inheritances from the past have constrained the outcomes of agency.'[110] As such, while situating understandings of civil society within discourses on neoliberalism may suggest a functionalist approach, my own analysis recognises this agency, the potential spaces for political change and for pluralism more broadly.

Conclusion

The nature of civil society as depicted by Hegel, Marx and Gramsci following the emergence of capitalism in the eighteenth and nineteenth centuries bears little resemblance to how civil society is understood in present discourses on international development and good governance found within neoliberal discourses. However, it could be argued that the actual nature and functioning of civil society, in particular during key transformative moments for the state when the stakes are higher, reflects the way these writers understood this dynamic field of actors. While Hegel characterised civil society as inherently replete with contradictions and conflict, necessitating the regulatory function of the state, Marx shifted the nature of the discourse to restore agency onto

---

[109] Bayat, *Life as Politics*, pp. 14, 22.
[110] Hinnebusch, 'Change and Continuity after the Arab Uprising', p. 12.

civil society, in particular for the marginalised and working classes. Hegel situated the power within the state to organise the internal disharmonies of civil society, while Marx located the agency within civil society itself to resolve its own inconsistencies and liberate itself from capitalist modes of production.

Gramsci, like Marx, also acknowledged the relationships of domination and hegemony within civil society; however, he broadens these different sets of actors to not only include the working classes and marginalised groups but also educational, cultural and religious institutions, where class and ideological battles are constantly being constructed and deconstructed. Both Gramsci and Marx reinstate agency unto these actors who are capable of self-regulation and self-organisation as well as being able forces to overthrow the state. However, for Gramsci, hegemony is never a final end point but rather a continual process embedded within the inter-relationships between the state and civil society. Gramsci's understanding of civil society was influential in the social movements in Eastern Europe, but in particular in Latin America among the region's new left during the 1980s. The concept during this period assumed a central role in new radical democratic theory and allowed civil society to become associated with a distinct self-management agenda emphasising the notion of the 'defence of freedom outside the state'. Within contexts of totalitarian and military rule, the concept of civil society transformed into an ideological tool to cultivate the transition to, and consolidation of, democracy in oppressive countries – consequently relocating civil society as the antithesis of authoritarianism. The concept, in part through its ideological association with the end of socialist societies, eventually became a vital instrument in the neoliberal architecture for the promotion of the minimalist state and for democratisation.

The 1980s witnessed an effective 'NGO boom', with funding for civil society organisations from some governments increasing significantly in just one decade. This significant increase in the prominence and legitimacy of civil society organisations was largely a result of policies outlined in the neoliberal Washington Consensus and the 'New Policy Agenda' advocating for the limited state in the promotion of macroeconomic stability. The principal efforts of the state were to be directed towards the creation of an enabling environment for growth rather than towards the provision of public services. Civil society, through the formalised entities of NGOs, emerged to fill this gap and to alleviate the often severe, socio-economic disruption caused by neoliberal policy through the form of structural adjustment packages. During a relatively short period of time, thousands of civil society organisations emerged to assume two primary roles – as cost-effective providers of welfare services and poverty-reduction initiatives and as torchbearers for democratic values and good governance. Despite mass mobilisations across lower- and middle-income countries against the austerity of neoliberal policies, many civil society organisations have indirectly (and at times directly) become instruments in sustaining these policies.

In contrasting the dynamic role directly assumed by civil society throughout the social movements in Eastern Europe and Latin America where Gramscian revolutionary thought featured prominently to the increasing instrumentalisation of these organisations by some donors and national governments, it is possible to situate the origins of such sharp divergences in how the concept of civil society is understood, in particular during transitions from authoritarian rule. During periods of sharp sociopolitical turmoil, specifically when there is an opportunity to radically reshape the direction of the state, the internal disharmonies of a society are brought into full relief. These vastly disparate understandings and historical transformations of the concept of civil society are a fundamental source of this critical shift where conflict, which was once considered as positive and productive, is now understood as destructive to democratisation. In particular, the Gramscian understanding of the concept that emphasises agency, instability and the reversible nature of hegemony stands in discernible opposition to the neoliberal understanding in which the role ascribed for civil society actors is generally functional and conflict is de-emphasised. At the root of the conflicts and contestations observed among civil society are two simultaneously operating but incompatible concepts of civil society influenced by the ideology of Communism on the one hand and the ideology of neoliberalism on the other. In looking to this sphere of actors following the downfall of an authoritarian regime, what can be discerned from the nature and quantity of these different contestations? Moreover, do these manifold conflicts indicate positive or negative outcomes for democratisation and sociopolitical change more broadly?

3 | The Consolidation of the Tunisian State

The security and stabilisation of the status quo in the Middle East and North Africa have often taken precedence for states over political and societal pluralism in the region. This has led over time to various consequences for civil society. One outcome is the expansion of the public sector by the state to such an extent that it has inevitably sought to incorporate civil society organisations directly into the state structure. This has had the effect of driving many alternative forms of collective activism and association underground, further fermenting dissent.[1] A second consequence is that the cost of maintaining an overstretched 'bureaucratic' state has led, in some instances, to the transfer of the social contract to civil society organisations to support social welfare interventions. To avoid contestations to the existing hegemonic order while simultaneously managing dissent, a degree of 'sanctioned' civil society is permitted to operate, often under the direct guise of the government's public sector.[2] Since Tunisia's independence in 1956, the symbolic and physical public spaces provided for civil society have regularly expanded and contracted to accommodate the disparate agendas of state and international entities. Through a strategy of what Eva Bellin describes as 'controlled *civisme*', Tunisian leaders 'have actively mobilised their citizens in parties and associations, but have subjected these parties and associations to very strict state control in an effort to limit their autonomy and their contestatory capacities'.[3] Under the leadership of Habib Bourguiba and Zine El Abidine Ben Ali, the Tunisian state cracked down routinely on perceived opposition and simultaneously fostered spaces for civil society to manoeuvre.

---

[1] See T. Ismael, *Middle East Politics Today: Government and Civil Society* (Gainesville: University Press of Florida, 2001), p. 72.
[2] E. Bellin, 'Civil Society in Formation: Tunisia' in A. Norton (ed.), *Civil Society in the Middle East: Volume I* (Leiden: E. J. Brill, 1995), p. 124.
[3] Ibid., p. 126.

To more fully understand the sites and areas of conflict among civil society actors and groups, as well as the consequences of these conflicts following the downfall of an authoritarian regime, it is important to examine the nature of the state prior to the regime change. As such, it is necessary to consider the space(s) afforded to civil society actors and groups prior to the downfall of the Ben Ali government. This involves a consideration of the nature of the pre- and post-independence Tunisian state and its approach to not only civil society but also more broadly to perceived or viable opposition.

Situating the Tunisian State

While descriptions of the political history of Tunisia often begin with the charismatic leadership of Habib Bourguiba following Tunisia's independence from French colonial rule in 1956, the origins of the Tunisian state in the Maghreb region have far deeper roots. In his book *Tunisie: Etat, Economie, et Société: Ressources Politiques Légitimation Regulations Sociales*, Mahmoud Ben Romdhane examines the various factors that could explain the persistence of authoritarianism in Tunisia more than a half century after its independence. He and other writers, such as Michael Willis and Christopher Alexander, trace the specific characteristics of the Tunisian state from even before the eighteenth century to explain some of the core features that continue to leave their historical residue on the country today.[4] Although there are several key factors and historical events that greatly influenced the nature of the Tunisian state that emerged following independence in 1956, two are considered here. These are Ottoman control from the sixteenth century and French colonial rule from 1881 to 1956 as these represent critical periods during which core structures and features of the Tunisian state began to materialise.

The Origins of the Tunisian State

Prior to Ottoman control, the Hafsid dynasty governed the majority of what is known as Tunisian territory from 1207 to 1574, with its

---

[4] M. Willis, *Politics and Power in the Maghreb: Algeria, Tunisia, and Morocco from Independence to the Arab Spring* (London: Hurst, 2012) and C. Alexander, *Tunisia* (London: Routledge, 2010).

control expanding in conjunction with the extension of trade ties with Europe. Alexander points out, 'More than any other pre-Ottoman dynasty, it is the Hafsids that modern Tunisians often regard as the founders of a Tunisian state.'[5] The Ottomans seized control of Tunis in 1574 and eventually appointed a *bey*, or a civil administrator, to maintain all executive, legislative and judicial authority over Tunisia. However, difficult climates and nomadic populations continued to pose challenges for political administration, thus constraining the bey's authority and ability to collect taxes and enforce the law in the central and southern areas as well as the northwest regions along the Algerian border.[6] To address this, the *bey* appointed chiefs to collect taxes and administer the law in their local tribes; these local chiefs are said to have maintained complete independence during this period.[7] While this allowed a more effective administration of these key functions in the more difficult-to-reach territories, authority over the disparate tribal populations remained fragmented in Tunisia for several centuries. In addition, the influence of the reform movement in Istanbul on similar reform movements in Tunisia, such as the 'Young Tunisians', moved the country closer to more established and centralised forms of government and a more consolidated state.[8] Nevertheless, the Ottoman period in Tunisia effectively exacerbated the coastal versus interior divide. It also carried with it the increasing importance of Islam as a 'central and legitimising aspect of political power'.[9]

Subsequently, French colonial rule at the end of the eighteenth century introduced a number of reforms that would eventually extend and consolidate the Tunisian state into well beyond the 75-year period of colonial rule. In 1881 France gained substantial control over Tunisia, and in 1883 it became a French protectorate. French colonialism had economic impacts that arguably continue today through the extraction of raw materials, exploitation of labour, the dislocation of agricultural labourers and the gradual process of the privatisation and centralisation of land. But the protectorate administration also established municipal governments, improved transport infrastructure and strengthened the central government's ability to extend into the more difficult-to-reach peripheral and tribal areas of the country. For many countries, such as neighbouring Algeria, the experience of colonialism

---

[5] Alexander, *Tunisia*, p. 12. [6] Ibid., p. 13. [7] Ibid.
[8] Willis, *Politics and Power*, p. 15. [9] Ibid., p. 18.

not only significantly disrupted economic dynamics but also damaged political institutions. Alexander contends, 'This experience of uninterrupted state-building and progressive centralisation marks an important difference between Tunisia and many other colonized countries ... Since Tunisia avoided this kind of profound disruption of its central governing institutions, the new government would not have to create a whole new order atop the rubble of the old one.'[10] In addition, French support for educational reforms allowed for the creation of a new educated elite whereby a significant number of young people from middle-class families, children of provincial landowners and small businessmen were able to access new educational opportunities at home and abroad.[11] With economic conditions worsening under French colonial rule and an emerging well-educated class, both the 'old indigenous elite' and the younger and more radical elements of Tunisian society returning from studies in France eventually formed the nationalist Destour party in 1920.[12] The party called for greater rights for Tunisians, but it did not make attempts to unite the different elements of the Tunisian population – such as traditional elites, students, workers and farmers – behind a collective united strategy for opposing French rule.[13] Concerned with the daily economic problems facing Tunisians across the rural–urban dichotomy, younger activists, including Habib Bourguiba, worked to establish a new party that could build a broad-based and unifying movement for Tunisians to support; as a result the Neo-Destour party was established in 1934. Neo-Destour, while not without conflicting elements inside the party, operated based on a moderate strategy of a negotiated transition to independence from the French.[14] It became evident that a unified nationalist movement could be effective and widely influential as an outcome of practices adopted under French rule. Willis points out, 'The full and effective subjugation of the rural areas and the tribes that lived there by the colonial powers, and their success in bringing them under the control of central political authority, had never previously been achieved.'[15] Effectively, prolonged efforts towards political centralisation in Tunisia became a tool to diminish the autonomy of the tribes but also to serve Neo-Destour in unifying

---

[10] Alexander, *Tunisia*, p. 21.   [11] Ibid., pp. 26–27.
[12] Willis, *Politics and Power*, p. 24.   [13] Alexander, *Tunisia*, p. 26.
[14] Ibid., p. 29.   [15] Willis, *Politics and Power*, pp. 32–33.

The Bourguiba Project: Modernisation and Secularisation

At independence in 1956, Tunisia was considered an 'established bureaucratic state'.[16] Bourguiba was considered the architect and father of Tunisian modernity as he carried Tunisia and the Neo-Destour Party through the tumultuous independence period to fight for liberation from the French, with the period from 1949 to 1954 manifesting in both guerrilla warfare in the countryside as well as student and worker strikes in the cities.[17] Ben Romdhane notes that for several years following the attainment of independence, Bourguiba was the target of numerous coups and threats against his regime, with many of these challenges directed by Salah Ben Youssef following his expulsion from the Neo-Destour Party in 1955. A key figure in the movement for Tunisia's autonomy from France, and for independence, Ben Youssef was influenced by the pan-Arab nationalism featuring across the region in Egypt, Syria and Iraq and therefore advocated more militant methods to achieve independence from the French, in contrast to Bourguiba's strategy of a transition in stages.[18] Ben Youssef and the Youssefists instigated attacks, sabotage (including the derailing of trains) and violence, where during a period of 'total chaos' the entirety of Tunisia was affected with more than 900 deaths.[19] These initial moments of state fragility and conflict over Bourguiba's national project eventually contributed to the nature of how he governed Tunisia, and it is argued, greatly influenced his more severe responses to perceived political opposition. Bourguiba's sustained strategy of building national support through the broader appeal to patriotism to achieve independence eventually succeeded in 1956. His politics of 'national unity' was aided through the post-colonial legacy of a highly efficient and highly centralised state apparatus.[20] For example, Alexander writes, 'Tunisia's struggle did not involve a fight over land or between two fundamentally

---

[16] L. Anderson, *The State and Social Transformation in Tunisia and Libya* (Princeton: Princeton University Press), 1986, p. 231, as cited in King, 'Regime Type, Economic Reform, and Political Change', p. 63.
[17] Alexander, *Tunisia*, p. 31.   [18] Ibid.
[19] Ben Romdhane, *Tunisie: Etat, Economie et Société*, pp. 66–67.
[20] Willis, *Politics and Power*, p. 34.

different political orders. Rather, it was largely a struggle over who would staff and lead the organs of a central government that developed steadily for more than a century.'[21] However, it is argued that Bourguiba's politics of national unity left minimal space for opposition. This, in addition to a country that historically was characterised by the absence of popular participation in politics, set the stage for authoritarian tendencies that would fully manifest at a later stage. Moreover, Ben Romdhane highlights the period of instability and insecurity in the years that followed independence as a series of key watershed moments that ultimately reinforced at the highest level of the state and the Party an 'authoritarian spiral'.[22] These initial experiences of both civil war preceding independence, and the years of violence in its consolidation, effectively eliminated the possibility for democratic pluralism in Tunisia for the decades that would follow.

During the 1956–1969 period, the Bourguiba regime entered into what Ben Romdhane refers to as a period of 'national construction' through a process of firmly establishing the state's sovereignty and legitimacy – politically, economically and militarily – alongside the further institutionalisation of solid state infrastructure and the implementation of modernisation measures.[23] With a French presence remaining on Tunisian territory even following independence (the French army had bases in both the northern and southern regions following independence), fragmented justice systems, French currency and limited education for the majority of the population, only the state could lead such significant reforms. Beji Caid Essebsi, a former minister under Bourguiba and, perhaps not without coincidence, the democratically elected president of Tunisia in 2014, remarked:

> It was through the mobilisation of the dual State–Party that Bourguiba was able to lead these reforms. It was by definition a reform from on high applied with a certain authoritarianism. It necessitated a strong state, a strong competence, and at its leadership, a man ... Habib Bourguiba was this man as a result of his incontestable legitimacy, the sacrifices he made for his country and his own personal strength. Bourguiba did not need pressure from a popular base nor democratic control to undertake these grand reforms.[24]

---

[21] Alexander, *Tunisia*, p. 34.
[22] Ben Romdhane, *Tunisie: Etat, Economie et Société*, p. 67. [23] Ibid., p. 69.
[24] Caid Essebsi's remarks cited in Ben Romdhane, *Tunisie: Etat, Economie et Société*, p. 71.

During the Bourguiba regime, political reform and social reform were also inseparable.[25] Article 1 of the 1959 Tunisian Constitution came to represent the 'spinal cord' of Tunisian political identity; it stated, 'Tunisia is a free state, sovereign and independent; its religion is Islam, its language is Arabic and its regime is a republic.'[26] Article 1 inevitably became the mechanism through which Bourguiba led and maintained an authoritarian regime in Tunisia. Article 1 was commonly referred to as the 'Bourguiba solution', with secularism featuring as an underlying ideology for Tunisia during this period.[27] More importantly, in his biography of Bourguiba, Samy Ghorbal explains that Bourguiba believed that a modern state would not hold in a traditional society and thus the building of the modern state involved not only the establishment of political structures but also the 'vigorous targeting of society'.[28] Integral to this was the Code of Personal Status (CPS) of 1956 that led Tunisia to become the first country in the Arab–Muslim world to ban polygamy and radically changed women's social position in the country.[29] As a result of these policies and strategies, at the end of the 1960s democracy seemed untenable as the top-down process of national construction left little room for the emergence of political parties. Concurrently, the institutions of civil society had become weak or non-existent as a result of a gradual process of co-optation into the broader Parti Socialiste Destourien (PSD) State–Party.[30] Ben Romdhane, citing Caid Essebsi, writes, 'A strictly democratic regime would have probably had to abandon all of these progressive, liberal and absolutely decisive reforms to come out of the archaic nature of Tunisian society of the 1950s.'[31]

Nevertheless, in contrast to the poor socio-economic indicators of the 1960s, which included extreme levels of poverty across the country, high levels of illiteracy, the majority of the population being located in rural or semi-urban areas or in overpopulated town centres, and with regular employment only available for a minority of the population, the 1970s saw a reversal of these trends.[32] Following a period of

---

[25] S. Ghorbal, *Orphelins de Bourguiba et Héritiers du Prophète* (Tunis: Ceres Editions, 2012), p. 24.
[26] Ibid., p. 11.   [27] Ibid., pp. 10–11.   [28] Ibid., p. 24.
[29] W. Zartman, *Tunisia: The Political Economy of Reform* (Boulder: Lynne Rienner, 1991), p. 3.
[30] Ben Romdhane, *Tunisie: Etat, Economie et Société*, p. 73.   [31] Ibid., p. 72.
[32] Ibid.

socialism under the direction of the Minister of Planning and National Economy Ahmed Ben Salah in the 1960s, in which there was a national endeavour towards import-substitution industrialisation accompanied by significant increases in foreign borrowing and consequently debt, the 1970s experienced a sharp shift towards market reforms.[33] With a concerted focus on export-oriented development strategies to attract domestic and foreign investment, Tunisia effectively became one of the first countries in the Middle East and North Africa to implement policies of *infitah* or 'opening'.[34] From 1970 to 1974, Tunisia's exports rose from 98.8 million dinars to 398 million dinars. Growth rates increased to 8–10 per cent, placing Tunisia among the world's top 10 countries for GDP growth per person during that period.[35] Significant injections of private sector resources in conjunction with increased international optimism for Tunisia's economic prosperity contributed to increases in the number of employees in both the private and public sector, generating an estimated 400,000 new jobs. This growth also raised per capita income by more than 70 per cent and reduced the overall poverty level to less than 13 per cent; also notable is the decrease in illiteracy from 84.7 per cent in 1956 to 47.5 per cent by 1980.[36]

Simultaneously there emerged a more radical and combative educated young workers movement, with the General Labour Union of Tunisia (UGTT) eventually becoming autonomous from the PSD, as well as an active and engaged student movement and nascent human rights advocacy culminating in the creation of the National Council for the Defence of Public Liberties. However, subsequent to economic deterioration at the end of the decade as a result of the European economic recession and state overinvestment in public sector enterprises in order to continue to provide employment, debt rose to 74 per cent of GDP in 1987.[37] A foreign exchange crisis prompted the government to eventually negotiate a structural adjustment package and initiate liberalisation measures with the IMF and World Bank in 1986.[38] Moreover, increasing disenchantment with the Bourguiba

---

[33] Alexander, *Tunisia*, pp. 71–75.   [34] Ibid., p. 76.
[35] Citing M. Ben Romdhane, 'Mutations Économiques et Sociales et Mouvement Ouvrier en Tunisie de 1956 à 1980' in Alexander, *Tunisia*, p. 77.
[36] Ben Romdhane, *Tunisie: Etat, Economie et Société*, pp. 74–75.
[37] Alexander, *Tunisia*, pp. 78–79.
[38] Durac and Cavatorta, *Politics and Governance in the Middle East*, p. 93.

regime and greater calls for more representative institutions and democratic processes led to a new wave of authoritarianism in Tunisia after discredited democratic elections in 1981. Ben Romdhane writes, 'The institutions that civil society took years to create – the syndicates, political parties, the League of Human Rights, etc. – were destroyed... As to those who were responsible for protecting society – the systems of justice and the forces of order, they were charged with silencing, arresting, imprisoning and torturing.'[39] This crackdown on political opposition, collective activism and secular as well as religious civil society actors eventually necessitated a space for political and civil alternatives to emerge.

The Manifestation of Political Islam

The exact role of religion in post-independence Tunisia was ambiguous. Conscious of the mobilising function of religion, Bourguiba continued to make public references to Islam. Ghorbal argues, 'Bourguiba very neatly refused to disassociate political categories from religious ones. To the contrary he in fact worked to aggravate and maintain this confusion.'[40] Ghorbal states that the Bourguiba regime was driven to domesticate religion, whereby the president interpreted and qualified religious text and law when necessary, using religious law to justify his secularising reforms. Ghorbal, in fact, goes so far as to term this '*Ijtihad Bourguibien*'.[41,42] Bourguiba eventually took control of the mosques and their personnel, integrated the Sharia courts into the secular legal system and combined the renowned University of Zaytouna – considered a dangerous obstacle ideologically and politically[43] – with Tunis University.[44] In 1960, the president even attempted, albeit unsuccessfully, to motivate people to abandon the Ramadan fast, alleging

---

[39] Ben Romdhane, *Tunisie: Etat, Economie et Société*, p. 78.
[40] Ghorbal, *Orphelins de Bourguiba*, p. 16.
[41] *Ijtihad* refers to a historical process in Islamic law in which the core sources were interpreted by religious scholars (*mujtahids*) to align with emerging practices within post-Medineen societies; for additional information see Hallaq, 'On the Origins of the Controversy about the Existence of Mujtahids and the Gate of Ijtihad', *Studia Islamica*, no. 63 (1986), pp. 129–141.
[42] Ghorbal, *Orphelins de Bourguiba*, p. 15.
[43] M. Hamdi, *The Politicisation of Islam: A Case Study of Tunisia* (Boulder: Westview Press, 1998), p. 13.
[44] Willis, *Politics and Power*, p. 158.

that fasting could be harmful to Tunisia's economic growth and efforts to modernise. He famously drank a glass of orange juice during Ramadan following a public rally in 1964.[45]

Tunisia's post-independence drive to modernise cultural practices was considered the most radical in the region, in large part because it came at the expense of the majority of the public, who remained relatively conservative.[46] Abdelkader Zghal explains that the Islamic movement inevitably became 'the product and the expression of this resistance to the modernisation policy of Bourguiba, a policy perceived as a mechanism of submission and alienation to the West'.[47] He contends that the core strategic direction of the Islamic movement was to 'deal carefully and tactically' with traditional Islam, to incorporate Salafist Islam into the Tunisian context and to eventually 'reconcile' Islam with modernity.[48] The principal Islamist party in Tunisia, Le Mouvement de la Tendance Islamique (MTI), struggled throughout the Bourguiba regime to definitively determine how politically engaged it should become and the degree to which it should become visible. The leadership of the Islamist movement in Tunisia was well educated and highly motivated to address the narrowly secular orientation of the Bourguiba government in particular.[49] One of the key figures throughout the life of MTI and eventually the Ennahda party, Rachid Ghannouchi, explained that Islam was a comprehensive methodology for liberation: 'It liberates humanity from the tyranny of dictatorship and exploitation; it is a call to unitarianism and its attendant values of equality, fraternity, freedom and the love of justice.'[50] However, the Tunisian Islamist movement did not necessarily adhere to the promotion of the classical model of Islam. Moreover, the Tunisian Islamist movement did not contain a reputable Islamist scholar, and over time, it moved away from 'non-political concerns such as morality, faith and social harmony' as it sought to increasingly engage in and influence political matters.[51] For example, in 1978 the movement

---

[45] Ibid.
[46] A. Zghal, 'The New Strategy of the Movement: Manipulation or Expression of Political Culture?' in Zartman (ed.), *Tunisia: The Political Economy of Reform*, p. 207.
[47] Ibid. [48] Ibid., p. 208. [49] Willis, *Politics and Power*, p. 156.
[50] Al-Ghannushi, Mahwair Islamiyya, cited in Hamdi, *The Politicisation of Islam*, p. 164.
[51] Hamdi, *The Politicisation of Islam*, p. 164.

began to publish a weekly news journal entitled *Al-Mujtama* ('The Society') through which Tunisian Islamists demonstrated their support for the Iranian revolution. Simultaneously, a widely growing Islamist student movement was developing, expressing the call for a pro-Islamic anti-Western revolution.[52]

In 1981, MTI organised a press conference to announce its intention to transform into a legal political organisation 'focused on restoring Tunisia's Islamic identity'.[53] From here Willis contends that the government response to discernible opposition became severe whereby the leadership of MTI was arrested, charged with forming an illegal organisation, publishing inaccurate information and defaming the president; many members were imprisoned and tortured, with some given life sentences and the death penalty.[54] This period of a contraction of public space also involved the routine arrest and imprisonment of MTI members throughout the remainder of the Bourguiba regime, with the president quoted as declaring, 'The eradication of the Islamist poison will be the last service I'll render Tunisia.'[55] Nevertheless, some consider this period of repression as a beneficial tool for MTI as it reaffirmed the unity of the Islamist movement, gave grounds for it to insist on formal recognition and 'confirmed its commitment to peaceful and democratic means of political action'.[56] Furthermore, throughout the 1980s in particular, Islamic activists were able to situate themselves as vital voices for economic discontent as well as champions of the politically marginalised. MTI was also able to benefit from growing popular dissatisfaction with the secular direction of the government and its elites.[57]

Despite scholars', international donors' and policymakers' aspirations for Tunisia to become one of the region's best hopes for liberalism with Bourguiba's earlier demonstration of pluralistic tendencies accompanied by economic stability, soon his regime's tacit attempts to

---

[52] Ibid., p. 33.   [53] Willis, *Politics and Power*, p. 164.   [54] Ibid.
[55] E. Hermassi, 'The Islamicist Movement and November 7' in Zartman (ed.), *Tunisia: The Political Economy of Reform*, cited in Willis, *Politics and Power*, p. 166.
[56] Al-Mansuri, *al-Ittijah al-islami wa Burqayba*, cited in Hamdi, *The Politicisation of Islam*, pp. 44–45.
[57] S. Waltz, 'The Politics of Human Rights in the Maghreb' in J. Entelis (ed.), *Islam, Democracy, and the State in North Africa* (Bloomington: Indiana University Press, 1997), p. 82.

manage any dissent overshadowed these potential gains.[58] For almost three decades the Bourguiba regime brought economic growth and stability while it concurrently increased crackdowns and human rights abuses against perceived opposition. For Bourguiba, the drive for ideological conformity towards an all-encompassing modernising agenda eventually overpowered forms of collective activism, including from among both religious and secular movements that did not align with his vision of post-independence Tunisia. In this instance, the almost total state endeavour towards secularism and modernity inevitably impacted upon the nature of Tunisian society. It also unwittingly permitted the forging of powerful counter-publics.

The Rise of Ben Ali and the Retrenching of Liberal Authoritarianism

In what was considered a bloodless 'medical coup' as a consequence of the deterioration in his health and popularity, Bourguiba was succeeded as president by Zine El Abidine Ben Ali, his former interior minister and prime minister, in November 1987.[59] With increasing hostility and repression against all forms of opposition accompanied by eventual drops in economic indicators and standards of living, Ben Ali's ascendency to the presidency was initially (and ironically) hailed by the media, members of the academic sector and donors as a Tunisian 'revolution'. For Ben Ali, political stability and the implementation of the neoliberal reforms through structural adjustment programmes previously negotiated under Bourguiba in 1986 became one of the regime's principal priorities.[60] During the 1990s, the government pursued strategies to stimulate private investment, including the privatisation of state-owned enterprises established in the 1970s and 1980s that previously benefited from heavy injections of state investment. And while Western financial institutions praised Ben Ali for his persistence in implementing market-oriented reforms, he was

---

[58] King, 'Regime Type, Economic Reform, and Political Change in Tunisia', p. 64.
[59] As a result of growing concerns over his ability to govern, Ben Ali organised a group of seven physicians to attest to Bourguiba's incapacity. On 5–6 November 1987, Ben Ali took over the presidency. See: Alexander, *Tunisia*, p. 52.
[60] Alexander, *Tunisia*, p. 79.

eventually criticised for the pace at which he implemented other key reforms such as these privatisation measures.[61] In particular in 2000 for example, socio-economic conditions in Tunisia deteriorated, bringing severe economic hardship to a significant proportion of the population. This included rapidly increasing household debt, high unemployment among undergraduates – rising from 8.6 per cent in 1999 to 44.4 per cent in 2009 – and widespread corruption at the centre of the Ben Ali regime.[62] As such, in an effort to maintain political stability and preclude social unrest, the goal of both the preservation and creation of new jobs was paramount for the regime.[63]

While Ben Ali was keen to demonstrate a commitment to neoliberal economic reform at home and abroad, he was equally committed to demonstrating his outward conviction in liberal political reform. As early as the 1990s, Ben Ali created perceptible openings for political liberalisation; accompanying these measures was an international enthusiasm for the democratic potential these new opportunities could offer Tunisian political society.[64] The new president pardoned opposition leaders, allowing them to return from abroad, and provided amnesty to a multitude of political prisoners;[65] liberalised press codes; inaugurated human rights reforms (Ben Ali was even awarded an international human rights prize in 1989); and loosened the 1959 laws of association (no. 59–154).[66] In 1988, the National Assembly passed a law authorising political parties (although it prohibited parties based on 'religion, language, race or religion'), and in 1989 presidential and parliamentary elections were held with the Constitutional Democratic Rally (RCD) party receiving a total vote of 80 per cent. William Zartman writes, 'The government announced its entry into the democratic era with understandable pride and enthusiasm, since Tunisia had its first free and fair, non-violent, competitive multiparty elections.'[67]

---

[61] Ibid., p. 80.
[62] Durac and Cavatorta, *Politics and Governance in the Middle East*, p. 23.
[63] Alexander, *Tunisia*, p. 80.
[64] See W. Zartman, 'The Conduct of Political Reform: The Path Toward Democracy' in Zartman (ed.), *Tunisia: The Political Economy of Reform*, pp. 16, 25; G. Geyer, *Tunisia: A Journey through a Country that Works* (London: Stacey International, 2003).
[65] Zartman, 'The Conduct of Political Reform', p. 16.
[66] S. Waltz, 'Clientelism and Reform in Ben Ali's Tunisia' in Zartman (ed.), *Tunisia: The Political Economy of Reform*, p. 36.
[67] Zartman, 'The Conduct of Political Reform', p. 23.

Ben Ali himself was elected with a nearly unanimous vote of support of 99.27 per cent, albeit only representing half of the total 4 million potential voters (only 2.1 million Tunisians voted).[68] Scholars such as Susan Waltz and Eva Bellin observed that despite these signs of optimism, the residue of personalist rule would soon re-materialise. Rather than creating a system of multiparty opposition, the regime was actually increasing its power and further embedding authoritarian and repressive practices.[69] This aligns with Steven Heydemann's analysis that regimes across the Middle East and North Africa during this period were 'upgrading' authoritarianism through the perfunctory adoption of liberalisation measures, providing the outward impression of regime change, whilst in reality, this allowed them to reinforce their own political and social control at home.[70]

Trends and events in neighbouring countries in the region also directly influenced the approach the Ben Ali regime would eventually adopt towards Islamist opposition, in particular as Ben Ali sought to further establish his legitimacy as Tunisia's leader. This included the victory of the Islamic Salvation Front (FIS) in Algeria in the first round of parliamentary elections in December 1991, Islamist demonstrations against the US military in Saudi Arabia following Iraq's invasion of Kuwait earlier that year and, more locally in 1991, the attack on the RCD's central offices in Tunis during which a security guard died and several were wounded (despite being blamed by the Ben Ali government, Ennahda consistently denied responsibility for event).[71] For example, MTI became a viable threat to the Bourguiba regime when it eventually attained significant representation in the 16th national conference of the UGTT; it had secured an executive committee position on the board of the Tunisian League of Human Rights; it featured regularly in the media; and MTI witnessed its student movement expand to more than 15,000 students petitioning to hold a general student MTI conference.[72] However, Ben Ali released several thousand MTI activists from prison and eventually released Rachid Ghannouchi

---

[68] Ibid., p. 24.   [69] See Bellin, 'Civil Society in Formation: Tunisia', p. 29.
[70] Heydemann, 'Upgrading Authoritarianism in the Arab World', as cited in Cavatorta, 'No Democratic Change', p. 142.
[71] J. Entelis, 'Political Islam in the Maghreb: The Nonviolent Dimension' in Entelis (ed.), *Islam, Democracy, and the State in North Africa*, p. 46 and Willis, *Politics and Power*, p. 168.
[72] Hamdi, *The Politicisation of Islam*, p. 50.

and the movement's core leaders in May 1988.[73] In a concerted attempt to develop a less confrontational relationship with the new regime, Ghannouchi made clear that MTI only hoped to attain 10 seats in the Assembly; and, in an effort to minimise explicit references to Islam, in 1989 MTI was renamed Hizb Ennahda, or the Ennahda party, in its application to establish a formal political party.[74] The results of the election to the National Assembly allocated all seats to Ben Ali's RCD party, and no seats to Ennahda. It is argued that Ennahda attracted at least 30 per cent of the popular vote in reality, and therefore Ennahda publicly contested the election.[75] From this point, the relationship between the Ben Ali government and Tunisia's Islamist movement began to take on the residue of the former regime's approach to all political opposition. In May 1989 Ghannouchi sought exile in Algeria and eventually the United Kingdom in protest against the election results. Eventually Ennahda was banned, and in 1992 its entire leadership was imprisoned.[76] The threat of Islamist 'extremism' as perceived more broadly in the Middle East and North Africa during this time effectively allowed the Ben Ali regime to repress significant sections of the population as well as any form of collective activism understood as potential opposition.[77] Mohamed Hamdi writes:

What followed later was a total attack on Ennahda and everything connected with it, in almost every political and social aspect ... The thousands of its leaders and members arrested were put on trial and given various sentences ranging from the death penalty ... to life sentences for most of the political leaders.[78]

---

[73] Willis, *Politics and Power*, p. 166.
[74] Willis, *Politics and Power*, pp. 166–167 and D. Gray, 'Tunisia after the Uprising: Islamist and Secular Quests for Women's Rights', *Mediterranean Politics*, vol. 17, no. 3 (November 2012), p. 288.
[75] Willis, *Politics and Power*, pp. 166–167.
[76] Gray, 'Tunisia after the Uprising', p. 288.
[77] It is important to note that there is disagreement in academic literature on Tunisia concerning how and why Tunisians lived under an authoritarian regime over several decades whereby extreme repression was applied against perceived opposition. This debate is poignantly explored by Ben Romdhane, *Tunisie: Etat, Economie et Société*, who details the economic, social and political explanations behind this phenomenon and who is critical of the analyses of writers such as Michel Camau and Beatrice Hibou.
[78] Hamdi, *The Politicisation of Islam*, pp. 72–73.

Despite routine crackdowns on perceived Islamic activity, the Ben Ali regime emphasised that such restrictive policies underpinned economic growth, improved living standards and 'protected social advances such as the integration of women into the public and economic life'.[79] The Ben Ali government also went to great lengths to associate Islamist movements with intolerance and violence. Susan Waltz argues that were it not for the moral panic shared in the perception of the 'dangers of the Islamist movements' among political leaders in the region as well as policymakers in the West, Western governments might have worked more diligently to underscore the ongoing human rights abuses against Islamists across North Africa. According to Waltz, 'As it is, thanks to a Western revulsion at the prospect of Islamists in power, assiduously cultivated by Algeria and Tunisia, the regimes were not only permitted to revert to their authoritarian ways, they were also paid for it.'[80] Some secular factions, including political parties and civil society organisations during this time, supported and collaborated with the Ben Ali regime in its repression of the Islamists because of their own fear of Islamism.[81] Consequently, these organisations began to distance themselves from Islamist organisations. As Islamist organisations de facto could not legally acquire the 'associational visa', organisations perceived as Islamist could not establish, even at a minimum, social welfare organisations in their communities. This ultimately had a direct impact on the nature of Tunisian society that would emerge during this period. Consequently, over time, civil society in Tunisia comprised mainly secular organisations operating in an almost entirely uncontested field. John Entelis writes, 'Sadly, many of the country's leading intellectuals, journalists and writers have collaborated in the governmental effort (actively or by their silence) despite the severe limitations this has had on basic civil and human rights including the freedom of expression.'[82]

Despite encouraging signs that the 'revolution' in 1987 would bring increased liberalism, freedom and tolerance, the residue of personalist authoritarian rule did indeed resurface and become further embedded

---

[79] Entelis, 'Political Islam in the Maghreb', p. 47.
[80] Waltz, 'The Politics of Human Rights', p. 138.
[81] G. Joffe, 'The Arab Spring in North Africa: Origins and Prospects', *The Journal of North African Studies,* vol. 16, no. 4 (2011), p. 519 and Willis, *Politics and Power,* p. 177.
[82] Entelis, 'Political Islam in the Maghreb', p. 49.

in Tunisia. Earlier efforts to foster the impression of broadening liberal democratic reforms – such as the lifting of restrictions on the media, in legal reforms, and the changes to the laws of association – did not actually lead to a more politically active society. With increasing crackdowns on the margins of space permitted for dissent, the Tunisian populace endured an oppressive regime in part for economic and national security. In the next section, the simultaneous process of expanding and contracting the symbolic and physical public spaces for civil society under Ben Ali is further described. It reveals in greater detail a regime that went to great lengths to stifle emerging counter-publics while often giving the outward appearance of fostering and nurturing spaces for these different groups.

The Consolidation of Civil Society

The Ben Ali regime understood fully the efficacy and usefulness of adopting liberalisation policies as this permitted the facade of government legitimacy domestically and internationally while allowing further control over perceived opposition. In particular, Ben Ali grasped the benefits of embracing discourses on human rights and in lifting restrictions on civil society, namely the formal laws of association. Tunisia was the first country in North Africa to apply a human rights discourse and it is even argued that the regime's legitimacy was intrinsically linked to his adoption of the human rights platform.[83] Waltz details that despite the arrest and detention of thousands of Islamists since the early 1990s, 'Ben Ali was openly commended for introducing reforms by Tunisia's western partners, and France went so far as to award him a prestigious human rights prize.'[84] These idiosyncrasies also manifested in the manner in which reforms were implemented in relation to civil society. Throughout the Ben Ali regime, amendments were made to the laws of association formerly implemented under Bourguiba in 1959. These amendments simultaneously permitted expansions for some civil society organisations while strictly contracting room to manoeuvre for others. For example, the law of 7 November 1959 on associations was amended in 1992 to establish a system of classification for the associations and again in 1998 to establish the

---

[83] Waltz, 'The Politics of Human Rights in the Maghreb', pp. 85–88.
[84] Ibid., pp. 86–87.

procedures for the 'declaration' of associations.[85] However, while the laws of association in Tunisia were being gradually loosened by the regime, human rights violations continued with Tunisia's prisons being more populated in 1991–1992 than during any period throughout colonial rule.[86] Furthermore, new freedoms in the media, such as the restoration in 1987 of an independent press, overshadowed the removal of religious literature in broader media. Eventually the political *Al-Mawkaf* (published by the Rassemblement Socialiste Progressiste (RSP))[87] and weekly independent journal *Realités* also had their copies temporarily removed.[88] Waltz argues, 'In the Ben Ali era, toleration in widely publicised cases of press and associational freedoms is in some measures offset by less well publicised but no less significant instances where the new freedoms have been abridged.'[89]

The Law and Life of the Associations

It is important to note that although Islamist movements and organisations were a primary target of repression throughout the two decades prior to the downfall of the Ben Ali regime in 2011, a number of secular civil society organisations also encountered the brunt force of the regime's repressive tactics against perceived political opposition. Some civil society organisations during this period, rather than serving as a means to consolidate democracy through the density of social capital growing in Tunisia, were being instrumentalised by the government to further embed authoritarian practices. The regime eventually used the laws of association, as well as the civil society organisations themselves, to bring a host of actors and groups under greater governmental control and to undermine their ability to function effectively.

---

[85] Euro-Mediterranean Human Rights Network, 'Freedom of Association in the Euro-Mediterranean Region' (2007), p. 83 and 'La Loi des Associations' Lo. 59–154, 7 November 1959, (Journal Officiel de la République Tunisienne (JORT) n° 63 du 22 décembre 1959 p. 1534). See: www.cnudst.rnrt.tn/index26e1.html?jort_fr.

[86] C. Henry, 'Post-Colonial Dialectics of Civil Society' in Zoubir (ed.), *North Africa in Transition: State, Society, and Economic Transformation in the 1990s*, p. 21.

[87] The RSP was a political opposition party legalised officially in 1988, which subsequently boycotted the 1989 Tunisian elections during which Ben Ali is reported to have acquired 99 per cent of the vote.

[88] Waltz, 'Clientelism and Reform in Ben Ali's Tunisia', pp. 38–39.

[89] Ibid., p. 38.

Clement Henry explains that for countries in North Africa, civil society and its relegated associations are not entirely distinct from the state. He writes:

Informal as well as formal intermediaries are shaped by laws, regulations, and ... by historical legacies of conflict and cooperation with authorities. It is the modern state, after all, that encourages or discourages intermediaries from becoming formal associations, makes them legal or illegal, and gives them public space or drives them underground.[90]

In 2007, there were 9,132 civil society organisations officially registered in Tunisia, with an estimated 9,600 at the end of 2010.[91] The majority of these civil society organisations were classed as artistic and cultural (6,005), sports (1,281), scientific (495) or social (579).[92] Among the thousands of civil society organisations established during this period, very few engaged in humanitarian development or the promotion of women's rights or broader human rights. The civil society actors and groups at the time were characterised as timid and were understood only to play a symbolic role to participate in public events and occasionally provide social/support services to certain groups of the population.[93] The laws of association throughout the Ben Ali regime were notoriously constrained. The procedure to legalise an organisation was cumbersome, and, for many, simply registering an organisation brought uncertain risk.

In August 1988 and April 1992, Ben Ali amended the law of 7 November 1959 that legally governed the formation and existence of civil society organisations in Tunisia.[94] After these changes there were eight 'associational' categories from which an organisation must choose when submitting a written request for official 'associational status' to the Ministry of the Interior; they were: women, sport, science,

---

[90] Henry, 'Post-Colonial Dialects of Civil Society', pp. 12–13.
[91] Euro-Mediterranean Human Rights Network, 'Freedom of Association', p. 83 and Le Centre d'Information, de Formation, d'Etudes et de Documentation sur les Associations (IFEDA): www.ifeda.org.tn.
[92] M. Majoub, 'La Gouvernance Environnementale Démocratique: Rôle et Place de la Société Civile', *Rapport National sur l'Etat de l'Environnement*, Edition Spéciale 2011, p. 8, citing the 2011 IFEDA statistics (based on 2010 data). See also: www.ifeda.org.tn/francais/statistiques.php.
[93] Majoub, 'La Gouvernance Environnementale Démocratique', p. 2.
[94] Euro-Mediterranean Human Rights Network, 'Freedom of Association', p. 83.

cultural and artistic, social, development, friendly/social (*amicales*) and general.[95] The categories appear broad; however, their actual application significantly limited the disparate kinds of organisations eligible to apply as the law prohibited organisations of a political nature. The changes to the laws of association during the Ben Ali era (in 1988 and 1992) also detailed that the Ministry of the Interior was required to consider applications by political parties and organisations within three months of receiving an application.[96] Once the Ministry of the Interior approved a request, the organisation could acquire its legal status. There was, however, no legal time limit to issue a receipt of declaration from the Ministry of the Interior, and some civil society organisations would argue that 'officials take advantage of that void to disrupt the process'.[97] This measure could consequently prevent the required and formal notice in the *Journal official de la République Tunisienne (JORT)* and hence the legal formation of an organisation.[98] The result was that a number of civil society organisations were then forced to operate outside the law as they were 'unrecognised associations' by the government; this left the organisations in a challenging situation.[99] The civil society organisations that remained officially unregistered also had limited access to the populations they sought to support.[100] The ministry could also refuse the application simply on the grounds of 'contrary to the law' without providing any further details. Moreover, the ministry could legally request the court to dissolve an organisation whose activities were perceived to contravene the laws of association. In practice, the ministry routinely closed associational premises and prevented members from meeting without having to seek permission from the courts. For example, the ministry closed 11 regional offices of the Tunisian Human Rights League

[95] See *Journal Officiel de la République Tunisienne*: www.cnudst.rnrt.tn/index26e1.html?jort_fr.
[96] Y. Bouandel, 'Human Rights in the Maghreb' in Zoubir (ed.), *North Africa in Transition: State, Society, and Economic Transformation in the 1990s*, pp. 130, 13.
[97] Euro-Mediterranean Human Rights Network, 'Freedom of Association', p. 84.
[98] The association could not begin to operate before the three-month period or before the publication of notice (of organisational establishment) in the JORT.
[99] Euro-Mediterranean Human Rights Network, 'Freedom of Association', p. 84.
[100] B. Hibou, *The Force of Obedience: The Political Economy of Repression in Tunisia* (Cambridge: Polity Press, 2011), p. 101.

(LTDH) from September 2005 without permission from the courts.[101] In effect, Moncef Ouannes argues that during this period the North Africa regimes, including under Bourguiba and Ben Ali in Tunisia, were never far from their ultimate distrust with regard to the public space.[102]

The implementation of neoliberal economic reform in Tunisia necessitated a high degree of political legitimacy on behalf of the Ben Ali regime. In order to secure and maintain this legitimacy, liberalising reforms were adopted to provide the national and international impression that genuine democratic pluralism was underway. To the contrary, authoritarianism was being further embedded through a combination of sustained oppression of perceived opposition and networks of neopatrimonial relationships, effectively allowing the regime to stifle public spaces for political and collective activism. Raymond Hinnebusch writes that Tunisia 'combined the most educated and socially mobilised population ... with the least open political system, where the Islamists and secular opposition were thoroughly excluded from the political arena, the press least free, and non-governmental organisations (NGOs) most controlled'.[103]

The Deployment of Surveillance and the Suppression of Civil Society

Between 1990 and 1992 the government is reported to have 'hauled in' and arrested more than 8,000 individuals following growing state crackdowns on perceived opposition.[104] Alexander explains, 'Most Tunisians tolerated the government's repression. As the press never ceased to remind them, a vigorous economy that could generate new jobs depended on Tunisia's ability to attract foreign investment.'[105] Strategies of infiltration and duplication were increasingly applied by

---

[101] Euro-Mediterranean Human Rights Network, 'Freedom of Association', pp. 84–85.
[102] M. Ouannes, *Le Phénomène Associatif au Maghreb* (Tunis: Les Editions Altier International, 1997), p. 28.
[103] Hinnebusch, 'Change and Continuity after the Arab Uprising', p. 23.
[104] S. Waltz, *Human Rights and Reform: Changing the Face of North African Politics* (Berkeley: University of California Press, 1995), p. 72, cited in C. Alexander, 'Back from the Democratic Brink: Authoritarianism and Civil Society in Tunisia', *Middle East Report*, no. 205 (October–December 1997), p. 35.
[105] Alexander, 'Back from the Democratic Brink', p. 35.

the government to further control or undermine civil society actors and groups that were kept under permanent surveillance. Laila Alhamad argues that a 'repertoire of tactics' was perfected to 'tie the hands of these organisations and prevent them from posing any important threat to the state'.[106] In Tunisia, force or coercion was mobilised when an autonomous organisation became a threat, for example through the direct manipulation of the organisation's elections or policy direction, or via the practice of government officials attending the organisation's general assemblies. Bellin notes, 'Consequently, the autonomy of associations in Tunisia is made strictly conditional upon their dedication to serving the "national interest", with the "national interest" defined by the regime itself.'[107] The civil society organisations perceived as threatening were also regularly subjected to harassment by the security apparatus, the judiciary and government officials.[108] Measures to silence opposition once again took on increasingly severe forms as mechanisms for repression became further embedded in the power of the state and shadow state. Beatrice Hibou quantifies the ubiquity of not only the police security apparatus but also the omnipresence of the significant number of RCD party members and cells across Tunisia during the Ben Ali regime in an effort to demonstrate the regime's efforts to deepen social control. She argues that after the police, the RCD cells were the most systematic means of surveillance – citing 7,500 local cells and 2,200 professional cells with more than 2 million members for Tunisia's 10 million inhabitants.[109] She states that many civil society associations effectively facilitated the government's ability to 'keep the country under surveillance' because they were heavily influenced by the RCD.[110] She contends, 'Matters are more complex when it comes to the very dense network of thousands of small associations of which hardly anything is known and whose creation was suggested or fostered by political circumstances ... The RCD has played a fundamental role in their creation or the way they have been subjected to surveillance.'[111]

Hibou also depicts a political economy of domination in Tunisia 'that mainly operates by means of the insertion of disciplinary and

---

[106] L. Alhamad, 'Formal and Informal Venues of Engagement' in Lust-Okar and Zerhouni (eds.), *Political Participation in the Middle East*, p. 38.
[107] Bellin, 'Civil Society in Formation: Tunisia', pp. 140–141.
[108] Euro-Mediterranean Human Rights Network, 'Freedom of Association', p. 83.
[109] Hibou, *The Force of Obedience*, p. 87.   [110] Ibid., p. 93.   [111] Ibid., p. 95.

coercive techniques of power into the most everyday economic and social structures and practices'.[112] The regime routinely practiced surveillance and phone tapping, threats against family members, passport confiscation and violence that included targeted assassinations.[113] Daily life in Tunisia was soon characterised by the populace's reluctant tolerance of a 'constant and intrusive police presence'.[114] For example, the number of police reported under the Ben Ali regime was between 80,000 and 133,000 for approximately 10 million inhabitants. In Tunisia the ratio of police to citizens at the higher end was 1:112 whereas in France during a similar period (considered the most heavily policed state in Europe) the corresponding ratio was 1:265.[115] Of the descriptions of techniques of intimidation and manipulation applied by the regime, Hibou manages to capture the repression inflicted upon associations at any given time:

> Officially or not, they can prevent or interrupt meetings, follow and harass militants, encircle meeting places, force their way into premises, attack militants physically, call the relevant people in for questioning in police stations or at the Ministry of the Interior, organise tendentious and defamatory campaigns in the press, launch prosecutions and institute proceedings, and organise break-ins into professional and private offices.[116]

The more extreme examples of government distrust and repression of civil society organisations in Tunisia were, for example, applied against the UGTT – its leadership structure was eventually penetrated and taken over by the government[117] – and against the LTDH, for which the 1992 law of association was amended in order to circumvent its perceived oppositional role.[118] However, from the moment of their initial establishment, many organisations experienced disparate forms and levels of harassment, intimidation and infiltration.

---

[112] Ibid., p. xiv.   [113] Alexander, 'Back from the Democratic Brink', p. 36.
[114] Hibou, *The Force of Obedience*, p. 81.   [115] Ibid.   [116] Ibid., p. 98.
[117] Under Ben Ali, the president appointed UGTT's secretary-general and often directly appointed members of the executive committee. See Cavallo, 'Trade Unions in Tunisia', pp. 239–266.
[118] The April 1992 law, allowing for greater political supervision, specifies that an association 'cannot refuse membership to any person who is committed in his principles and his decisions'. Hibou, *The Force of Obedience*, pp. 98–99. See also Euro-Mediterranean Human Rights Network, 'Freedom of Association', pp. 84–85 and Waltz, 'The Politics of Human Rights in the Maghreb', pp. 75–92.

The experience of Naila, a woman who worked within the main headquarters of a women's rights organisation that operated during both the Bourguiba and Ben Ali regimes, also underscored the ability of the surveillance apparatus to infiltrate the micro-level. She described the incredible propensity among the population for 'auto-censure' and how potent this was on the minds of the women they tried to work with. Naila stressed how the Ben Ali regime managed to penetrate the mind of the individual and that these techniques were remarkably effective. 'Ben Ali était partout et dans les têtes des gens.' ('Ben Ali was everywhere and in the minds of the people.')[119] George Joffe contends that although the state was able to maintain ultimate control over 'this partially liberalised social space', autonomous groups and organisations that were not directly controlled by the state were able to emerge. These organisations addressed primarily social concerns and at times took on more political activities.[120]

Moreover, political participation exists in every political system regardless of regime type.[121] This participation can take the form of informal or formal organisations engaging in human rights, advocacy or social welfare support. Individuals often explicitly acknowledge the risks involved in engaging in a civil society organisation, in particular if the regime is authoritarian and the nature of their work is perceived as 'political'. However, an indeterminate component deep within the inner resolve of the individual also accepts these risks in exchange for the ability to engage in autonomous social action. Alhamad stipulates, 'When the state, through its formal institutions, represses, excludes, or fails to listen or respond to people's needs, people resort to the informal realm.'[122] The next section demonstrates that even for legalised and formal civil society organisations, by accepting and internalising these risks, some groups and actors were able to choose from an amalgamation of tactics to advance their sociopolitical agendas.

---

[119] Interview in Tunis (42), 16 March 2012.
[120] Joffe, 'The Arab Spring in North Africa', p. 514.
[121] H. Albrecht, 'The Nature of Political Participation' in Lust-Okar and Zerhouni (eds.), *Political Participation in the Middle East*, p. 15.
[122] Citing E. Lust-Okar, 'Taking Political Participation Seriously' in Lust-Okar and Zerhouni (eds.), *Political Participation in the Middle East*, p. 8.

Manipulating the Rules of the Game: Moving through an Authoritarian Regime

Discourses on civil society often attempt to differentiate conceptually and empirically between the state and society, the formal and informal realms and between what is political and apolitical. In fact, by looking specifically to civil society in Tunisia prior to the 2010–2011 uprising, it is possible to observe that many of these actors habitually drifted through and among these different domains via regular interaction with state and non-state entities. Furthermore, civil society actors also simultaneously engaged in activities that were formal (i.e., accepted under the eyes of the regime) and informal interventions, such as those that had to be kept under the radar to reach more vulnerable groups. Moreover, it can be argued that by choosing to work with marginalised communities and engaging in a formal or legalised civil society organisation, these actors inherently chose to act on political ground and were, in effect, political actors.

Here I explore two sets of organisations: the rights-based organisations such as women's rights and the broader human rights organisations that operated during the Ben Ali regime and the HIV/AIDS-related organisations engaging in both service provision and advocacy that were established soon after Ben Ali took office in 1987. In exploring these two sets of organisations I highlight the different strategies these sets of actors and organisations utilised to manoeuvre tactically under an authoritarian regime. This includes a range of strategies including negotiation, discretion, invisibility, hyper-visibility and targeted advocacy to signal and address key issues for these actors. It is important to emphasise that these organisations encountered disparate experiences with the Ben Ali government – some were intensely repressed and ostracised while others, comfortably ignored by the state, faced their main challenges at the sociocultural level rather than from the heaviness of the state security apparatus.

Rights-Based Organisations: Confronting a Dictator

There were only a handful of organisations that worked overtly in rights-based programming in Tunisia during the Ben Ali regime. These organisations deliberately chose to operate despite heavy crackdowns by the security apparatus. They included (but were not limited to) the

Tunisian Association of Democratic Women (ATFD), the Tunisian League of Human Rights (LTDH) and Amnesty International. Much has been written on these organisations in the sociopolitical literature on Tunisia, so here the purpose is to reiterate the degree of repression these groups experienced and to determine how they manoeuvred through an authoritarian regime. I interviewed a number of individuals working specifically with human rights organisations during the Ben Ali presidency as well as individuals who explicitly chose not to establish an association during this period. For example, Najeeb, an individual who worked with a bilateral development agency in Tunis, stated that before the revolution in 2010–2011 he had always been involved in volunteer activities but had consistently refused to work with others under the umbrella of a civil society organisation. He admitted that he was discouraged by the organisations that formed under the RCD party, which he said 'controlled these associations to such a degree that they became extensions of the party itself'.[123] Najeeb explained:

Very few associations were able to resist this control and those which did resist (ATFD and LTDH) suffered ... They were able to resist in the long run but their work was rendered very difficult. The space for associative action was very constrained and the government even had the habit of imposing members onto the association, obliging the association on political occasions to sign something showing publicly their support of the government. And financially these resources were very controlled and virtually non-existent ... you were either with the system or against it.[124]

The Tunisian Association of Democratic Women (ATFD), for example, began as an informal club to promote female autonomy where women came together each Saturday to speak about issues related to women through the creation of a space for reflection and discussion. As the meetings grew (to more than 80 women attending each week), the principal founders of the club began to consider a strategy to allow women to participate more fully in public life. Naila, a member of the association, observed that at the time there were two discourses – the 'formal feminine discourse', which was the feminist discourse under Bourguiba on the CPS, and the 'informal feminine discourse', which was much larger and even called into question the

---

[123] Interview in Tunis (38), 6 March 2012 and March 2013.   [124] Ibid.

CPS. Naila remarked, 'We called everything into question and most importantly this question of power ... From the beginning the role and the rights of women and the issue of democracy were always intrinsically linked – how can you effectively have a democracy without half the population?'[125] Soon after Ben Ali came to power in 1987, the '7th November Declaration' did not refer to women specifically, so ATFD produced its own declaration on the issue. This also coincided with ATFD's first visible activities on solidarity with Palestine after the Israeli attack on the Palestinian Liberation Organisation (PLO) base in Lebanon in 1987. Naila noted, 'We were working internationally on issues of liberation and solidarity with the women engaged on this.'[126] It was after these decisions and efforts to increase their own visibility that the group of women decided to formalise their association in 1989.

After acquiring legal associational status, the organisation worked increasingly on issues central to women (rights, education and health) through national, regional and international entities. However, the organisation chose to openly challenge and confront the government in 1992 following the growing attacks by the Ben Ali regime against the LTDH – in response to which, as aforementioned, the laws of association were explicitly amended in order to infiltrate the group's membership. One of the roles of ATFD soon became the larger defence of associations and civil society in Tunisia under Ben Ali. Naila remarked further, 'We took on the issues of civil society at the time and this was not easy as even internally this was a huge debate in terms of how political our association would be.'[127]

ATFD soon experienced the gamut of surveillance and intimidation mechanisms applied by the government. Branches of ATFD opening outside of Tunis stopped their work as staff members were harassed and intimidated by the police. Naila stated, 'Everything was done on their part (the government) to discourage and they managed to do this at a very "personal level" even at the level of the family.'[128] I asked Naila how the association eventually was able to operate during the Ben Ali regime and how she and her colleagues managed to work more than two decades in Tunisia in such a restrictive environment. She remarked:

[125] Interview in Tunis (42), 16 March 2012. [126] Ibid. [127] Ibid.
[128] Ibid.

When we have solidarity and are unified and clear on our aims (internally) we can make these gains. It is because of our strong unification internally that we were able to do this with strong organisational leadership. We showed that the rights of women are also political – the private sphere is indeed public ... It is our association's perseverance on these issues that has allowed us to work more than 20 years under a dictator ... Everything we did was legal and we survived by sticking to what is legal.[129]

The experience of Wail, who worked with a smaller human rights organisation (and who eventually went on to work with a larger international human rights organisation in Tunis) before 2011, also highlighted the Ben Ali regime's predisposition towards the repression of civil society organisations working in human rights related initiatives. Wail explained that he was imprisoned in 2009 for acts he considered apolitical, involving more than 150 recordings and the documentation of human rights abuses committed by the regime.[130] The documentary he orchestrated featured poor living conditions in Nabeul (a small town approximately 60 km (40 miles) from Tunis) with exceptionally high pollution levels, a situation pointing to failures in the regime's urban development projects; he was imprisoned for four months. Wail contended that the associations working in human rights always had problems and remained in conflict with the state. Many of these associations were assumed to have other political agendas as 'l'opposition politique dans les habits des droits de l'homme' ('political opposition dressed in the clothing of human rights'). He noted, 'All of the civil society organisations were held in suspicion for this reason.'[131]

ATFD and other actors engaging in human rights advocacy openly challenged the government but also had a strong constituency base as well as a support structure of regional and international networks they could work through. These organisations alternated between strategies of visibility and hyper-visibility, corresponding to perceived openings such as the Israel–Palestine conflict and the attack on LTDH. In effect, these organisations understood early on the 'rules of the game' enforced by the regime but also pushed these boundaries when they were cognisant they were working within a larger support structure, either in solidarity with other national associations or with regional and international advocacy bodies. Rather than strategies of

---

[129] Ibid. [130] Interview in Tunis (41), 13 March 2012. [131] Ibid.

negotiation or discretion, these actors at times operated on the side of hyper-visibility, openly challenging the government to respond.

The Materialisation of the HIV/AIDS Organisations

Prior to 2011, there were a handful of organisations working throughout Tunisia with people living with and affected by HIV/AIDS.[132] This work began officially in 1987 when the National AIDS Programme (NAP) was created and a few small bio-behavioural studies were conducted.[133] The Ben Ali government and the Ministry of Health routinely reported (nationally and internationally) that the country was experiencing 'low epidemics' among key populations at higher risk of HIV exposure, with HIV prevalence only 'approaching' a concentrated epidemic among some groups.[134] This was against mounting evidence that Tunisia's key populations were in fact experiencing concentrated epidemics in some areas at or above 5 per cent.[135] Despite lack of official acknowledgement of the actual scale of the HIV/AIDS epidemic in the country, the HIV/AIDS organisations were able to carry out prevention and education work mainly targeted to the general population. From 1985 to December 2011, there were 1,706 officially registered cases of HIV in both adults and children in Tunisia. Of the 1,706 registered cases, 982 individuals acquired AIDS, and 540 died during that period.[136] Although HIV prevalence was less than 0.1 per cent of the population in Tunisia, there were concentrated epidemics among Tunisia's key populations. For

---

[132] Interviews: 5, 11, 16–26, 28, 30, 31, 32, 36, 39, 45, 46, 48, 52 and 54–57.
[133] Le Programme National de Lutte Contre le Sida et les Maladies Sexuellement Transmissibles, UNAIDS. 'Rapport d'Activité sur La Riposte au SIDA – Tunisie', *UNGASS Report*, République Tunisienne Ministre de la Santé Publique, Programme Nationale de Lutte Contre le SIDA et les MST, March 2012, p. 8.
[134] The terms 'key populations' or 'key populations at higher risk of HIV exposure' refer to those most likely to be exposed to HIV or to transmit HIV. In all countries, key populations include people living with HIV. In most settings, men who have sex with men, transgender persons, people who inject drugs, sex workers and their clients and seronegative partners in serodiscordant couples are at higher risk of exposure to HIV than other people. See: UNAIDS, 'Terminology Guidelines', October 2011, p. 18.
[135] J. Bastin, 'La Révolution Militante', *Transversal*, no. 58 (May–June 2011), p. 11.
[136] Le Programme National de Lutte Contre le Sida, p. 38.

example, bio-behavioural surveys conducted in 2009 and again in 2011 indicated 0.43 and 0.61 per cent prevalence, respectively, in sex workers, 3.1 and 2.4 per cent in people who inject drugs and 4.9 and 13 per cent among men who have sex with men (MSM).[137]

From the mid-1990s there emerged three 'HIV-thematic'[138] organisations working specifically in the domain of HIV/AIDS with a formal 'associational visa' to do this work. They were L'Association Tunisienne de Lutte Contre les Maladies Sexuellement Transmissible et le SIDA (ATL MST/SIDA), created in 1990; L'Association Tunisienne d'Information et d'Orientation sur le SIDA (ATIOS), established in 1993; and L'Association Tunisienne de la Prévention de la Toxicomanie (ATUPRET), launched in 1995. The three organisations were initially established under the associational category of 'scientific' (and so linked to the Ministry of Health) and led by medical doctors. At the time the organisations were established, there was a weak tradition of local and private sector funding in Tunisia, and while the government gave some financial support in the form of unrestricted grants, the funding for this work was minimal. During this period there was also considerable scrutiny of international donors and contributions to NGOs; all funding had to be directly channelled through the government before dispersal to the association.

There were increasing instances during this period of intentional co-opting of organisations by the government, infiltration of the association by government staff posing as volunteers and significant levels of harassment by the government and corruption. However, the HIV-thematic organisations were allowed to continue with their work virtually uninterrupted during the Ben Ali regime within Tunis and throughout various sections across Tunisia (Sfax, Nabeul, Sousse, etc.). This was due in part to the technocratic staff within the Ministry of Health and the National AIDS Programme, who saw the need for this work, and because this work was perceived as apolitical and so therefore was understood to pose a minimal threat to the government. Most of the work of the three organisations fell under the rubric of 'prevention and public health', as this was the only *porte d'entrée* to be

---

[137] Ibid., p. 8.
[138] 'HIV-thematic' refers to those organisations whose exclusive remit is to work in HIV/AIDS as opposed to some organisations such as the Red Cross or National Scouts that engage in a range of activities, with intermittent HIV/AIDS awareness-raising interventions.

able to work legally in HIV/AIDS in Tunisia. So in effect, the state sought to control and thereby limit sanctioned elements of the HIV/AIDS interventions but also relied on these organisations to reach communities with key populations at risk of acquiring HIV.

In 2006, the three organisations extended their scope beyond awareness – raising campaigns among the general population to work with more marginalised groups known as 'key populations', specifically men who have sex with men, sex workers and people who inject drugs. This adaptation in the organisations' programmatic target groups also corresponded simultaneously with the receipt of a sizeable grant (more than US$17 million) from the multilateral health organisation the Global Fund to Fight AIDS, Tuberculosis and Malaria (an initiative proposed by the former UN Secretary General Kofi Annan at the African Leaders Summit in 2001 and created shortly thereafter) to further engage in interventions with key populations and sexual minorities in 2007.[139] It is within this work in particular that the organisations began to adopt more covert strategies in their outreach work and where there was a distinct evolution in the strategies for reaching these groups, from negotiation and coordination to discretion. Nevertheless, it is also in part as a result of this new and sizeable funding that the organisations began to interact more regularly with state entities. Kareem, a former staff member and consultant for ATL, explained that the additional resources from the international financing institution permitted the organisations to maintain offices, acquire vehicles and pay salaries to their staff and in general brought a degree of 'professionalism' to these organisations. At this stage he explained that the government was always engaged with a certain level of goodwill towards the work they were doing. He said, 'The Ministry of Health and even the military were engaged and respected the work of the associations at this time.'[140]

The government sanctioned this work, albeit within limits – as it did not fund the work directly it could avoid perceptions that it was explicitly endorsing this work. Kareem noted further, 'There were never any blockages in trying to do this work, and the government was always aware of what we were doing. There was always a certain

---

[139] For more information and grant agreement details see: http://portfolio.theglobalfund.org/en/Grant/Index/TUN-607-G01-H.
[140] Interview in Tunis (28), 1 February 2012.

laisser allez by the government in terms of their approach to these associations, but the associations worked with discretion.'[141] The experience of Walid, a human rights lawyer working in HIV/AIDS, also highlighted that the scientific and health nature of HIV/AIDS allowed the actual work of the organisations to proceed without much scrutiny by the state. According to Walid:

> ATL had a lot of courage as they were doing this work under the umbrella of HIV and the fight against AIDS. The government was naturally aware of the work they were doing but was okay with this work because it was not open and more importantly it was not the state institutions which financed this work. We were always working with the angle of HIV so this did not catch their attention.[142]

These civil society organisations implicitly adopted a strategy of discretion bordering on invisibility in their peer education and outreach work as well as in the distribution of condoms and clean syringes to populations at risk of HIV/AIDS exposure. For example, in 2010, among the 188 sex workers working in *maisons closes* in Tunis, Sousse and Gabes, approximately 99 per cent had at least one marker of a sexually transmitted infection (STI), with a current infection found in 86.7 per cent of cases.[143] This signified not only that this was an incredibly high-risk group for acquiring HIV/AIDS but also the extent to which the greater population, in particular the clients of sex workers and their families, were at risk for spreading STIs and HIV. Two HIV/AIDS organisations worked with the women inside the *maisons closes* with the permission of the Tunisian government to provide free STI examinations and condoms; moreover, tests for HIV were administered intermittently when funding permitted. In addition to sex work that was legally sanctioned, staff members from the different HIV/AIDS organisations reported that Tunisia was also home to a number of women who engaged in clandestine sex work. Prior to the 2010–2011 uprising, it was reported that clandestine sex workers were often paid more money and had more flexibility in choosing their clients and when they engaged in sex. However, they were also more

---

[141] Ibid. [142] Interview in Tunis (36), 16 February 2012.
[143] A. Znazen, O. Frikha-Gargouri, L. Berrajah et al., 'Sexually Transmitted Infections among Female Sex Workers in Tunisia: High Prevalence of Chlamydia Trachomatis', *Sex Transm Infect*, vol. 86, no. 7 (2010), pp. 500–505.

exposed to physical violence as there was no *matronne* overseeing the exchange. The experience of Moazzam, whose remit was to engage in peer education with clandestine sex workers, underscored the vital strategy of negotiation to reach the different women. He explained that he worked through counterparts in the community who would introduce him to different women who might be open to doing peer education work. He became well recognised by the women as someone who accompanied them to different centres for treatment or testing. He met the women in cafes and explained he himself had never felt a sense of personal risk in doing this work with the women but that often the women themselves were targeted by the police and arrested.[144] It is important to note that there were very few, if any, reportable statistics on clandestine sex work in Tunisia so it was not possible during the research for this book to determine just how widespread this issue was. Nevertheless, for the organisations that worked with sex workers, either within the *maisons closes* or with clandestine sex workers in different communities, whilst the state was aware of this work, they were obliged to adopt tactics of discretion, invisibility and where necessary, negotiation.[145]

Another example concerns the experiences of the HIV/AIDS organisations that chose to work with injecting drug user populations. Bio-behavioural HIV surveillance studies conducted among populations at higher risk of acquiring HIV in 2009 and 2011 indicated HIV prevalence among individuals who injected drugs of 3.1 and 2.4 per cent, respectively.[146] During the Ben Ali regime, the trafficking of drugs was reported to have increased, and eventually injecting drug use became a significant issue in and outside of the main capital in Tunis. The main drugs were Subutex (a drug typically used for opioid addiction) and Temgesic (pain tablets), followed by heroin and cocaine.[147] From the year 2000, the civil society organisations in neighbouring Morocco began to increase work with people who inject drugs. Not long after,

---

[144] Interview in Tunis (23), 24 January 2012.
[145] While Tunisia has also been associated with sex tourism among men and male sex workers, the organisations interviewed did not cite working with male sex workers or this phenomenon in Tunisia.
[146] Minister of Public Health and the National Programme to Fight HIV and STIs, 'National Strategic Plan to Respond to HIV and STIs in Tunisia 2012–2016' (Tunis, 2012), p. 10.
[147] Ibid., p. 22.

Morocco became the first country in the Middle East and North Africa to introduce 'harm reduction' programmes, including methadone maintenance therapy and needle-syringe programmes.[148] The HIV/AIDS associations that worked in Tunisia at the time participated in a series of workshops and conferences on the issue of harm reduction in North Africa, and in 2009 began advocacy work targeted to the government to introduce similar programmes to those being implemented in Morocco.[149] Drug use outside the capital, however, began to increase and eventually in 2007 the association ATUPRET received a grant from the Global Fund along with land from the Ministry of Agriculture to open Tunisia's first in-patient drug rehabilitation centre in the town of Sfax (it remains the only centre of its kind in the country). Since its opening in 2007, the centre hosted more than a thousand individuals who were addicted to drugs (many of whom were injecting drug users).[150] ATUPRET continued to work with drug users on the street through outreach work and HIV/AIDS-prevention messaging; however, because drug use was illegal in Tunisia, some of the outreach workers were arrested and threatened by the police. The experience of Fajr, a former staff member who conducted outreach work with people who inject drugs in Tunis, also underscored the challenges outreach workers that worked with key populations encountered. She remarked:

They (outreach workers) were distributing clean syringes and condoms with the approval of the government, but this does not necessarily mean the police knew about this or were well informed ... the peer educators were confronted with this risk and were all along encouraged to do this work as discreetly as possible. We were doing something that was supported by the law and the government, but the police would challenge this, especially with condoms.[151]

---

[148] See: UNAIDS, 'Morocco Launches New National AIDS Strategy', 4 April 2012.

[149] 'Harm reduction' is used to describe a range of interventions designed to decrease vulnerability of acquiring infection among people who inject drugs. Interventions include the provision of clean needles and syringes, condom distribution, substitution drug therapy, HIV/AIDS testing and STI diagnosis and treatment in affected communities. For additional information see: World Health Organization (Europe), 'Status Paper on Prisons, Drugs and Harm Reduction', May 2005.

[150] Interview in Sfax (31), 9 February 2012.

[151] Interview in Tunis (32), 10 February 2012.

In addition, the Ministry of the Interior considered drug abuse a 'security' problem at the time. Therefore, working in prevention and treatment with people who use drugs was deemed intrinsically a problematic issue for the police. Dr Malik, who was the executive director of one of the HIV/AIDS associations in Tunisia, explained, 'So it was decided ATUPRET would do work in prevention only, and this was in fact the only way they could secure their associational visa at the time, and so as not to upset the minister.'[152] As a result of their decision to work with key populations at higher risk for acquiring HIV, the HIV/AIDS organisations eventually also had to adopt a strategy of communicating more with the local police in Sfax and Tunis to be able to conduct their work. Consequently, in order to reach drug users, they had to simultaneously move the core distribution of clean syringes into the drug rehabilitation centre and away from the streets (in Sfax) – off the radar almost entirely. Finally, Dr Tawfiq, who worked as a medical professional for ATUPRET, highlighted further the disregard by the government of increasing intravenous drug use at the national level. He explained, 'There has been in general significant denial at the national and political level of drug abuse in Tunisia up until now, with politicians saying there is no drug use in Tunisia.'[153] Before 2011, he reported there had not been a national government strategy to address drug use in Tunisia. Several of the HIV-specific research organisations confirmed that to work with key populations, the associations were in fact obligated to go through the issue of HIV to receive funding and government consent.

For the three organisations there were two primary challenges. The first was the legal environment in which they operated – the majority of behaviours of key populations were legally penalised through existing national penal codes, such as bans on same-sex behaviour and sex work. Nasser, who worked with men who have sex with men, highlighted the restrictive legal context in which the HIV/AIDS organisations worked. He explained that, consequently, vulnerable groups simply want to know, 'If I am put in jail, what can you do for me?'[154] The second greatest challenge was the sociocultural environment or 'la réalité du terrain'. During this period there were high

---

[152] Interview in Tunis (18), 13 January 2012 and 5 March 2013.
[153] Interview in Sfax (31), 9 February 2012.
[154] Interview in Tunis (25), 27 January 2012 and 14 March 2013.

degrees of stigma by communities against people who were vulnerable to acquiring HIV/AIDS, and this stigma could have the effect of hindering the progression of the work, either through inflammatory articles in the press or from discrimination among community caregivers. Organisations knew they would have to take their work forward in a more underground and informal manner to advance at either of these levels. Strategies of caution became vital to the work of the organisations at this time. Nasser stated:

> We are successful in doing our work in part because we are courageous and in part because of our discretion ... We know that there are risks, but we also want to live as equal citizens in Tunisia; this is primordial for me. We are conscious of these risks but we have to go far and advance. We have the will to go above and beyond these risks. However, I also realise that I do not want to put others in danger. We try to measure these risks and take precautions.[155]

The individuals working in this domain were open to varying degrees about difficult experiences they or their colleagues encountered at the political and sociocultural level in Tunisia as employees of the HIV/AIDS associations or as individuals engaging in policy and advocacy in this domain during the Ben Ali regime.[156] They highlighted the risk of conducting this work but also described the multiplicity of strategies they used to be able to manoeuvre through what was often perceived to be uncertain terrain.

Conclusion

The overall vigour with which the Bourguiba regime implemented economic and social reforms effectively allowed the project of national construction to supersede opportunities for political pluralism and liberalism. Over time, the legitimacy of the Bourguiba regime became increasingly tied to economic stability and success. Growing authoritarian and repressive measures for state social control soon came to overshadow possibilities for genuine democratic pluralism in Tunisia and inevitably influenced the nature of Tunisian society that would develop from this period. However, under Ben Ali, from 1987 to 2010 more than 9,000 civil society organisations were established through

---

[155] Ibid. [156] Interviews 18–26, 30, 31, 32, 36, 45, 48 and 57.

Conclusion

the 1959 laws of association modified under his regime, allowing a range of human rights and organisations working with marginalised groups to be created. Tunisia's laws of association were regularly amended, expanded and contracted to correspond to the degree to which the regime sensed potential opposition as well as to create the impression of legitimacy, nationally and internationally. This was as opposed to attempts to genuinely create spaces for civil society to play a consequential role in the way Tunisia was governed. Actors looking to engage in civil society organisations often knowingly accepted certain risks to engage in even benign activities, including the risk of harassment, intimidation and repression. The eventual cumbersome laws of association, practices of co-optation and infiltration and the frequent obligation to declare one's allegiance to the RCD party not only aimed to instrumentalise these actors and groups but also discouraged many individuals from engaging in collective activism. More importantly, a body of individuals, namely the Islamists, were denied the opportunity to be active in public spaces at any level. These authoritarian and exclusionary practices of some segments of the population eventually left their residue upon Tunisian society. Moreover, over time these practices restricted many civil society organisations to the role demarcated for them within neoliberal policy – as providers of social welfare services.

The civil society organisations that chose to formally legalise their work had to outwardly accept and abide by the 'rules of the game' set by the regime. The organisations that engaged in women's rights and broader human rights took greater risks than the groups working in HIV/AIDS as their work was often more visible, but more importantly, the issue of human rights represented a significantly contentious issue at the political level. However, these organisations also had arguably more support from national, regional and international bodies. The rights-based organisations were also strategic in linking their activities and advocacy to other broader issues such as solidarity with Palestine and the greater defence of human rights in the region. Despite the often brutal encounters with the regime, these external links offered the organisations a degree of protection, but more importantly, a principal means to subvert state control. For the HIV/AIDS organisations that later sought to support and work with key populations at higher risk of acquiring HIV, the challenge was not necessarily the overt, brunt force of the government or security apparatus. Instead, the greatest barrier was often the local police and communities through which outreach workers, researchers and medical staff needed to manoeuvre to reach clandestine and illegal communities.

The symbolic and physical public spaces for civil society actors became increasingly constrained throughout the five decades following independence, a period during which both an intolerance for political opposition, against both religious and secular movements, and a predilection for the implementation of 'modernising' reforms nearly transformed civil society into a homogenous entity of secular-liberal actors. Here and throughout the remainder of the book, I underscore how the manner in which both the Bourguiba and the Ben Ali regimes manipulated spaces for civil society to manoeuvre has left its durable residue on these actors today. Nevertheless, the Bourguiba and Ben Ali regimes unwittingly provided the conditions for independent social action to arise through the simultaneous adoption and implementation of liberalisation measures and the repression of emerging counter-publics. What materialised following the Tunisia uprising in 2010 was a virtual breathing space and unrelenting momentum to participate in Tunisia's public spaces, or what many referred to as the rebirth of *muwatana* or *citoyenneté*, following the revolution.

4 Civil Society and the Opening Up of the Public Space

Before Ben Ali, people were not free to do this (establish an association) for fear of engaging directly or indirectly in the political system with the regime; but now this spirit of 'electorism' is resurfacing and in a way, the creation of all these associations is a symbol of resisting a dictatorship.
— Director, United Nations human rights organisation, Tunis[1]

This space was wide open – there were no police, no government, the political groups were not structured, anything was possible.
— Journalist, TunisiaLive.Net[2]

The downfall of a dictator following almost three decades of authoritarian rule in Tunisia opened a space. In the months that followed the departure of the Ben Ali regime, this space swelled, harnessing a multitude of visions and priorities for post-revolution Tunisia. From the moments of national solidarity of having brought down a dictator to the redefining of national priorities, numerous battles unfolded in Tunisia's public spaces, unmasking the complex and unstable nature of democratisation. During this period one witnesses the moments of the 'popular upsurge' in which thousands occupied the historic public spaces of Tunis such as in front of the Ministry of the Interior along Avenue Bourguiba, the almost instantaneous measures for political liberalisation put into effect under the transition governments and finally the 'resurrection of civil society' described in the literature on transitions from authoritarian rule. However, what are often absent from this literature are accounts of the conflicts and contestations taking place among these actors and groups manoeuvring within these different spaces. Following the Tunisia uprising, numerous

---

[1] Interview in Tunis (34), 15 February 2012.
[2] Interview in Tunis (27), 30 January 2012.

sociopolitical conflicts manifested alongside the unattainable expectations among many for a higher or different standard of democracy.

From 2011 to 2013, the landscape for civil society actors in Tunisia expanded with the establishment of several thousand new and legally registered civil society organisations. Following the deregulation of the former laws of association, initially promulgated under Bourguiba and later amended by Ben Ali, civil society organisations were able to work more openly in a wider range of activities, including civic activism, human rights, social welfare initiatives and direct outreach work with deprived communities across the country. From January to October 2011 it is estimated that 1,700 new organisations were created, with a further 600 civil society organisations registering between October 2011 and March 2012.[3] The new organisations were also acting alongside the more than 9,000 civil society organisations established during the Bourguiba and Ben Ali regimes, termed soon after the revolution the 'historic' associations. As Tunisia moved to initiate political liberalisation measures following the departure of Ben Ali in January 2011, the symbolic and physical public spaces for a multitude of actors and groups critically widened.

One also began to observe a powerful sense of *muwatana* or *citoyenneté* emerging not only among the various civil society groups but also among the broader population following the uprising. As the numerous civil society actors moved to the forefront, spaces for political liberalisation opened with fresh avenues for civic participation. The organisations and the actors that inhabited these expanding spaces interacted with each other through a web of relations and confrontations. It is not surprising that every opening also brought competing agendas and visions for who exactly should fill the public space and what nature this changing domain should take. Through an examination of the effects of the opening up of the public space during the two years following the downfall of an authoritarian regime, it is possible to locate the different conflicts that emerge among civil society groups. In addition to locating the specific areas of these conflicts during what is often characterised as a tumultuous period of the transition, the actual consequences of these contestations become more apparent. This chapter examines the first core theme of the book, namely the 'illiberal' effects of the opening of the public space(s).

---

[3] Union Européenne, 'Rapport de Diagnostic', p. 5.

It looks specifically to the moments when this space opened in Tunisia as well as to the actors who were included and excluded as a result of the expansion of this space. The initial opening of the public space offers the opportunity to explore the overall function of conflict within civil society. This is with a view to understanding the broader consequences of these contestations during a transition from authoritarian rule. As such, this chapter depicts the 'resurrection of civil society' in Tunisia when thousands of new organisations were legally allowed to register through the newly expanded laws of association. And in so doing, it also considers whether civil society reflected the self-determination and self-management agendas present in the social movements of the 1980s or in the neoliberal understandings of good governance in donor-led development discourses.

Political Liberalisation and the Expansion of Space

With the disappearance of fear, Tunisians who previously would have characterised themselves as politically apathetic would express their newfound interest and thirst for news, information and political engagement. Sami Zemni, tracing the moments following the departure of Ben Ali, contends that from January 2011 political developments were largely shaped by tensions between the desire for 'institutional continuity' by the legal government and the 'revolutionary legitimacy of the popular mass mobilisations'.[4] In what Zemni describes as a moment of 'extraordinary politics', Tunisia entered into the 're-constitutive phase of the political'.[5] This process started with the creation of the 'Front of January 14th', involving already existing and newer political parties, young people who participated in the revolution and civil society actors. The Front articulated the demand for elections in order to form a constituent assembly within the year and argued for the suspension of political parties linked to the Ben Ali regime.[6] By 4 March, the Tunisian Constitution was suspended and later that same month Tunisia officially recognised 45 political parties, in

---

[4] Zemni, 'The Extraordinary Politics of the Tunisian Revolution', p. 4.
[5] The High Authority was created through the fusion of two institutions established immediately after the revolution, the Committee for Political Reform and the National Council for the Protection of the Revolution (CNPR). See Zemni, 'The Extraordinary Politics of the Tunisian Revolution', pp. 2, 6.
[6] Zemni, 'The Extraordinary Politics of the Tunisian Revolution', p. 4.

comparison with only 8 prior to January 2011.[7] By May, an electoral committee was put in place (L'Instance Superieure Independante pour les Elections (ISIE)) to hold elections for members to serve on the National Constituent Assembly. The space for political participation was opening and Tunisians were embracing their commitment to shape a different Tunisia. During the period from the 2010 to 2011 uprising until May 2011, when the dates for elections to the National Constituent Assembly were announced, Tunisia experienced several weeks of temporary political appointments characterised by frequent ministerial and RCD party member resignations. Zemni argues against the notion that this period was marked by political instability:

> Looked at from the perspective of the revolutionary effort to radically change the regime, the high levels of collective mobilisations, the demand for fundamental change, the emergence of informal public political spaces and even the emergence of extra-institutional movements ... should be seen as a phase of extraordinary politics.[8]

Approximately three months after the Tunisia uprising, two institutions that were created following the revolution merged. The Committee for Political Reform and the National Council for the Protection of the Revolution (CNPR) joined to initiate the first phase of the transition by establishing the High Authority for the Realisation of the Objectives of the Revolution, Political Reform and Democratic Transition. Led by the renowned scholar Yadh Ben Achour, the High Authority was created to oversee the transition from revolution to elections and was charged with drafting new laws to organise the October 2011 elections. Moreover, Zemni observes, 'The High Authority claimed co-decision on all governmental matters.'[9]

On 23 October 2011, Tunisia became the first country to hold democratic elections following the uprisings in the Middle East and North Africa. Total voter turnout on the day was 52 per cent of eligible voters (86 per cent of registered voters and 16 per cent of unregistered voters), and the Ennahda party won 37.04 per cent of the vote and 89 (41.01 per cent) of the 217 seats on the National

---

[7] M. Camau, 'La Disgrace du Chef: Mobilisations Populaires Arabes et Crise du Leadership', *Mouvements des Idées et des Luttes*, no. 66 (Summer 2011), p. 29.
[8] Zemni, 'The Extraordinary Politics of the Tunisian Revolution', p. 5.
[9] Ibid., pp. 6–7.

Constituent Assembly.[10] In addition, 58 women secured seats on the Constituent Assembly (39 of whom were members of Ennahda) to hold 27 per cent of the total number of seats.[11] Despite a relatively low voter turnout, the National Democratic Institute final report on the National Constituent Assembly elections concluded, 'Although no party won a majority of seats, Ennahda emerged as the strongest political force in the country, winning more votes than the next eight parties combined and garnering a plurality of seats in the NCA.'[12] Issandr El Amrani and Ursula Lindsey note, 'Not only did the party win a plurality of seats nationwide, it won a plurality in almost every district in the country, including in Tunis ... In other words, not only is Ennahda clearly Tunisia's strongest party, it appears to have deeper support, more evenly spread across the country, than any other party.'[13] It is argued that a significant proportion of the voters for Ennahda were located in the marginalised regions of Tunisia in the centre, south and west of the country and were mainly composed of the lower-middle classes. This included unemployed youths and employees of the service sectors, who, Habib Ayeb remarks, were 'mostly conservative and non-Francophone, and have strong ties to traditional values and religion'.[14] However, he argues that the voter choice of Ennahda was based less on ideological conviction but rather in line with the 'social expectations' of the revolution and against the immorality and corruption associated with the former regime. According to Ayeb, 'It seems the vote has been precisely against leftists and liberals more than it was for Ennahda. One can argue that it was largely a protest vote, or a vote of resistance.'[15] Following the election, Rachid Ghannouchi, co-founder and president of Ennahda, was quoted as saying, 'This is an historic day. Tunis was born again today. The Arab Spring is born again today – not in a negative way of toppling dictators but in a positive way of building democratic systems, a representative system which

---

[10] National Democratic Institute, 'Final Report of the Tunisian National Constituent Assembly Elections', 23 October 2011, pp. 15–19.
[11] Ibid., p. 17.   [12] Ibid., p. 19.
[13] I. El Amrani and U. Lindsey, 'Tunisia Moves to the Next Stage', *Middle East Research and Information Project* (8 November 2011).
[14] H. Ayeb, 'Understanding the Rise of Tunisia's Islamists', *Egypt Independent*, 1 February 2012.
[15] Ibid.

represents the people.'[16] Eventually, Ennahda formed a coalition with two secular parties – the Congress for the Republic (29 seats) and Ettakatol (20 seats) – to secure a majority, creating what would come to be known as the 'Troika'.[17] The eventual compromises required by all participants in a coalition involving secular and religious parties would become a critical source of tension within the government whereby a virtual stalemate between the parties continued until the October 2014 parliamentary elections.

The principal task for the National Constituent Assembly was in effect to remodel and package Tunisia's post-revolution national identity. This would not be an easy task given the manner in which the country appeared to be increasingly divided between the secular elements of the population and a vast range of religiously oriented actors. Maaike Voorhoeve observes, 'While the first slogans of the revolution invoked employment and dignity, the relationship between the state and religion quickly came to the fore in debates on what "the new Tunisia" should look like, and the future constitutional reference to religion played a crucial role.'[18] Consequently, one of the main issues for the National Constituent Assembly was Article One of the previous 1959 Constitution, which stated, 'Islam is Tunisia's religion.' The National Constituent Assembly chose to copy Article One from the previous constitution – a choice that Voorhoeve argues reflected 'continuity' over 'transformation' and in effect, for Ennahda, represented a political strategy to avoid an exacerbation of tension between religious and secular factions.[19] Nevertheless, one of the contentions concerning Article One was the vagueness with which it was applied in the past and with which it could be potentially applied through an Islamist majority;[20] of particular focus for some secular factions was the issue of whether there was a role for Sharia in the Tunisian Constitution. Voorhoeve, citing a Tunisian Law professor, argues, 'Although

---

[16] *BBC News*, 'Tunisia Votes in Historic Free Election', 23 October 2001.

[17] See: National Democratic Institute, 'Final Report of the Tunisian National Constituent Assembly Elections', p. 19 and H. Redissi, 'Tunisia: The Difficulties of the Coalition', Tunisia-Live.net, 3 March 2012.

[18] M. Voorhoeve, '"Islam is Tunisia's Religion": Continuity and Change in Article One of the Tunisian Constitution', *Journal for Politics and Religion* (2014), (unpublished), p. 3.

[19] Ibid., p. 5.

[20] See W. Khefifi, 'L'Expression "Système des Valeurs Islamiques" Remplace la Chariaa: C'est Ambigüe', *Le Temps* (Tunis), 9 March 2012.

the text of Article One has remained the same, its meaning may change significantly as new governments interpret it.'[21] The Ennahda party in fact embodied a host of disparate interpretations of Islam, some of which were moderate and others that represented stricter understandings of Sunnism.

For example, in March 2012 thousands of Salafi demonstrators called for the implementation of Sharia into Tunisia's Constitution. Protesters voiced cries of *'takbir'* – an affirmation of the greatness of god – and 'the people want the implementation of Sharia'.[22] A female protester remarked, 'Sharia is what we need. It is our salvation. Secularists know so little about Sharia; they only hear how men are allowed to marry four women or how thieves' hands are cut. This is not what Sharia is about, it is a way of life.'[23] Moreover, more than 100 associations under the umbrella organisation of the Tunisian Front of Islamic Associations delivered a formal petition calling for Islamic law.[24] Opponents were also active. Approximately one week later, on 20 March 2012, Tunisia's day of independence, thousands of self-identified secular Tunisians marched to demonstrate in favour of a 'civil state'. One of the protesters with a Tunisian flag wrapped around her waist asserted, 'We will not allow a minority that was not even present before January 14th to impose its views on us; it is wrong that after 56 years of independence we are still here calling for a civil state.'[25] From 2011 to 2013, a range of similar demonstrations and protests across Tunisia's public spaces exposed the different priorities and visions for post-uprising Tunisia.

Expectations for the Transition

The perception of disorder or chaos following the downfall of an authoritarian regime can eventually transform former sentiments of mutual solidarity and unity into what can be conflictual and consequential 'us' versus 'them' distinctions. These distinctions in Tunisia manifested in both the political debates of the National Constituent

---

[21] Voorhoeve, '"Islam is Tunisia's Religion"', p. 1.
[22] S. Ajmi, 'More than 4,000 People Descend on Constituent Assembly to Call for Shariaa Law', Tunisia-Live.net, 16 March 2012.
[23] Ibid.   [24] Ibid.
[25] T. Amara, 'Tunisian Protesters Reject Calls for Islamic State', AlArabiya.net, 20 March 2012.

Assembly as well as within the public space(s) among civil society. The 'us' versus 'them' demarcation perhaps most sharply emerged in debates regarding the free press and media, the status of women and key national symbols such as the Tunisian flag. These debates underscored, more importantly, the perception of a growing divide between Islamist and 'liberal' elements of Tunisia's post-uprising population as well a moral panic manifesting among disparate civil society activists. Effectively, these tensions had the effect of undermining earlier alliances made both before and immediately after the uprisings and, as Francesco Cavatorta argues, eventually affected the trust necessary to build solid institutions together.[26]

Tunisians debated a host of issues during the two years following the 2010–2011 uprising, including several issues that some thought had been resolved in the period immediately following independence in 1956. These issues included discussions on the veil, polygamy, traditional (or temporary) marriage, a woman's right to divorce, single mothers, abortion and even female genital mutilation.[27] Political discourses concentrated on, for example, the status of women at a time when many thought urgent political debates should focus instead on the state of the economy, rising food prices and unemployment.[28] In 'The Uprisings Will Be Gendered', Maya Mikdashi notes, 'Such a selective focus on sexual and bodily rights obfuscates power dynamics and contexts that are always also at play when discussing a particular political, historical, or economic issue.'[29] This sudden shift in discourse invoked a sustained moral panic among many secular-liberal women who grew up in the era of the Code of Personal Status (CPS). The CPS outlawed polygamy, set an obligatory minimum age for marriage (15 years of age for women and 18 for men), stipulated consent of both spouses for the validity of the marriage and created a more rigorous divorce procedure required in court.

---

[26] Cavatorta, 'No Democratic Change', p. 141.
[27] See K. Meziou-Dourai, 'A Propos du Mariage Coutumier: Attaque Frontale Contre le Code du Statut Personnel' *Le Temps* (Tunis), 4 February 2012, and R. Khalsi, 'Excision . . . ou les Prédictions d'un Psychopathe', *Le Temps* (Tunis), 14 February 2012.
[28] Gray, 'Tunisia after the Uprising', p. 285.
[29] M. Mikdashi, 'The Uprisings Will Be Gendered', Jadaliyya.com, 28 February 2012.

This moral panic was also accompanied by an overarching sentiment of being 'let down by the revolution', in particular among women who participated in the Tunisian uprising alongside men in very public spaces. With their male counterparts, they called for 'freedom, dignity, and employment', but following the revolution they perceived they could be at risk of losing some of the rights they had acquired through the former regimes.[30] Many secular-liberal women were arguably angry and fearful over the future direction of post-revolution Tunisia. Some women were also nervously looking over their shoulders to Iran and Afghanistan for examples of what could happen to the status of women after an 'Islamic Revolution'.

This fear of 'moving backwards' not only invoked anxiety but also a degree of disdain among secular-liberal women towards Islamist women demonstrating a visible commitment to Islam, such as by wearing the *hijab* or the *niqab*.[31] Mikdashi points out that as Islamists gained increasing support in Egypt, Tunisia and Syria, concerns over gender policies increasingly manifested. She argues:

Gender equality and justice should be a focus of progressive politics no matter who is in power. A selective fear of Islamists when it comes to women's and LGBTQ rights has more to do with Islamophobia than a genuine concern with gender justice. Unfortunately, Islamists do not have an exclusive licence to practice patriarchy and gender discrimination/oppression in the region.[32]

It is important to point out that it was not simply the secular discourse on the status of women igniting debate, but a range of voices equally came to the fore to advocate against the CPS in favour of a more Islamist system to guarantee the rights of women. For example, just before International Women's Day in March 2012, three women were interviewed by the new online journal *Tunisia-Live*. Nesrine Bouthafi, a member of Hizb Ettahrir (reportedly a legally unrecognised Islamist party), argued, 'We condemn the CPS. Women in Tunisia are suffering because of this code – it is the source of their pain now ... The code's principles are not derived from Islamic ones, and are only harming Tunisian women.'[33] In the post-revolution discourse, the issue of the

---

[30] Gray, 'Tunisia after the Uprising', p. 290. [31] Ibid., p. 289.
[32] Mikdashi, 'The Uprisings Will Be Gendered'.
[33] S. Ajmi, 'Tunisian Women Question Future and Role of Personal Status Code', Tunisia-Live.net, 7 March 2012.

status of women and the CPS became 'fully politicised'.³⁴ As such, conflicts over the future of Tunisia's national identity grew during the two years following the uprising. Contestations over some of the more critical issues for Tunisia, at times, resulted in public confrontations and even violence between activists.

Uncomfortable Confrontations: Persepolis *and* Manouba University

On 7 October 2011, only weeks ahead of the first post-revolution election for Tunisia's National Constituent Assembly, the private television station *Nessma TV* broadcast the animated film *Persepolis* dubbed into Tunisian dialect. The 2007 film was based on the writer and co-director Marjane Satrapi's autobiographical graphic novel, which followed a young girl as she and her family experienced the consequences of the Iranian revolution. Subsequent to its release, the film was labelled as 'blasphemous' by a number of Islamic critics for its depiction of a representation of Allah in a dream sequence where the film's protagonist imagines a conversation with God. The immediate outcome of the broadcasting of the film involved a firebomb attack on the head of the station's home on 14 October 2011 as well as protests by several hundred Salafis in front of the station's offices.³⁵ More importantly, soon after these events, the station head went on trial for 'undermining' sacred Islamic values and 'disturbing the public order', thus placing him at risk for three years in prison. A suit filed by more than 130 lawyers called for the persecution of the head of the station as well as two of his employees, who were eventually required to appear in court. The Court of First Degree of Tunis announced that it would open a criminal investigation.³⁶ After arriving at the courtroom in November 2011, the head of the station, Nabil Karoui, said, 'I feel an immense sadness because the people who wanted to destroy the channel are free and I am here because I broadcast a film.'³⁷

---

³⁴ Gray, 'Tunisia after the Uprising', p. 285.
³⁵ Human Rights Watch, 'Tunisia: Drop Criminal Investigation of TV Station for Airing Persepolis', 13 October 2011.
³⁶ Ibid.
³⁷ Associated French Press, 'TV Boss Goes on Trial for Showing "Persepolis"', France 24.com, 17 November 2011.

The fallout from the broadcasting of the film involved a number of attacks on journalists and violent confrontations outside the courtroom and the Ministry of the Interior. For example, in January 2012 Tunisian journalist Zied Krichen and university professor Hamadi Redissi were physically and verbally assaulted outside the courthouse. Krichen responded, 'If the physical safety of journalists is jeopardised, we cannot start talking about freedom of the press. The priority is to protect the individuals and pursue the offenders.'[38] These acts of aggression, which invoked limited initial response from the government, led many in the press and greater population to conclude a complicity of Ennahda with more conservative groups such as the Salafis. Moreover, the arrest of Nabil Karoui and his employees sparked a more vicious debate concerning the future of a liberalised press in Tunisia and greater questions regarding freedom of speech in the post-revolution environment.[39] The arrest and eventual prosecution of the head of *Nessma TV* (in May 2012 he was officially charged with 'undermining sacred Islamic values' and obliged to pay a fine of 2,400 Tunisian dinars)[40] sparked further public concerns over the nature of post-uprising Tunisia where the future was uncertain and difficult to predict.

The next event that came to occupy considerable public space across the media and among civil society actors and groups was in fact a series of events, demonstrations and public confrontations at the University of Manouba in Tunis. From the end of 2011 well into 2012, groups of students chose to occupy the university to protest a stipulation that banned female students from wearing the *niqab* on campus and a student union by-law that prohibited the wearing of the *niqab* during the sitting of exams. While it was argued that only a handful of students post-revolution would have chosen to wear the *niqab*, the demonstrators occupied the university for several months and distributed leaflets proclaiming, 'Sister, what is preventing you

---

[38] A. Ghribi, 'Tunisian Journalists Subject to Recent Wave of Violence', Tunisia-Live.net, 24 January 2012.

[39] See D. Mamelouk, 'The Rocky Road for Freedom of Press', *Tunisia Live*, 4 March 2012, and Human Rights Watch, 'Tunisia: Drop Criminal Investigation'.

[40] F. Belaid, 'Tunisia: Persepolis Trial Verdict Signals "Erosion" of Free Speech', Amnesty International, 3 May 2012.

from wearing the Niqab?'[41] The University of Manouba events culminated when two female students wearing the *niqab* attacked the school's dean by throwing books at this face and breaking his nose.[42] In response, secular-liberal members of the national students' union organised a demonstration. This demonstration was simultaneously met with a Salafist counter-demonstration calling for the right for females to wear the *niqab* during exams; the protesters brandished the black Salafist flag inscribed in Arabic with 'la ilaha illa Allah Muhammad rasul Allah' ('There is no God but God and Muhammad is His Prophet').

In March 2012, a young male Salafi student climbed to the rooftop of the university and removed the Tunisian flag, replacing it with the Salafist flag. Soon after, a female student climbed the wall to replace the Salafist flag with the Tunisian national flag. Before she could change the flag, she was pushed off the wall by the male student (she did not suffer any critical injuries). This public confrontation took place the day before International Women's Day during which thousands of women marched on Avenue Bourguiba, underscoring the importance of the CPS. The young woman was celebrated on International Women's Day and praised by politicians, including the general secretary of the Progressive Democratic Party (PDP), who stated, 'I salute the bravery of this young lady, who did not hesitate for a second to defend her nation's flag.'[43] The same week members of the National Constituent Assembly placed small Tunisian flags on their desks to express their displeasure with the mistreatment of the flag.[44]

For many Tunisians, symbols of identity such as the flag assumed greater importance following the 2010–2011 uprising. These acts of identity recovery could not only be witnessed in the re-appropriation of certain symbols but also in the dis-appropriation of symbols and institutions associated with the former regime. In the two years following

---

[41] N. Suleiman, 'The Disintegrating Fabric of Tunisian Politics: The Niqab Ban and Tunisian Flag Desecration at Manouba University', Jadaliyya.com, 13 April 2012.

[42] *Associated Press*, 'Islamist, Leftist Students Clash in Tunisia over Right to Wear the Veil', Haaretz.com, 7 March 2012.

[43] A. Ghribi, 'Tunisians Erupt in Anger over Desecration of Flag', Tunisia-Live.net, 9 March 2012.

[44] Ibid.

the revolution, this sense of identity recovery manifested in various forms at the level of the street. Not only was the subject of women through the symbols of the headscarf and the *niqab* 'strategic terrain' for national identity recovery, but marginalised groups also became targets for purifying the nation of the 'impiety' associated with the former regime.[45] For example, in addition to the attacks on the *maisons closes* in February 2011,[46] the power of the street was also responsible for the closing down of bars and stores as Salafis gathered in Sidi Bouzid in May 2012 to burn down bars and to physically threaten the owners in protest against the sale of alcohol in the town.[47] Moreover, it was reported that between 2012 and 2013 more than 100 cases of fire and looting were targeted at *zawiyas* (Sufi lodges) by Salafist forces.[48] These instances, led by members of communities rather than a formal government authority, resonated with many Tunisian communities (secular and religious) who before were afraid of the police but were now more concerned by the power of the mob, which arguably faced no visible consequences for its actions. In September 2012, the public opinion and marketing firm 3C *Etudes* highlighted in its press release the results of its political barometer survey entitled 'Neuvième Vague', indicating at the time that 60 per cent of Tunisians were dissatisfied with the security situation in the country, with 42 per cent indicating 'total dissatisfaction'.[49] This study reflected in part the increasing sense of insecurity being felt across the country by individuals and communities from 2011.

Finally, in February 2013, Chokri Belaid, a Tunisian politician and lawyer who was a key opposition leader with the secular-left Democratic Patriot's Movement, was assassinated outside his home in Tunis. Only five months later in July 2013, Mohamed Brahmi, the founder

---

[45] R. Haugbolle and F. Cavatorta, 'Beyond Ghannouchi: Islamism and Social Change in Tunisia', *Middle East Research and Information Project*, vol. 42, no. 262 (Spring 2012).
[46] Bensaied, 'Les Islamistes S'Attaquent aux Maisons Closes'.
[47] A. Ltifi, 'Salafists Burn Down Bars, Liquor Stores while Police are Passive in Sidi Bouzid', Tunisia-Live.net, 20 May 2012.
[48] Middle East Online, 'Tunisia Salafists Take Aim at Sufi Shrines', 15 October 2012, featured in F. Blibech, A. Driss and P. Longo, 'Citizenship in Post-Awakening Tunisia: Power Shifts and Conflicting Perceptions', *Euspring* (February 2014).
[49] 3C Etudes communiqué de presse, neuvième vague, September 2012; www.3cetudes.com.

and former leader of the People's Movement, was also shot (14 times) outside his home.[50] As the two men were vocal critics of Ennahda, many not only considered the assassinations a direct attack on political liberalism but also a perceived re-manifestation of authoritarian rule in post-revolution Tunisia. The prime minister at the time, Ali Larayedh, blamed the Salafist organisation Ansar al-Sharia for the two murders.[51] From the time of the elections in October 2011 when Ennahda gained power through the formation of the 'Troika' to the murder of Belaid 15 months later, increasing intolerance between the secular and religious factions could be perceived at the political and sociocultural levels throughout Tunisia. The mounting tension between the two sides provided the impression of a country mired in sociopolitical stagnation in the critical phase of the transition two years later. The assassinations of two very public members of the opposition only served to aggravate the intense transition climate.

Reflecting on events that took place during this tumultuous period, it becomes a challenge to untangle instances that were directed by political factions and those which were being instigated by sociocultural actors and groups. This haziness or *flou* reflects the notion that during a transition from authoritarian rule a country not only experiences a remarkable political transition but, arguably, the changes that appear to be happening at the sociocultural level merit equal scrutiny. These events, and the rumours accompanying them, take on even greater importance in particular within the context of loosened state capacity associated with transitions away from authoritarian rule. It is worth highlighting that the security apparatus and the judiciary systems had been crippled from January 2011. Moreover, conflicting statements on the government's post-uprising priorities were often exacerbated by the fact that for many years the leadership and members of Ennahda were either imprisoned or in exile in Europe and therefore experienced more than a decade of limited, if any, communication. Articulating a coherent stance or policies on critical national issues following the 2010–2011 uprising undoubtedly reflected this lack of cohesion.[52] Therefore, popular perceptions of inadequate responses to these

---

[50] *BBC News*, 'Tunisian Politician Mohamed Brahmi Assassinated', 25 July 2013.
[51] *Associated Press*, 'Ansar al-Sharia Blamed for Tunisia Killings', AlJazeera.com, 27 August 2013.
[52] Ennhada was banned in Tunisia from 1991 to 2011; See Gray, 'Tunisia after the Uprising', pp. 291, 293.

events, accompanied by hostile confrontations and – on some occasions – violence, evoked suspicions of a 'silent complicity' rather than encouraging more open opportunities for genuine dialogue on how to repair incapacitated infrastructure fraught by decades of abuse by those in power. Inevitably, the impact of the events occurring at the political and sociocultural levels and which manifested in Tunisia's expanding public spaces fostered a terrain of uncertainty, suspicion and at times even hostility among and between its actors, alongside the multiplicity of emotions unleashed after the revolution.

The next section examines in more detail the specific actors and groups that emerged to fill the expanding public spaces following the amendments to the laws of association. Throughout this period, one can observe not only the self-management, self-organisation and agency-centred approaches adopted by civil society actors in the social movements in Eastern Europe and Latin America but also evidence of the hegemony of the neoliberal understanding of the dual role of civil society organisations as service providers as well as key agents in democratisation.

The Resurrection of Civil Society

Almost immediately after the revolution, during the first phase of the transition, the High Authority for the Realisation of the Objectives of the Revolution, Political Reform and Democratic Transition was established to oversee the transition from revolution to elections.[53] Among its many remits, in addition to the drafting of the legal framework and constitution for the next elections, was modifying the text on the laws of association in Tunisia.[54] These measures for political liberalisation, implemented before the elections to the National Constituent Assembly, came as a result of critical and sustained pressure from the popular masses following the downfall of the regime on 14 January 2011.[55] Moreover, the amendments to the laws of association would allow a

---

[53] The High Authority was created through the fusion of two institutions established immediately after the revolution, the Committee for Political Reform and the National Council for the Protection of the Revolution (CNPR). See Zemni, 'The Extraordinary Politics of the Tunisian Revolution', p. 6.
[54] See decree laws no. 14 of 23 March 2011 and no. 27 of 18 April 2011 and Guellali, 'Pathways and Pitfalls'.
[55] Zemni, 'The Extraordinary Politics of the Tunisian Revolution', p. 4.

new range of organisations to be formally and legally established in Tunisia. In March 2012, the newly appointed Minister for Women and the Family, Sihem Badi, stated, 'The goal of an association is to defend certain rights and liberties, and to allow for the consolidation of democracy. In effect, it (the association) permits a citizen to be better informed of his rights and his obligations.'[56] In early 2013 the Foundation for the Future presented the results of a study that concluded that at the end of 2010, a total of 9,969 associations were formally registered with the government. At the end of 2012, this number rose by approximately 5,000 to 14,966.[57,58] Figures for the number of new civil society organisations established in the two years following the revolution range from between 2,000 and 5,000. And although qualitatively it is a challenge to evaluate the effectiveness of these newer organisations from the existing mappings, quantitatively the increase in the number of these kinds of organisations within a short period of time is noteworthy.[59]

Reshaping the Framework for Civil Society

The 2011 amendments to the 1959 law of associations allowed a civil society organisation with as few as six members to be created without authorisation, accompanied by a simple letter 'to inform' that the

---

[56] A. Nemlaghi, 'Associations et Embrigadement', *Le Temps* (Tunis), 21 March 2012.

[57] For additional information, see D. Ben Salem, 'Flagrant Deficit au Niveau des Capacités', *La Presse de Tunisie*, 26 March 2013.

[58] Although there are a number of mappings on the quantity and quality of civil society associations in Tunisia for the period from January 2011 to July 2013, the mappings/inventories have limitations as most were conducted in an unsystematic manner, focusing on only certain typologies of organisations or done within disparate contexts. Therefore, existing mappings are only able to capture a fraction of the associative environment during this period.

[59] Mappings of civil society organisations conducted during this period include: l'Institut Francais de Tunisie; the British Council; UNICEF; Enda Inter-Arabe; International Cooperation Agency of the Association of Dutch Municipalities (VNG International); Centre d'Information, de Formation d'Etudes et de Documentation sur les Associations (IFEDA); the European Union Delegation; the office of the prime minister; the Ministry of Agriculture; and the mapping initiatives conducted by two NGO initiatives: Center of Arab Women for Training and Research (CAWTAR), Middle East Partnership Initiative (MEPI) and Mercy Corps; and le Réseau Euro-Méditerranéen des Droits de l'Homme (REMDH). Cited in Union Européenne, 'Rapport de Diagnostic', p. 10.

association has been established. Newer organisations that did not receive a response to their application within three months could interpret this as a positive outcome for their 'associational visa'. Furthermore, the eight categories previously necessary for an associational application were dismantled. The newer organisations could be political and could represent or directly support political parties. In addition, in September 2011 the laws of association were once again amended, this time to allow civil society organisations free access to information and judiciary representation (whereby the association could go before the justice tribunals themselves). Following the 2010–2011 uprising, a key transformation for many aspiring organisations was that the associational remit, formerly situated within the obscure crevices of the Ministry of the Interior under Ben Ali, moved to become the responsibility of the Office of the Prime Minister under the Centre d'Information, de Formation d'Etudes et de Documentation sur les Associations (IFEDA). This could be interpreted as a symbolic shift towards an increased openness and transparency in approach towards civil society. Table 1 sets out the modifications to the law of association 59–154 (7 November 1959), finalised September 2011.[60]

As a result of these changes, civil society organisations were also able to create larger networks of organisations working along similar domains or with similar interests, something that was not allowed before 2011. Furthermore, smaller civil society groups could also be legally created, for example support groups and associations for people living with HIV, which were previously denied access to the associational visa. These changes in the legal framework were adopted almost immediately after the revolution and were revised and made more pliant again in September 2011. This phase could be described as the initial post-revolution stage whereby a window of opportunity was perceived allowing disparate actors to pass the maximum number of reforms.

The Rebirth of Citoyenneté

Tunisian's post-revolution 'resurrection of civil society' following the amendments to the 1959 laws of association was accompanied by a

---

[60] Table featured in the report Union Européenne. 'Rapport de Diagnostic', pp. 7–8.

Table 1 *Modifications to the Law of Association (59–154)*

Law 59-154	Law 2011-88
Declaration of association made to the Ministry of the Interior	Declaration made to the secretary-general of the government
The Ministry of the Interior can reserve up to three months to announce the acceptance of the creation of the association.	The prime minister has 30 days to announce the acceptance of the creation of the association.
The law provides eight associational categories and applies limits to their field of intervention.	There is no longer any classification or limitation for the field of intervention of the association.
The associations falling under the rubric of 'general' character are not permitted to refuse any demand for membership; if so, they can be pursued juristically.	The association itself is permitted to establish criteria for membership.
No age limit for the founders or members of the association	Individuals under the age of 16 cannot establish/found an organisation, and members have to be at least the age of 13.
Implicitly, associations can only be constituted by Tunisians (as the state demands the national identity card to open a new application for associational status).	Associations can be created and constituted by Tunisian nationals or residents of Tunisia.

renewed understanding and application of the concept of *citoyenneté*. The word *citoyenneté* means 'citizenship' in French, and through its Arabic understanding with the word *muwatana* (المواطنة), 'fellow citizens/compatriot' is a concept that embodies Tunisia's intrinsic spirit of volunteerism alongside a profound commitment to support the communities denied dignity and humanity under the former regimes. The concept itself represents a fundamental drive among the population towards reshaping a more inclusive post-revolution Tunisia. Of the approximately 15,000 associations formally registered through IFEDA, 30.9 per cent were schools or educational programmes, 15.4 per cent represented artistic or cultural NGOs and 12.2 per cent were social welfare and charity organisations.

While there are likely a multitude of explanations for the robust post-revolution sense of Tunisian *citoyenneté* that many individuals referred to during the writing of this book, two reasons are noted herein.[61] The first explanation relates to the levels of force, intimidation and repression applied by the former regimes, in particular against religiously oriented actors who were denied a public or associational role in Tunisia for several decades. The second explanation for this renewed sense of *citoyenneté* stemmed from the conditions under which Tunisia's revolution took place, i.e., following an immediate state of emergency and consequently a complete vacuum in political power in the weeks following the revolution. Tunisia was considered the only country in the region to fall into a political power vacuum during the Arab uprisings following the departure of Ben Ali and his family on 14 January 2011. After Ben Ali fled for Saudi Arabia, Tunisia experienced several weeks of temporary political appointments characterised by frequent ministerial and RCD party member resignations.[62] For approximately three months (from 14 January to 3 March 2011, when the date was announced for the elections to the National Constituent Assembly) there were very few active police or security forces. El Amrani and Lindsey provide this account:

In the days immediately after the 14 January departure of Zine El Abidine Ben Ali ... the country's future did not look so promising. Ben Ali's former ministers attempted to provide continuity without popular legitimacy, the economy was in shambles, and protests and insecurity continued. It took three months for a government more representative of the revolution to be appointed, the former ruling party disbanded, and the former regime elements sniping at passers-by rounded up.[63]

With the police absent from the streets, citizens took it upon themselves to set up local security checks and blockades into and out of the different neighbourhoods; they organised community patrols and occasionally arrested looters to hand over to the military.[64] Therefore, members of communities soon assumed this responsibility and accountability themselves at the local level to safeguard their own

---

[61] The French word *citoyenneté* is featured more in this research rather than the Arabic *muwatana* as most of the interviews were conducted in the French language.
[62] El Amrani and Lindsey, 'Tunisia Moves to the Next Stage' and Zemni, 'The Extraordinary Politics of the Tunisian Revolution', p. 4.
[63] El Amrani and Lindsey, 'Tunisia Moves to the Next Stage'.
[64] Beinin and Vairel, 'Afterword: Popular Uprisings in Tunisia and Egypt', p. 241.

neighbourhoods. Could this indeterminate period have contributed to the nature of civil society that forged ahead with this sense of total citizen engagement, or *citoyenneté*, seen in Tunisia after 14 January 2011? Najeeb, a founder and member of several different associations, noted the following, 'The rights of individuals have had an extraordinary advance. Now there is everything – young people, women, political associations, charities ... everything.' He added, 'With this new climate of liberty, everyone has the right to an association, from the extreme left to the extreme right.'[65]

Different civil society actors and groups soon emerged to exhibit a long-repressed spirit of volunteerism and *citoyenneté*, further served by the immediate expansion of the 1959 laws of association. However, for numerous reasons the terrain upon which these groups and actors operated following the revolution was uncertain. This uncertainty was aggravated by crippled state institutions, a sudden influx of new international donors, an inability to ascertain the relationship between the newly elected government and more 'conservative' actors operating at the sociocultural level as well as the complexity of rumour and myth-making that can manifest during sociopolitical transformations following authoritarian rule. This murkiness not only clouds the political landscape but also renders it a challenge to determine the genuine nature, disparate groups and functioning of civil society acting in both symbolic and physical public spaces.

The following two sections examine the various actors who considered themselves members of civil society in the two years following the 2010–2011 Tunisia uprising. The first section looks to the experiences of some of the historic civil society organisations established during the Bourguiba and/or Ben Ali regimes. The second section looks to the newer organisations formed as a result of the loosening of the laws of association, including their perceived expectations and challenges, as they too operated on indeterminate terrain. Both sets of civil society actors were affected (and responded) in distinct ways to this unfolding environment.

Past Meets Present: Historic Actors and New Spaces

Before the Tunisia uprising, many civil society organisations were the instruments of power of the Ben Ali regime and many were simply

[65] Interview in Tunis (38), 6 March 2012 and March 2013.

perceived as democratic decoration.[66] Mounir Majoub writes, 'In this mode of statist governance, civil society played a relatively timid role ... the organisations of civil society were often forced to play a rather symbolic role whereby the essential consisted in the participation of events and sporadic sensitisation of certain groups of the population.'[67] After the 2010–2011 uprising, a number of historic civil society organisations, in particular those that legally acquired their associational visa under the Ben Ali regime, shifted their focus to democratisation, civic education, the election process and engagement in political advocacy directed towards the various political parties. However, despite the new opportunities afforded by the opening of the public space, many historic civil society actors in Tunisia were limited by the heavy authoritarian inheritance from the former regime. For example, Amaney Jamal contends that the overall political context in which the organisation has come to operate shapes the manner in which they may or may not produce democratic change.[68]

With the perception of an immediate change in how business is conducted for the historic organisations in particular, many organisations found themselves on competitive terrain with the newer associations – as they were also required to establish fresh relationships with the new government and to cultivate existing and new donors for financial support. Many civil society organisations had previously adapted to working in their own domain without considerable competition from other organisations. Some were unaccustomed to partnering with organisations or competing alongside similar associations for donor funding. This perception was shared by Fajr, a woman who recently began working for a German-funded NGO in Tunisia to support transparency in the democratic process, and who previously worked for one of the larger historic civil society organisations; she emphasised the challenge of competition between the different organisations. She remarked, 'Some [historic associations] were harassed by the political regime under Ben Ali but now they find themselves in a situation where there is no real fear of the political environment but in a much more competitive environment with the newer associations;

---

[66] Le Réseau Euro-Méditerranéen des Droits de l'Homme, 'Contribution de la Mission du Réseau Euro-méditerranéen des Droits de l'Homme en Tunisie a la Description du Nouveau Paysage Associatif Tunisien', October 2011, p. 3.
[67] Majoub, 'La Gouvernance Environnementale Démocratique', p. 2.
[68] Jamal, *Barriers to Democracy*, pp. 9–10.

for many this is a destabilising and new terrain.'[69] She further noted that before the uprising they were working in a less than favourable environment, but one in which these organisations knew and understood the 'rules'. With the proliferation of NGOs following Ben Ali's departure, many of the groups had not been able to adapt as quickly and were not used to working with volunteers (due to past fears of infiltration by government officials). These organisations were now required to evolve rapidly. This view was also shared by Mohammed, a policy adviser from a recently established UN initiative in Tunis, who stated:

We are in a way faced with a dire reality, there is this division of civil society in Tunisia, and so this is hard to bring them together ... We are having a hard time bringing them together under the same action. The organisations now are working in isolation from each other and even if their work is the same there is a resistance to this collaboration.[70]

The degree of paralysis that affected some of these historic organisations stemmed from two possible factors. The first was the relationship of the civil society organisations to the donors and the overall donor climate following the 2010–2011 uprising. The second was the transformation(s) occurring at the sociocultural level and the subsequent sense of insecurity this brought as both individuals and organisations attempted to gauge the environment they would now manoeuvre in.

Donors in Transition

The events of the 'Arab Spring', which featured a swift domino effect of uprisings across parts of the Middle East and North Africa, caught many international donors by surprise. Some existing donors cautiously maintained their activities after the Tunisia uprising while waiting to see how events in the wider region would unfold. However, given Tunisia's positionality between Algeria and Libya – two countries perceived as potentially volatile – many international donors also saw Tunisia as a new opportunity to 'support the process of democratic transition'.[71]

---

[69] Interview in Tunis (32), 10 February 2012.
[70] Interview in Tunis (34), 15 February 2012.
[71] B. Hibou, H. Meddeb and M. Hamdi, 'Tunisia after 14 January and Its Social and Political Economy: The Issues at Stake in a Reconfiguration of European Policy', Euro-Mediterranean Human Rights Network (2011), p. 17.

For example, in March 2011, the Commissioner for Enlargement and European Neighbourhood Policy committed to doubling the financial aid provided by the European Commission, with the objective of strengthening civil society and supporting the development of underprivileged regions. Furthermore, in April of the same year, the European Union announced a pledge of €258 million (US$355 million as calculated at the end of 2013) between 2011 and 2013.[72] Beatrice Hibou, Hamza Meddeb and Mohamed Hamdi point out the haste with which a range of donors made commitments so early after the Arab uprisings, with no real or genuine assessment of the effectiveness of donor policies pursued up until that point. They argue that this:

> ... demonstrates a certain confusion among European institutions when confronted with the new situation. More worryingly, it seems that there is a drift to a mere continuation of the policies already being pursued, with a few day-by-day adjustments to cope with future eventualities; and that many of the announcements presented as support for the "new Tunisia" are in actual fact the (new) presentation of previous commitments already ratified.[73]

In addition, following the elections in October 2011, several newer donors arrived in Tunisia – some with no experience of working in the country and with no clear strategies or mandates. So while there were newer donors coming into Tunisia, there was also the perception that the traditional international donors were paralysed, including the multilateral donors who seemed to have adopted a 'let's wait and see' approach. Dr Saqib, the director of a UN initiative established in Tunis after the Tunisia uprising, stated, 'Many are waiting to see what happens at the end of the transition period ... This reluctance among donors to engage is not helping, because mainly if you are looking to see a strong democratic presence these organisations must be engaged ... at the moment there is no funding.'[74] Moreover, Tawfiq, a programme manager and medical doctor with an HIV/AIDS organisation in Sfax, also highlighted the challenge of an indeterminate donor climate. He said, 'The environment is favourable for associations but the main problems now are the economy and financing, especially with a very weak state ... The associations look to the state to give but the state cannot give a budget to associations when it is in economic crisis.'[75]

---

[72] Ibid. [73] Ibid. [74] Interview in Tunis (34), 15 February 2012.
[75] Interview in Sfax (31), 9 February 2012.

After the Tunisia uprising, the amendments to the laws of association also stipulated changes in the regulation of the financing of civil society organisations. This followed a previously constrained environment in which the international donors operated during the Ben Ali regime. Kristina Kausch claims, 'Before the uprisings, Tunisia had not been a favourite destination for international donors due to both its narrow strategic significance and the limited impact potential in a heavily repressive political environment.'[76] Decree-law 88 of 24 September 2011, however, permitted associations to receive membership fees, public subsidies and financial and material donations, including from foreign countries. In addition, the Tunisian state was obligated to set aside an unspecified amount of funding to NGOs, even though it has been argued that this funding was minimal.[77] More importantly, from 2011, donations to civil society organisations, including foreign donations, required no prior approval by the government.

The historic organisations were also at a disadvantage because many had evolved over time from activists to providers of services. This can be attributed to the decline of the social contract under Ben Ali and the functionalist role assigned to civil society through neoliberal policies adopted by the regime. This contributed to the sense of destabilisation and hesitation some of the historic organisations experienced in not only being able to solicit support from new donors but also in articulating the specific direction their organisation would take after 2011. Kareem, who served as a volunteer and eventual consultant with one of the HIV organisations based in Tunis, stated:

> NGOs now are mainly the providers and deliverers of services rather than involved in advocacy ... They are losing their ability to do this kind of work because they are so busy delivering services ... if they continue only to deliver services they will lose the place they have gained next to the government. They need to learn to do this advocacy again.[78]

Conflicting Priorities, Divergent Visions

The Arab uprisings not only brought political regime change across a number of countries in the Middle East and North Africa, it also

---

[76] K. Kausch, '"Foreign Funding" in Post-Revolution Tunisia', AFA, Fride and Hivos, 2013, p. 2.
[77] Ibid., p. 3.   [78] Interview in Tunis (28), 1 February 2012.

carried with it a tide of sociocultural change, with disparate attitudes and behaviours rising to the surface. Radi, an activist and sociologist based in Sfax who undertook a series of HIV bio-behavioural surveys across Tunisia, noted, 'The major issues now are not just Tunisia's issues, but larger regional issues concerning the liberals and the conservatives, happening all around us, and this has a big effect on what we do.'[79] What were also actual and perceived changes across this terrain forced some of the historic civil society organisations to revert back to strategies of caution, discretion and invisibility – strategies that served them well under the Ben Ali regime.

During periods of sociopolitical turmoil, the changes taking place at the political level can often overshadow the rapid transformations occurring at the sociocultural level. Rikke Haugbolle and Francesco Cavatorta describe a revival of the practices of Islam in Tunisia that began more explicitly in the early 2000s as a rejection of the practice under both Bourguiba and Ben Ali of excluding Islam from public life. They explained, 'Since public space was monopolised by the regime, there was a greater emphasis on personal morality and comportment ... Crucially, pious Tunisians also became more involved in public activism, which was perceived as ... an ethical choice implicitly condemning the regime as unethical.'[80] The revival at the sociocultural level deepened further after the revolution as individuals and communities were able to overtly condemn the corruption and immorality associated with the Ben Ali regime.

The combined challenges of a broken post-revolution economy (and global economic crisis), disrupted state systems and infrastructure, uncertain donor commitment and what were perceived as mounting (more flagrant) 'conservative' attitudes that were not always favourable towards marginalised groups and minorities marked expectations for the post-revolution period in Tunisia. Of immediate concern to the historic organisations working in, for example, HIV/AIDS, and for those who were largely dependent upon the support of the government (i.e., for treatment of HIV, including procurement of drugs), was whether the gains they made in effectively reaching the most at-risk populations could be maintained and if the work to date could be sustained amid a multiplicity of governmental and donor priorities

---

[79] Interview in Tunis (30), 7 February 2012.
[80] Haugbolle and Cavatorta, 'Beyond Ghannouchi'.

in the transition and post-revolution context. Kader, who worked as the supervisor of key populations and outreach workers for one of the HIV/AIDS organisations in Tunis, spoke of how the dilemma of both not having assured funding from international donors after 2013, and of no immediate signs of commitment from the newly elected government, left the work of his organisation in a precarious position. He noted, 'This is a real problem and so far it is not a priority for the state to take forward this work; sustaining this work is going to be very difficult.'[81] This perception was also shared by Ouroub, a country officer for one of the UN offices in Tunis, who stated, 'It will be more difficult than before. We could say before "we have a public health problem", but now all that work done before has to be redone. They (the government) might surely have other priorities. It is a worry. We hope to be able to convince them but there is now a predominance for the conservative.'[82]

This concern over the future of working with marginalised groups affected by HIV in Tunisia also trickled over to international donors and regional multilateral organisations who shared the pessimism of some of their civil society colleagues. Of the donors who spoke of future HIV-specific interventions in Tunisia for the research, some were explicit about concerns over the priority HIV would have with the new government in comparison to other post-revolution transition priorities. For example, Dr Hajjar, a leading HIV/AIDS activist and former director of one of the largest UN led HIV/AIDS programmes in the Middle East and North Africa, observed the following:

I am not at all optimistic for the next few years. The whole political context with the Arab Spring has meant that, of course, HIV/AIDS is no longer a priority. AIDS is not a priority now on anybody's agenda and I would even have trouble getting anyone to talk about HIV. In addition, there is almost no more funding, there is less and less now and this has had an impact on everyone's work ... There are also new political players now in all of these governments and they have no clue on HIV, so we almost have to start from scratch again! ... But the UN no longer has the luxury to go to the government to speak about HIV as a priority. This is why I am not optimistic, it is not easy.[83]

[81] Interview in Tunis (26), 30 January 2012.
[82] Interview in Tunis (20), 16 January 2012 and 13 March 2013.
[83] Telephone interview (55), 10 May 2012.

So in effect, the historic organisations working in HIV/AIDS became increasingly cognisant that global health and non-communicable diseases would not remain a priority as donors might be more interested in securing big 'public' wins to satisfy constituents at home rather than over perceived peripheral issues such as HIV/AIDS. Second, with an uncertain sociocultural terrain, the government would not necessarily be in a position to overtly fund work with vulnerable and marginalised populations in an increasingly divided society. The secular historic civil society organisations perceived the divergence as situated directly between the conservative 'extreme' right and the secular (at times equally as extreme) left. For example, the supervisor of outreach work with key populations, Kader, posited, 'The opening will come but Tunisian society will divide itself between the progressives and the conservatives who are very closed. The Salafists here are now really showing their power but the progressives are also trying to show that they have this power' (referring to the demonstration for freedom of expression in which 8,000 Tunisians participated on 27 January 2012).[84] This implicit pessimism for post-revolution Tunisia was also underscored by Dr Malik, the executive director of one of the associations working in HIV/AIDS in Tunis, who remarked:

To see one's own country regress several centuries in just a few months is very difficult. This is going to take time ... When you have such a large number of people living in poverty, they are not really free. This level of poverty and the choices people will make in this situation will not lead to genuine democracy.[85]

Not only was there a polarisation between the secular elements of the population and religiously-oriented factions, but emotions were also divided between the euphoria of being able to bring down a dictator and fear over how the country would be governed in the future. Dr Malik further observed:

Religion has become the most important – and this understanding of religion is an obstacle for HIV/AIDS. If the government were now secular it would be much easier ... I predict that our work will not be very easy. Not because of the government but because of the people. Before, it was enough to be

---

[84] Interview in Tunis (26), 30 January 2012.
[85] Interview in Tunis (18), 13 January 2012 and 5 March 2013.

correct with a certain number of people; we were tolerated. Now, it is less obvious ... there is an intolerance which is being manifested.[86]

The civil society organisations established before the Tunisia uprising in 2010–2011 faced challenges that many of the newer organisations would likely be spared. In particular, the historic organisations previously manoeuvred in a comparatively constrained public space – they either learned to adapt to the rules of the game or risked encounters with the full weight of the security apparatus often intolerant to perceived opposition. These organisations also operated during a time in which religiously oriented associations and overt Islam as a political discourse was largely restricted. Therefore, the public terrain was relatively isolated from competing views and counter discourses. Following the Tunisia uprising, the historic civil society organisations stood in a problematical position as they inadvertently continued to apply the same strategies they used under Ben Ali of discretion and invisibility while they waited for the nature of the post-revolution landscape to reveal itself. As the newer civil society organisations emerged to claim both old and new spaces, the historic associations appeared to be at a clear disadvantage based largely on the authoritarian residue they inherited and whereby there was a gradual predominance of service provision over civic activism. Nevertheless, among many of the historic civil society organisations, there was a discernible acceptance that with the complete rupture from decades of repressive authoritarian rule, genuine political liberalisation would take time. Many were experienced actors who aspired for a higher standard of democracy in Tunisia following the uprising. Nasser, the supervisor of peer education with one of the HIV/AIDS associations, speaking of post-uprising Tunisia, said, 'Eventually this will lead us to something more democratic and real. It's a long process, but this is our process.'[87]

The Emergence of the New

Tunisia not only experienced an almost total re-composition of civil society actors but also individuals and groups were genuinely trying to set up a system of local democracy. Many new associations focused on national solidarity and mobilising citizens; moreover, they were not

[86] Ibid. [87] Interview in Tunis (25), 27 January 2012 and 14 March 2013.

waiting for the state to determine their role. Soraya, a woman who helped to create an association in Kef (a deprived region of Tunisia), said that her group organised meetings in her garage since it first received its associational visa.[88] Following the uprising, she spent most of her time in Tunis attending civil society strengthening workshops and training meetings. Several of the newer associations were involved in citizen mobilisation and the promotion of democracy. The newer associations also engaged in service provision and social welfare/humanitarian initiatives, both within Tunis and in the poorer regions outside the major urban areas.

This section looks to three new organisations that acquired their associational visa after January 2011: Al Madanya, Femmes et Citoyenneté and L'Association de Recherches sur la Démocratie et le Développement. It describes the perceptions and expectations of these newer organisations following the downfall of the Ben Ali regime. Subsequently, this section also presents some of the key identified issues and challenges for the newer organisations, including significant capacity and skills gaps as well as the relatively recent emergence of a counter-public in Tunisia's expanding public spaces.

Citoyenneté *in Practice*

The three organisations could be characterised as secular-liberal organisations. They were created in the immediate post-revolution environment and, approximately one year after the revolution, were still in the process of refining their strategic objectives, in particular how their work would sit in relation to the newly elected government. Similar to the historic associations, the newer civil society organisations also situated conflicts within civil society between their envisioned activities and what they perceived as mounting political as well as sociocultural 'conservative' discourses. Some civil society actors were antagonistic to emerging counter-publics that were religious in nature, while others accepted with reluctance that the new public space was by its nature a contested space with varied ideologies and perceptions of how post-revolution Tunisia should be modelled.

---

[88] Interview in Tunis (47), 22 March 2012.

Al Madanya

The association Al Madanya was established immediately after the revolution by Uday and his brother. Uday explained that he had previously lived in the United States, in Florida, and worked in business management (trade in textiles from Morocco and Tunisia) for more than 10 years. After the uprising in 2011 he returned to Tunisia to become more engaged in his country following the departure of the Ben Ali regime. He remarked that he and his brother had always wanted to establish a similar kind of organisation, but 'had no interest in engaging in the Ben Ali system'.[89] Despite their admitted lack of experience in humanitarian development, Uday and his brother travelled throughout Tunisia to conduct an informal needs assessment of lower-income communities outside of Tunis. Based on the needs assessment, they developed the ideas and priorities for their organisation, such as helping unemployed young people qualify for their driving license (as this is something still quite expensive and the lack of which prevents many people from qualifying for employment), a skills transfer programme in agriculture and a cultural heritage programme with a website for all the different sections across Tunisia. The aim was to support and reinforce the sociocultural aspects they felt were lost over the last few decades in Tunisia. Uday remarked that he was hoping this work would in fact make people's daily lives easier. Although Uday continued some of his work in business management, his humanitarian work in Tunisia following the uprising was what he considered his full-time employment. As he and his brother were 'well-connected' to the business community both inside and outside of Tunisia, they were able to rely on financial donations from diaspora overseas. At the time of the research they had also been able to acquire some funding from the United States, Germany and Scandinavian countries.

When I spoke to Uday a little more than one year after the revolution, he and his organisation had already been able to sign an agreement to support the transport costs for young people to attend school in rural areas outside Tunis with the Ministry of Development for their work. I was conscious that the historic organisations working in HIV/AIDS had not had this opportunity to meet with the new members of government at the time. Uday acknowledged that there was a significant amount of competition already among the newer organisations.

---

[89] Interview in Tunis (33), 13 February 2012.

He said, 'I perceive that these organisations want more power... There are problems with bureaucracy and many people are still perceiving NGOs as political entities.'[90] I asked him how they were being received in the different communities they worked in. He explained that overall the communities were very positive because of the need to improve the available services there – such as transport to schools for their children.

Femmes et Citoyenneté

What began as a book club between women soon transformed into an organisation to support greater rights for women in Tunisia based on the spirit of helping others. Femmes et Citoyenneté received its associational visa in April 2011 and immediately began providing support to lower-income communities in Kef (a poorer region in the country's North West), in particular to women who had experienced domestic violence, individuals affected by the heavy snowfall and floods in that region in 2011–2012 and communities in need during Eid al-Fitr. Nevertheless, supporting the greater rights of women was the primary focus of the organisation. Soraya, one of the officers of the organisation, explained that the association felt the rights of women were threatened following the revolution, and that the issue of equality was very important during this transitionary phase for Tunisia. She stated, 'We are really balancing on the line of inequality at the moment... we feel seriously threatened.'[91] I spoke with Soraya, whose mother established the organisation, together with her younger sister who was applying to university at the time, at a busy cafe in Tunis on Avenue Bourguiba. They stressed that the issue of the rights of women was paramount to them as the younger sister claimed, 'There is this risk that extremists could take away our rights and we have never had this or experienced this here.' Soraya followed on her sister's words, acknowledging that with democracy she should be tolerant of all views and extremism but adding that she refused to be 'threatened verbally or physically, this is not democracy'.[92]

Only two weeks before I met with Soraya and her sister, the organisation's headquarters were based in their home garage. They had since acquired an office in Kef. Soraya explained that the association had a horizontal structure and that through this they tried to exercise democracy and democratic principles throughout their

[90] Ibid.   [91] Interview in Tunis (47), 22 March 2012.   [92] Ibid.

organisation – 'Everything we do is put to a vote.' They remarked that they had a good relationship with the other organisations and that network associations were being created to allow smaller organisations to become stronger. Soraya noted that increasingly they were becoming connected with other organisations doing similar work and that the Internet helped them to find out what is going on, stating, 'Word of mouth is essential at the moment.' They were primarily working on issues concerning violence against women, the incarceration of women, leadership and training for women from low-income environments and microcredit projects for young people out of school. One of the main goals for the organisation was to create a safe space for women who had suffered domestic violence as well as services for psychological follow-up with the women, children and their spouses. They also explained that they had recently acquired funding from the Spanish and German bilateral institutions to fund some of their organisational activities. In addition, alongside initiatives to support the rights of women, Femmes et Citoyenneté organised smaller activities, such as a recent collection of books, school supplies and clothes for poorer areas in Kef. Soraya stated, 'We put up posters to mobilise people and everyone became engaged. There was no resistance to our activities; where there is a will one can find all means to succeed, and this can be done without a lot of money.'[93]

L'Association de Recherches sur la Démocratie et le Développement (ARDD)

ARDD was established immediately after the Tunisia uprising in February 2011. Ghilzlan, one of the founders of the organisation, explained, 'We all lived the revolution and cried out for our dignity and liberty, as we engaged ourselves then in the future of our country. We suffered years under the family of Ben Ali as they betrayed the social and political objectives of the country.'[94] Ghilzlan and her colleagues established the association with the aim of wanting to open the consciousness of individuals and to expand opportunities for them in what she considered a period of emergency for the country. Early in the life of the organisation they held a conference on the 'democratic transition'. She explained that following the conference, their work intensified as people started to become more and more aware of the

[93] Ibid. [94] Interview in Tunis (53), 3 April 2012.

repression applied under the former regime. She described how, during her former humanitarian work before the uprising, the police often visited her as her work was thought to tread on political areas. Now she believes, 'It is necessary that civil society is present in all of these domains, that they are present in all of these institutions so that finally things change.'

ARDD also organised events on 'the media and the revolution', 'the environment and the revolution' and the rights of women, each of which involved a series of roundtable discussions with different experts from political and civil society. The organisation also prioritised work with young people, in particular on how they themselves perceived the aftermath of the uprisings. ARDD also held a seminar on the 'issue of Islamists' following the October 2011 elections. Ghilzlan acknowledged, 'Now we learn we will have to live together. As a woman I felt threatened in my personal as well as associational life, as all this now comes into the public life ... Even if the results of the elections are not what I wanted, I also do not want to lose my liberty; we feel a bit cornered at the moment.' She raised the issue that the CPS was at risk in Tunisia and gave the example of emerging debates on temporary marriage at the time, noting, 'We are seeing things we have never seen here before. Religion is something personal that no one can oblige of the other.' Despite her personal feelings concerning Islam, Ghilzlan acknowledged that the Islamists suffered enormously under the former regime. She passionately declared, 'No to repression, no to making judgements of them; yes to freedom and the diversity of opinion!' In what she considered 'l'apprentissage de la démocratie', she expressed, 'We are learning to live together.' ARDD has since organised roundtables to bring together 'Islamists' and oppositional political figures to discuss emerging issues for the transition from authoritarian rule in Tunisia. Despite her and the organisation's general efforts towards inclusion, she remarked, 'It is a mutual and reciprocal apprenticeship but I am from the left – yes to the separation of the state from religion.'[95]

Many of the newer organisations (including the three aforementioned examples) expressed a remarkable enthusiasm to be able to engage fully in the expanding public space as well as a sense of urgency and conviction for the work they were doing. The objectives of the

[95] Ibid.

organisations in many ways evolved around the shaping of a more inclusive and supportive environment, in particular for many marginalised and deprived groups living across Tunisia. For the newer organisations, the role of the state was rarely discussed as it appeared that post-uprising civil society sought to vigilantly protect itself from the intrusions of the state. The ethos described by the different organisations points to the self-management and self-organisation agendas explicit in Baker's description of the new Latin American left, with the notion of the 'defence of freedom from outside the state' present during the social movements across Eastern Europe and Latin America. Here one perceives a set of civil society actors filling the social contract the state was arguably not able to provide during the transition from authoritarian rule. Finally, several of the organisations suggested a 'civil society utopia' with a strong underlying normative suggestion that at the least the post-revolution public space would be a domain of solidarity, voluntarism and altruism.

Following the Tunisia uprising, some members of civil society were also relatively antagonistic to newer emerging counter-publics representing disparate ideologies and visions for the emerging public space(s). Some of the newer associations expressed degrees of concern or opposition with regard to religiously oriented organisations also manoeuvring within public spaces (this will be further explored in Chapter 5). They expressed reluctance to sharing new spaces with organisations whose visions and objectives were perceived as disparate to their own. This point was stressed by Muammar, an online media journalist, who remarked that 2011 was a good time to 'push the agenda'. He further observed, 'Everything is changing really fast and for those who manage to occupy that space first, after that it's hard to keep them out. There will be more difficult times for the liberals here in Tunisia as they are not organised politically at all and they are not infiltrating the organisations which are active.'[96]

Emerging Issues for the Newer Associations: Freedom from the State?

While one could argue that civil society, and the newer organisations in particular, operated within a climate of relative freedom following the

---

[96] Interview in Tunis (27), 30 January 2012.

2010–2011 uprising, they also began to encounter challenges. These challenges were compounded by fragile state infrastructure, a crippled economy and political deadlock aggravated by in-fighting among the political parties. Apart from these exogenous factors, however, civil society was also impacted by the indeterminacy of the transition itself that affected some organisations' ability to mobilise resources from private, regional or international donors. More importantly, newer civil society organisations had to evolve from a singular or insular focus on democratisation to more strategic longer-term objectives for their organisational activity. The synthesis mapping conducted by the European Union indicated that many of the organisations were at a rudimentary stage of development with few members, reduced capacity in financial and human resources, a lack of strategic vision of their role and limitations in achieving sustainability in their work.[97] A number of organisations were created to respond to the precise needs of the transition from authoritarian rule, such as the fostering of citizen engagement, monitoring the election process and participation in the development of the new constitution. These organisations would eventually be inclined to shift their focus to further engagement in economic and humanitarian development activities.[98]

The two core challenges for the newer civil society organisations were issues associated with organisational capacity and a lack of experience, both of which were perceived to exacerbate susceptibility to political co-optation and instrumentalisation. Fajr, a former member of a larger historic association now working with a new German-funded democracy strengthening initiative following the Tunisia uprising, underscored the perception that the newer organisations held a relatively narrow focus at the outset. She perceived that the newer NGOs were inexperienced structurally and strategically. She stated:

Before the elections all the interest was focused on the first democratic elections in Tunisia but this was time limited and everyone could rally and focus on this. And now they are having to think much more long term and they see they do not have the capacities necessary or the strategic

---

[97] Union Européenne, 'Rapport de Diagnostic', p. 12.
[98] Le Réseau Euro-Méditerranéen des Droits de l'Homme, 'Contribution de la Mission'; Majoub, 'La Gouvernance Environnementale Démocratique'; and Union Européenne, 'Rapport de Diagnostic', p. 12.

vision... Everyone is still in the post-revolutionary euphoria... we are only just planning now.[99]

Some attributed the lack of capacity and strategic vision to the residue of the former regime, during which period many NGOs were dependent on financing from various embassies and bilateral donors. Dr Saquib, the director of a recently established UN initiative in Tunisia, also remarked:

The strategic skills required for obtaining and managing funds with both the NGOs of before and now are not strong – and this inability to reach out to donors is a consequence of severe repression under the Ben Ali regime. This is the nature that 95 per cent of the NGOs are currently operating in. All of them are badly in need of capacity building. They are also badly in need of internal democracy building as they are used to being a one man or one woman show ... The civil society organisations have no experience in capacity building and therefore this spirit of volunteerism ends with the distribution of services and material items.[100]

One additional area of contention for the newer organisations as well as the historic associations was in determining the role of the state in social welfare and humanitarian development – in particular as Tunisia was undergoing an economic crisis. The remarkable spirit of volunteerism that emerged after the revolution overshadowed the necessity for the state also to redefine its role. For example, in February 2012 the North West region of Tunisia – a relatively deprived region – experienced unusual degrees of heavy snowfall whereby entire communities were left without food, water or heating; a host of associations rushed to deliver aid to these communities before the state could act. Fajr expressed frustration that the newer organisations were not pursuing a long-term vision for social welfare and humanitarian development. She argued:

At the moment the NGOs should be advocating that the state takes on its proper function and roles with regard to social services, but instead it's the NGOs themselves taking on these services; and this is not a stable situation or sustainable. They seem to be directed by emotions at the moment ... The

---

[99] Interview in Tunis (32), 10 February 2012.
[100] Interview in Tunis (34), 15 February 2012.

NGOs are supporting these communities [in the North West] rather than pressuring the state to act.[101]

However, given the historical residue left on civil society by the Bourguiba and Ben Ali regimes, it was perhaps understandable that the newer organisations in particular would be pursuing self-management agendas and would not be waiting for the state to act. Najeeb, an employee of a bilateral organisation and civil society member, sympathised with the seemingly haphazard approach the associations seemed to be taking, noting:

The country lived under the total control of the state – a centralised state – and during this period the 'local collectivity' or associational actors had no authority or autonomy of resources ... they were primarily there to accompany the action of the government and of the party [RCD]. It was a relation of subordination. These associations could not organise themselves without permission from the state previously.[102]

Therefore, given the tangible remains of repression, it is possible to comprehend the need for civil society to act autonomously as well as its caution towards both state institutions and Ennahda in the expanding post-uprising public space. In the two years subsequent to the downfall of the Ben Ali regime, Tunisia was on course for the incorporation and, moreover, acceptance of two parallel systems in which the state and civil society would act independently from one another.

The sudden emergence of a new and vibrant civil society immediately following the 2010–2011 uprising highlighted the dynamic spirit of volunteerism and *citoyenneté* embodied deep within Tunisians despite decades of repression under authoritarian rule. Uday, the director of Al Madanya, observed, 'In a way, it was a huge step for the NGOs to come forward and be able to overcome these historical precedents and barriers to their participation.'[103] Nevertheless, the newer organisations were also beginning to encounter challenges of their own, those which were both endogenous and exogenous to their organisations. Internally, they had to adapt their core activities to more realistic expectations beyond strategies of hyper-visibility for activities such as citizen mobilisation for elections and monitoring of the National

---

[101] Interview in Tunis (32), 10 February 2012.
[102] Interview in Tunis (38), 6 March 2012 and March 2013.
[103] Interview in Tunis (33), 13 February 2012.

Constituent Assembly. They also had to reflect strategically on how to engage domestic and international donors in a competitive and uncertain transition climate as well as to anticipate organisational capacity needs. Externally, the newer associations had to manoeuvre within the context of fragile state institutions, a delicate economic landscape and in-fighting between secular and religious political parties. Overall, a number of civil society actors who participated in the research accepted that democratisation would take time and that many uncomfortable debates and contestations would, by necessity, be had. Many also highlighted in a positive manner that the current landscape for civil society in Tunisia at the time was exceptional, something that could have never been imagined in the previous decades of authoritarian rule. Therefore, they recognised that the transformations occurring in the political as well as public spaces would incur both gains and losses.

Conclusion

Following the departure of the Ben Ali regime in January 2011, the High Authority instituted measures for political liberalisation that included the expansion of laws permitting political parties to register and amendments to the formal laws of association allowing for the creation of thousands of new civil society organisations. The sociopolitical space expanded and a range of actors and groups emerged to claim their right to participate in post-uprising Tunisia. Simultaneously, a multitude of views and priorities were tabled for discursive contestation, such as issues concerning freedom of the press and media (or the limits of), issues regarding the status of women, support and recognition of vulnerable populations and, finally, a key symbol of national identity, the Tunisian flag.

During what could be considered as the 'resurrection of civil society', thousands of new civil society organisations were legally created to not only provide support to deprived communities in the different regions of Tunisia but to also participate in Tunisia's efforts towards democratisation. The thousands of newer organisations would also be acting alongside and sharing the same symbolic as well as physical public spaces with Tunisia's historic civil society organisations, created in the decades prior to the 2010–2011 uprising.

The historic civil society organisations, formed prior to the downfall of the regime, encountered challenges that many of the newer associations would likely be spared. For example, after the revolution donor funding from bilateral and multilateral institutions became temporarily uncertain as a result of the regional uprisings and the overall global financial recession. While it was argued a 'tsunami' of donors flocked to Tunisia after January 2011, some previously existing donors halted their activities until a more stable political climate could emerge. Alternatively, some newer donors committed to initiatives without fully comprehending the wider implications of Tunisian's political and developmental inheritance. In addition, the sociocultural terrain became murky as a range of debates and attitudes proliferated, in particular what were conceived as more 'conservative' discourses around the future role of Islam in the country. Uncertain financing and a contentious environment contributed to many historic organisations' sense of paralysis with regard to their former activities in various communities across Tunisia. In addition, these organisations were unaccustomed to competition for resources, having operated in a relatively restricted public space under Ben Ali. Prior to the downfall of the regime, this space was largely modelled based on neoliberal policies that afforded legitimacy to these organisations as primarily cost-effective providers of services. The consequence for many of the historic civil society organisations would be their limitation to engage in Tunisia's post-uprising public spaces beyond the provision of social welfare services.

More importantly, before 2011 the historic civil society organisations manoeuvred in a relatively limited public space where the regime was intolerant to perceived opposition. These organisations also operated during a time in which legal Islamist associations and political Islam were restricted. They inhabited a space relatively isolated from competing views and counter discourses. After January 2011, some historic civil society organisations, in particular those working with vulnerable communities, faced a dilemma as they inadvertently continued to apply the same strategies of discretion and invisibility used under Ben Ali. As the newer organisations charged to the forefront to claim both old and new spaces, the historic associations appeared to be at a clear disadvantage based in part on the political residue they inherited. Accustomed to strategies of discretion and negotiation, some understandably maintained caution as the customary *modus operandi*.

And while one could argue that the newer organisations operated within a more fertile expanding public space, some also began to encounter their own set of challenges. These challenges were only compounded by fragile state infrastructure, a dwindling economy and political in-fighting between the 'liberal' and the 'conservative' members of the National Constituent Assembly. Civil society was also impacted by the indeterminacy of the transition period itself, affecting some organisations' ability to mobilise resources from private, regional or international donors. More importantly, civil society organisations had to evolve from a singular or insular focus on democratisation, in large part led by the euphoria of the revolution, to more strategic longer-term objectives for their activities. With many organisations lacking in organisational experience and capacity, developing clear visions and goals in a turbulent environment became problematic. In addition, similar to the historic associations, some of the newer members of civil society situated a conflict between their envisioned activities and mounting political as well as sociocultural 'conservative' discourses. Some civil society actors expressed resistance to emerging counter-publics that were religiously oriented. Others reluctantly accepted that Tunisia's widening public spaces would be contentious with varied ideologies and perceptions of how post-revolution Tunisia could be modelled.

Finally, the newer civil society organisations, in particular, exhibited the self-determination and self-management agendas underscored by the new Latin American left in the 1970s and 1980s, described in Chapter 2. Moreover, following the downfall of the regime, these actors came to closely resemble the nature of civil society as understood by Gramsci. Civil society emerged as an entity believing itself capable of restoring agency through self-rule but also in subverting the hegemony of the state. This was most evidenced in the materialisation of the concept of *citoyenneté* reminiscent of the popular upsurges and social movements in Eastern Europe and Latin America in the 1980s. Some of these actors, consequently and perhaps unwittingly, alluded to a civil society utopia, free from the state following the uprising, without necessarily acknowledging the limitations of a self-determination agenda. Alternatively, under Ben Ali in particular, the concept of civil society reflected a Hegelian understanding in which the state was ultimately responsible for the ordering of the disharmonies within civil society and whereby these actors were reliant on the state for their existence. Following the 2010–2011 uprising, the historic civil society organisations carried with them this residue of decades of authoritarian rule, but perhaps more importantly, a neoliberal inheritance. Were the 'illiberal' battles unfolding in Tunisia's expanding public spaces the result of the incompatibility between these two very disparate ideological understandings and manifestations of civil society?

5 Social Divisions and the Re-Manifestation of Social Islam

They were nowhere and they were, in effect, forbidden to lead their lives and gain a living – they could not be in the media and they could not be in the private sector, they could not be represented anywhere – they were only allowed in small commercial activities. Ben Ali emptied the social and economic structures of the Islamists.

– Association member, Tunis[1]

In 2013, two vocal critics of Ennahda, Chokri Belaid and Mohamed Brahmi, were assassinated within the span of only a few months. Many Tunisians not only considered the assassinations of the two men a direct attack on efforts towards democratisation but also a perceived re-manifestation of authoritarian rule. From the time of the democratic elections in October 2011 to the murder of Belaid just over one year later, increasing intolerance between secular and religious viewpoints could be perceived at the political and sociocultural levels in post-uprising Tunisia. The mounting tension gave the impression of a country mired in sociopolitical stagnation in the critical phase of the transition from authoritarian rule two years on. John Voll, alluding to the fall of the one-party state in Algeria in the early 1990s and the secularist state of Habib Bourguiba in Tunisia in the 1980s, in a sense foretells the challenge once again facing the region. He writes, 'The crisis is not only one of trying to decide which group will control existing structures; the battle is to decide which worldview will define the fundamental structures of the social and political order.'[2] One outcome of the 2010–2011 Tunisia uprising was that a multitude of unstable and reversible hegemonies gave rise to a host of visible as well as less perceptible publics and counter-publics emerging to fill Tunisia's

---

[1] Interview in Tunis (38), 6 March 2012 and March 2013.
[2] J. Voll, 'Sultans, Saints, and Presidents: The Islamic Community and the State in North Africa' in Entelis (ed.), *Islam, Democracy and the State in North Africa*, p. 3.

new public spaces. The different publics each sought to control the dominant discourse within these spaces where now a multitude of ideological and political affiliations could co-exist.

There were two simultaneously occurring processes leaving their mark on the sociopolitical transformations following the Tunisia uprising. The first was a battle for political space and control over hegemonic discourses as Tunisia endeavoured to re-determine the nature of the 'modern' state after the revolution. This concerned questions of identity, religion and the Arab-Muslim nature of the nation.[3] The second process was the battle emerging among secular and Islamist civil society actors and groups. These battles mirrored the rivalries and divergences manifesting in the political arena among Ennahda representatives, other members of the National Constituent Assembly and oppositional political parties.

This chapter examines the second core theme of the book, namely the emerging sociocultural and socio-religious divisions, including the rise of associational or social Islam following the downfall of the Ben Ali regime in 2011. It analyses in more depth the emerging conflicts and divisions between the secular and religious actors to further determine the function of conflict within civil society – in particular, the consequences of these divergences for understandings on civil society. The chapter begins with a narrative of the emergence of Salafism in Tunisia and the historical approach of the Ben Ali regime to Islamist opposition, namely the Mouvement de la Tendance Islamique (MTI) that eventually evolved into the Ennahda party in 1989. This context, in conjunction with the historical materials from Chapter 3, demonstrates how over several decades the regime endeavoured to detach Islam from the public imagination. The chapter then examines the different civil society actors manoeuvring in Tunisia's public spaces following the uprising – for example, Islamist actors who were denied the opportunity to engage in legal civil society organisations under Ben Ali who now chose to participate in the momentum of post-uprising Tunisia.

The Making of a Counter-Public

In the run up to and following the social protests in the Middle East and North Africa in 2010 and across 2011, Islamist actors and groups

[3] Ghorbal, *Orphelins de Bourguiba*, p. 9.

were not the primary force behind the demonstrations. According to Jane Kinninmont, 'They were not absent but rather constituted just a part of the much broader social and political coalition that came onto the streets to demand political change.'[4] Nevertheless, due to decades of visible and invisible political manoeuvring and organisation accompanied by sweeping liberalisation measures following the uprisings, Islamist organisations and political parties were able to mobilise mass support in Tunisia to eventually gain the political majority in the elections after the uprising. Historically, the path of political Islam in Tunisia was met routinely with contestation by the government. Accompanying each rise in public support for the Islamist agenda was repression, including imprisonment, torture, exile and a comprehensive political campaign to turn public opinion against Islamists across different levels of society. Aziz Al-Azmeh explains that the eventual means by which the concept civil society was used by state and non-state intelligentsia was related directly to the rise of Islamism. In Tunisia, the notion of civil society increasingly became applied as an exclusionary term, which by 1989 directly marginalised political Islam on the grounds that it was 'at variance with national civil consensus'.[5]

The Revival of Islam in Tunisia

Subsequent to and perhaps in conjunction with post-independence and pro-nationalist movements, Islamists movements began to play the principal oppositional role across North Africa in Morocco, Tunisia and Algeria. In each of these countries, Islam represented what Michael Willis considers 'the most significant political challenge' the three regimes encountered since independence given the ability of Islamist organisations to mobilise the population, in particular marginalised and deprived groups, across each country.[6] Two main factors account for the rise in popularity of Islam following independence movements in North Africa. The first was the concurrent emergence of Salafiyyah

---

[4] J. Kinninmont, 'The Next Fight Will Be among Islamists', *The World Today* (February and March 2012).

[5] A. Al-Azmeh, 'Populism Contre Democracy: Recent Democratist Discourse in the Arab World' in G. Salame (ed.), *Democracy without Democrats: The Renewal of Politics in the Muslim World* (New York: I. B. Tauris, 1994), pp. 122–123.

[6] Willis, *Politics and Power*, p. 155.

or Salafi movements in the nineteenth and twentieth centuries, with prominent Islamist thinkers such as Mohammed Abdu visiting Algeria and Tunisia during this period.[7] Salafist ideas at the time represented a return to the teachings of Islam to address European colonialism. Willis says they 'provided a vital ideological and organisational strand to the anti-colonial movement in both countries'.[8] Furthermore, many of the Islamist movements in the Maghreb were strongly influenced by the model and practices of the Muslim Brotherhood in Egypt. Salafi movements rose in response to both external antagonism and perceived threats to local culture and beliefs.[9]

The second factor responsible for the emergence of Islamist movements simultaneously with post-independence movements was the ambition and extent to which the Bourguiba regime sought to adopt and impose secular modernising reforms in Tunisia. While Islam was established as the official state religion at independence in Tunisia, significant areas of life were secularised during this period. The state effectively took control 'over issues and tasks that had traditionally been the reserve of independent religious institutions'.[10] Moreover, Abdelbaki Hermassi analyses the situation as follows:

Of all the Arab countries, Tunisia was unique in the public manner in which its modernist elites attacked institutional Islam and dismantled its basic institutions in the name of systematic social and cultural reform – the result was to dismantle the whole old cultural order ... accompanied by a very negative and contemptuous position toward traditional Islam.[11]

This position against Islam in the name of modernisation and political liberalisation reinforced an entire counter-movement dedicated to safeguarding Arab-Muslim identity and the stronghold of traditional Islamist institutions in Tunisia.

The ambition of the government to rid the country of what was considered to be 'radical' Islam persisted throughout the Bourguiba and Ben Ali regimes both as a drive to uphold the 'modern' nation-state based on secular values and to eliminate perceived political opposition to the incumbent regime. At various points during the governance of both regimes, the main Islamist party in Tunisia,

---

[7] Ibid., p. 156.   [8] Ibid.
[9] Entelis, *Islam, Democracy and the State in North Africa*, p. xiv.
[10] Willis, *Politics and Power*, p. 157.
[11] As cited in Hamdi, *The Politicisation of Islam*, p. 16.

Le Mouvement de la Tendance Islamique (MTI), which eventually evolved into Hizb Ennahda or the Renaissance Party, experienced political openings with opportunities for more visibility as well as contractions in the space to manoeuvre in the political arena. The routine repression and exclusion of the Islamists from most political and social domains in Tunisia over time led to a growing Islamist counter-public looking to restore human dignity for redress to human rights abuses, including the routine torture and harassment of family members and, more importantly, to put forward an alternative view for the post-revolution Tunisian state.

What existed for decades as a counter-public with limited power soon began to emerge into a group of heterogeneous actors looking to design and influence Tunisia's national identity. While the Bourguiba and Ben Ali regimes acted to detach Islam from the political and sociocultural imagination, several formal and informal Islamist groups continued to manoeuvre before 2010. Haugbolle and Cavatorta describe a 'religious awakening' from even the early 2000s in Tunisia during which a new identity model was being formed. This model was, they write:

> A rejection of both Bourguiba's, which excluded Islam from public life, whether policymaking or regular communal prayer, and the Ben Ali regime's, which seemed to celebrate conspicuous consumption and corruption in the name of progress ... Crucially, pious Tunisians also became more involved in social activism, which was perceived not only as a religious duty, but also as an ethical choice implicitly condemning the regime as unethical.[12]

Concurrently, Ennahda relocated its structure and leadership overseas. From this period, the movement concentrated on maintaining the organisation, providing support to its imprisoned members in Tunisia and campaigning to underscore human rights abuses and the lack of genuine democracy in Tunisia under the Ben Ali regime. The movement also established social welfare networks, an internet site and a satellite television channel.[13] In addition, from the late 1990s the television news network *Al Jazeera* went into operation and featured a range of political opponents of existing Arab regimes, including Tunisian dissidents.[14] Achcar writes, 'Millions of viewers saw, for the

---

[12] Haugbolle and Cavatorta, 'Beyond Ghannouchi'.
[13] Willis, *Politics and Power*, p. 196.
[14] Achcar, *The People Want*, pp. 135–137.

first time, the faces of opponents of their governments who had been forced into exile. Some even learned for the first time of the existence of these dissidents, their compatriots.'[15] This effectively allowed a multitude of groups, including Ennahda, a political as well as public platform, to promote their social welfare and reform agendas. After the events of the Tunisia uprising, various networks of Tunisian Islamist diaspora materialised to reveal a motivated group of actors seeking to become more formally involved in Tunisia's civil society. From December 2010 to January 2011, these counter-publics acquired the freedom to emerge and claim new spaces.

After Ennahda gained the post-election majority in the National Constituent Assembly through the 'Troika', many Tunisians grew concerned over what role Islam would play in the country's future political and sociocultural identity. The post-revolution debates in Tunisia were often polarised between the secular and religiously oriented factions of the population, whereby the 'middle ground' appeared to have evaporated.[16] Considerable academic as well as media attention following the election in October 2011 was also devoted to understanding the relationship (if any) between Ennahda and the Salafi movement in Tunisia.[17] In an article entitled 'The Terrorist Threat is Not High in Tunisia, but...', a professor of contemporary history argued that approximately 50 per cent of Ennahda was composed of the more conservative Salafist elements.[18] He wrote, 'And this explains in part the accusations of a double language which often surrounds Ennahda.' This and subsequent articles that effectively underscored the tendency for liberal-secular bias such as 'Que mijote Ennahda?' ('What is Ennahda plotting?') advocated the need for Ennahda 'to make clear their relationship with the Salafis'.[19] Some members of the public voiced concern through the media of a 'silent complicity' between the majority party Ennahda and the Salafis, assumed by virtue of Ennahda's silence on instances of disorder and violence occurring after the uprisings (these specific instances are

---

[15] Ibid., p. 137.   [16] Suleiman, 'The Disintegrating Fabric of Tunisian Politics'.
[17] See El Amrani and Lindsey, 'Tunisia Moves to the Next Stage' and Ayeb, 'Understanding the Rise of Tunisia's Islamists'. See also Kinninmont, 'The Next Fight Will Be among the Islamists'.
[18] The original French title: 'La Menace Terroriste n'est pas Très Elevée en Tunisie, mais...'
[19] A. Nemlaghi, 'Que Mijote Ennahdha?' *Le Temps* (Tunis), 4 February 2012.

detailed in Chapter 4). Mehrez Bensaid, who wrote about such issues in an article featured in *La Presse*, stated:

It is necessary that the government take firm decisions and apply the law in a way that dissuades those who want to bring harm to our identity. Liberty has its limits and one should not be lax in the face of those who behave like brutes ... We do not need these apostles coming from elsewhere to sow confusion and to bring peril to our union through their particular way of conceiving our tolerant religion. The Tunisian society is horrified by extremes, ladies and gentlemen, our people are moderate, and no one can deceive them.[20]

In February 2012, thousands of Salafis marched to protest the government's negative comments regarding a visit by the Egyptian Imam Wajdi Ghonaim, who reportedly advocated the introduction of female excision; the Tunisian president at the time, Moncef Marzouki, referred to the imam as a 'microbe'.[21] The size of the protest signalled the discernible presence of Salafis in Tunisia at the time.[22]

The imagined (or real) complicity of Ennahda and the Salafis, alongside perceptions that acts of violence were going unpunished, could as aforementioned be attributed to damaged internal security systems and the judicial systems in Tunisia at the time or to the lack of communication among its leadership and members (due to imprisonment or exile) in the decades prior to the downfall of the regime. Therefore, what was publicly perceived as complicity could also have been a consequence of weakened state institutions and nascent communication platforms following more than two decades of authoritarian rule and an abrupt revolution in which many of these institutions were temporarily abandoned.

Situating Power: The Manifestation of Salafism

By virtue of the perceived complicity on the part of Ennahda, there was a belief among some that power was situated in a minority that was

---

[20] Bensaid, 'Le Gouvernement Progresse'.
[21] 'Tunisie: Marzouki S'Excuse pour Avoir Traite Wajdi Ghanim de "Microbe"', Kapitalis.com, 16 February 2012.
[22] C. Baeder, 'Controversial Cleric, Advocate of Female Genital Mutilation, Challenges Tunisian Critics', Tunisia-Live.net, 15 February 2012, and N. K., 'Le Prédicateur Wajdi Ghonaïem Annonce: La Tunisie Appliquera Prochainement la Chariaâ', *Le Temps*, 18 February 2012.

neither legally legitimate nor acting on behalf of the majority. However, this minority occupied a considerable amount of physical, social and media space in the two years following the revolution, and therefore perhaps power was imagined in what was visible – the Salafis. Salafis are associated with a strict or literalist adherence to and application of Sunnism and had become more present in Tunisia's symbolic and physical public spaces since the 2010–2011 uprising. The liberalisation of the political landscape, the end of repression and the release of hundreds of political prisoners created the opportunity for a range of different ideologies and political platforms to emerge. As such, Stefano Torelli writes, 'This opening led to the entrance into Tunisian public life of actors that had been previously banned. Among them were many radical Islamists who had been imprisoned for their ideological leanings and activities.'[23] From January 2011, individuals were more perceptibly able to indicate which form of Islam they supported through their dress and social behaviour. A more 'visible' Islam could be observed in increasing numbers of both younger and older men, often branded simply as 'Salafis' because they wore loose trousers and longer tops, accompanied by long beards. In addition, a growing number of women were seen in the streets wearing the *niqab* and full *burqa*.[24] Members of the Francophone Tunisian press expressed alarm at these very discernible forms of Islam they would now see in Tunisian everyday life. For example, articles in two Tunisian journals – 'To Those Who Still Persist on Wearing the Burqa',[25] in *Le Temps*, and one in *La Presse*, 'The Rights of Women Are a Red Line',[26] which was written by the secretary general of the General Labour Union of Tunisia (UGTT) – underscored the dangers of more conservative understandings of Islam to women's rights.

Since the Tunisia uprising, Salafism had also become increasingly synonymous with the rejection of modernity, violence and extremism. For example, in an article entitled 'The Return of an Occupation not

---

[23] S. Torelli, 'The Multi-Faceted Dimensions of Tunisian Salafism' in F. Cavatorta and F. Merone (eds.), *Salafism after the Arab Awakening Contending with People's Power* (London: Hurst and Company, 2017), p. 61.
[24] Gray, 'Tunisia after the Uprising', p. 286.
[25] S. Khalfi, 'A Celles qui s'Obstinent Encore a Porter la Burqa', *Le Temps* (Tunis), 29 March 2012.
[26] S. Cheffi, 'Les Droits de la Femme Sont une Ligne Rouge', *La Presse de Tunisie*, 12 March 2012.

like the Others', the author wrote, 'The Salafis recognise neither negotiation nor mediation. They are adept at force ... they derive their existence through a rejection of modernity and the democratic matrix ... and thus in the name of a totalising religion, a process of the "Talibanisation" of our society has begun.'[27] In addition, politically controversial decisions taken by Ennahda, such as the decision in February 2012 to evict the Syrian ambassador from Tunisia, raised questions concerning Ennahda's relationship with the West, in particular with France, in influencing its post-uprising positions on key political matters.[28] Unfortunate, however, was the conflation among some members of civil society and media between the myriad Islamist actors, given this was a remarkably heterogeneous group of organisations and individuals.[29] Torelli underscores that Tunisian Salafism is incredibly heterogeneous, advocating that, 'We have Salafi political parties that wish to participate actively in the political and institutional life of Tunisia, next to anti-systemic movements who refuse to interact with existing institutions and even with al-Nahda itself.'[30] For example, it is important to make the distinction between the 'scientific-Salafis' and the 'jihadis Salafis', whereby the former invest in associative activities with vulnerable communities and seek to influence the political realm while the latter are more predicated upon armed resistance against non-Muslim military and political forces.[31] It is estimated that the number of either 'scientific-Salafis' or 'jihadis Salafis' in Tunisia during this period was approximately 50,000; these individuals were not necessarily part of a formal organisation or based within a political group.[32] However, two weeks after the departure of Ben Ali, the interim government released prisoners incarcerated under the anti-terrorist law of 2003; it was estimated that 1,200 Salafis – of whom 300 fought in Afghanistan, Iraq, Yemen or Somalia – were liberated at this time. Moreover, several Tunisian Salafi imams (both scientific and

---

[27] J. Sayah, 'Retour sur une Occupation pas Comme les Autres', *La Presse de Tunisie*, 12 January 2012.

[28] A. Warren, 'Tunisia Steps Out', ForeignPolicy.com (23 February 2012).

[29] See International Crisis Group, 'Tunisie: Violences et Défi Salafiste', *Rapport Moyen-Orient/Afrique du Nord*, Crisisgroup.org, no. 137 (13 February 2013).

[30] Torelli, 'The Multi-Faceted Dimensions of Tunisian Salafism', p. 158.

[31] See N. Jebnoun, 'Salafi Trouble in Tunisia's Transition', Jadaliyya.com, 13 July 2012, and International Crisis Group 'Tunisie: Violences et Défi Salafiste', pp. 9–10.

[32] International Crisis Group, 'Tunisie: Violences et Défi Salafiste', p. 10.

jihadis) who had been living in Western Europe during the Ben Ali regime returned to Tunisia after January 2011.[33]

It is also argued that a new generation of young Islamists between the ages of 15 and 35 was emerging across Tunisia, composed of unemployed men who did not necessarily know Ennahda but who saw themselves as participants in a resistance movement across the region, alongside their Chechen, Iraqi or Afghan counterparts.[34] While spectacular, the instances of violence attributed to Salafis in Tunisia from 2011 to 2013 were of relatively low intensity. Overall, of the individuals harmed in the various events, most casualties were among Salafis themselves (there were 14 Salafi casualties, two of whom were as a result of hunger strikes).[35] And although these and similar acts of violence raised important questions in Tunisia around the unauthorised circulation of weapons and juvenile delinquency, Islamists and their Salafist counterparts were routinely blamed for a host of incivilities and wrongdoing whether or not these acts were politically, religiously or socially motivated. Often these acts served to underscore the governing party's limitations rather than to advance genuine dialogue on democratic and economic reforms.

It could be argued that power was situated everywhere but within the party in the government majority. Following the uprisings, Ennahda took the deliberate decision to institutionalise the party and to subscribe to tenets of liberal democracy such as pluralism and the protection of the rights of citizens. Some factions of the wider Islamist movement in Tunisia did not necessarily see themselves in Ennahda's post-revolution political project, nor did all elements of the movement implicitly support democracy.[36] This led to the creation of splinter Salafist movements, such as Ansar al-Sharia, which eventually publicly criticised and stood in opposition to Ennahda. Perceptions of the weakness of the Party were exacerbated by a perceived fragility of individual members of Ennahda as many party members were known to have suffered extreme physical and psychological torture in prison under the Ben Ali regime.[37] Following the 2011 election, while some could argue that political authority rested with Ennahda, a multitude of political projects were playing out across Tunisia. As such, was real

---

[33] Ibid., p. 15.   [34] Ibid., p. i.   [35] Ibid., p. 6.
[36] Torelli, 'The Multi-Faceted Dimensions of Tunisian Salafism', p. 157.
[37] J. Dridi, 'Pourquoi Ennahdha Rencontre un Succès Populaire en Tunisie?', Kapitalis.com, 18 October 2011.

power in the hands of those who were occupying Tunisia's symbolic and physical public spaces such as the institutions associated with the state? Was it situated in the democratically elected majority of the National Constituent Assembly? Or was this power most potent in an imagined form entangled in rumour and myth-making within greater society? A transition from authoritarian rule can also be characterised by the rapidly shifting power relations between state and society during this period – and the ultimate obscurity by which these relationships are typified.

Finally, Tunisia's leaderless revolution highlighted common economic grievances such as high rates of unemployment, low wages, high rates of inflation and significant income disparities between the rich and the poor whereby the social and economic inequalities created under neoliberalism were arguably to blame.[38] It is argued that the revolution was promulgated by the stifled aspirations of unemployed young people under the age of 30 as well as by the 'left behinds' of the northern interior regions of the country.[39] After the October 2011 elections, despite the economic crisis having been a primary and foremost feature of the Tunisian uprising, the interim government was reluctant to develop definitive policies on socio-economic issues. Two years after the revolution, declining growth and growing inflation and food prices continued to destabilise the economy. Inflation rose to 6.5 per cent in March 2013 and GDP growth flat-lined in the first quarter of 2013 at 2.7 per cent.[40] Furthermore, following the October 2011 elections to the National Constituent Assembly, Tunisia was governed through the Islamist-secular coalition, the 'Troika'.[41] Tasked with drafting a constitution and forming an interim government until presidential elections could be held, the National Constituent Assembly was destabilised by oppositional infighting and prolonged negotiations. Hamadi Redissi argued through one of many of Tunisia's new online press sites, 'All of a sudden, political life has become polarised.

[38] Aarts and Cavatorta (eds.), *Civil Society in Syria and Iran*, p. 8.
[39] Beinin and Vairel, 'Afterword: Popular Uprisings in Tunisia and Egypt', pp. 238, 248.
[40] Blibech, Driss and Longo, 'Citizenship in Post-Awakening Tunisia'.
[41] Following the October 2011 elections, Ennahda formed a coalition with two secular parties – the Congress for the Republic (29 seats) and Ettakatol (20 seats) – to secure a majority, creating what would come to be known as the 'Troika'.

At the Assembly, the Troika has imposed a "mini-Constitution," organising public powers until the next elections ... Hence, the malaise: the Troika believes that it has been mandated to govern, while the opposition continues to criticise its divisiveness.'[42] The assassinations of the two prominent oppositional political figures, Chokri Belaid and Mohamed Brahmi, in 2013 served to exacerbate the tensions between Tunisia's secular parties and the 'Troika' over the national economic crisis and the emerging Salafist movement(s). One of the principal challenges for Ennahda in the two years following the uprising was that it regularly found itself ensnared between Salafist contestations and the secular opposition's drive to accentuate the party's inability to govern.[43] Moreover, the growing divisions manifesting at the political level reflected across to the emerging social divisions between the multitude of civil society actors manoeuvring in Tunisia's public spaces.

Social Islam: Claiming New Spaces

While even two years after the revolution it is a challenge to disaggregate the data on the orientations of the different registered organisations, individuals interviewed for the book cite that several hundred religiously oriented associations were established from 2011. Many of these organisations were charitable or humanitarian organisations working in poverty alleviation directly with deprived communities. A number of Islamist associations during this period were also educational and cultural; for example, there existed a range of organisations providing classical Qur'anic education and literacy to women in mosques across the country, such as the Saheb Ettabaa Association of Islamic Culture in Tunis. Evie Soli and Fabio Merone reflect as follows:

The opening of this social space was the chance for many new actors to come onto the Tunisian scene. Tunisian classical social entrepreneurs, mostly secular and western-oriented, discovered that a large and highly motivated new group of actors were now occupying a space in society, provoking widespread suspicion regarding these organisations.[44]

---

[42] Redissi, 'Tunisia: The Difficulties of the Coalition'.
[43] International Crisis Group, 'Tunisie: Violences et Défi Salafiste', p. 8.
[44] Soli and Merone, 'Tunisia: The Islamic Associative System', p. 1.

Soli and Merone contend that this new social activism developed through a 'dual process of internal and external networking' that allowed for these emerging organisations to nourish a resource base to undertake this work in Tunisia's expanding public spaces.[45] Many of these actors and groups worked in deprived areas, operating at the local level to supplant broken state systems. In the International Crisis Group report 'Tunisie: Violences et Défi Salafiste', it was reported that Salafist militias in particular became essential actors in the economic life of post-revolution Tunisia, providing academic support to young scholars, conflict resolution between neighbours and help with local administrative problems. In many villages and neglected urban areas, these groups had 'inserted' themselves in the informal and underground economy.[46]

Social Activism and Associational Islam in Post-Revolution Tunisia

Dr Dema, together with 10 female colleagues and friends, received the formal associational visa to establish the association Al-Usra al-Amina (The Secure Family) in June 2011. She perceived that for many years the population in more deprived areas outside of Tunis lacked information on education, health and hygiene. She said because she was a medical doctor she liked helping individuals in need. She remarked, 'During those years when we were not free at all we could not start an association because everything had to pass through the party; everything had to pass under "them" and in "their" name. We were Islamists and so otherwise we were marginalised. We never tried to work under them.'[47] The organisation worked during Ramadan and Eid to help poorer families with food, clothing and material support. Dr Dema and her colleagues also maintained their full-time roles in the medical profession. She acknowledged that having never worked in a humanitarian organisation she was relatively inexperienced, so with her friends and colleagues 'we are learning'. The association also relied on some 60 volunteers because they were dependent on small local private donations from the community.

---

[45] Ibid., p. 3.
[46] International Crisis Group, 'Tunisie: Violences et Défi Salafiste', p. ii.
[47] Interview in Tunis (49), 28 March 2012.

A core part of the work of Al-Usra al-Amina focused on the family at the health and psychosocial levels, such as on conflict resolution and issues for young people. Dr Dema noted, 'The areas outside Cap Bon are particularly poor areas – just the infrastructure of the houses, how people are living ... absolutely catastrophic situations.'[48] The principal activities of the organisation as set out in its constitution stipulated the following: to give social, material and educational aid to families; to educate stay-at-home women and heads of household; to help prepare young women for their future role as mother and head of the family; and to undertake sociocultural sanitation and environmental interventions. In researching the constitution and aims of the association, it became a challenge practically and conceptually to delineate precisely what makes an association such as Al-Usra al-Amina 'Islamist' and aforementioned organisations such as Femmes et Citoyenneté, secular. The organisations each carried out several of the same activities in deprived communities with a particular focus on women, although it could be argued the Islamic associations were employing a 'moral value system' entrenched in the core values of Islam. Furthermore, these organisations considered themselves Islamic because they relied on the application of different Islamic values, including *zakat* and religious piety.[49]

Dr Dema explained that her understanding of Islam was not just through the five pillars of *ibadat* (religious obligations) but also as a way of life. Her commitment to working with deprived communities, she perceived, comes from her religion. She explained, 'We do this for God – *Fee Sabeel Allah* – or for the pleasure of God. When we work as volunteers we do this for a moral satisfaction. We do not know why they do it, but we know God will be very pleased with us.'[50] The notion of the 'us' versus 'them' social divide was also underscored by Najeeb, who himself established his own civil society organisation after the uprising. He spoke already of this divide between the activities and core target populations of the newer associations. In his analysis, secular organisations were doing more information and awareness-raising meetings (concerning democratisation) and the religiously

---

[48] Ibid.
[49] Soli and Merone, 'Tunisia: The Islamic Associative System', pp. 1–4.
[50] Interview in Tunis (49), 28 March 2012.

oriented organisations, such as the Islamist associations, were doing more 'on-the-ground' work. He stated:

> The Islamist associations are much less visible from the point of view of the media, and are engaging in work on the ground and more of a social-focused work with poorer populations, the unemployed, and they are the ones who are now occupying the terrain with the people themselves ... They are doing outreach work and gaining the sympathy and favour of these populations.[51]

However, he contested the notion advocated by members of the population who claimed these organisations 'are buying the favour of the people'. He also recognised that following the Tunisia uprising, the understanding of the concept of civil society, or *al mujtama al-madani*, was called into question. He argued:

> This notion was put in place by the regime and was almost presented in opposition to the Islamists and even this discourse on terrorism. This was on the side of security, cultural, economic and social and they all came out (the media and the administration) with this notion of civil society in opposition to all things religious and religion (*al-mujtama al-dini*). But this was a political distinction between politicians trying to draw a line under the state and religion ... This in fact lasted over twenty years and has definitely marked the spirit of the population. This sense of civil society was without religious organisations. The churches and the mosques are civil society but whether or not people accept them is another question.[52]

Najeeb, whose sister also founded an Islamist association, directly attributed the post-revolution polarisation between the secular and Islamist organisations currently operating in Tunisia's public spaces to decades of concerted repression under the Bourguiba and Ben Ali regimes. He further explained:

> The Islamists and their ideology on politics were banned and all activities related to the social, political, economic and cultural sphere in Tunisia were banned, and the individuals involved were put in prison or exiled for more than 20 years – even under Bourguiba. So in a way, how do you expect them to be well represented in societal structures now?

Najeeb expressed a clear sympathy for Ennahda as well as a significant admiration for the different civil society actors emerging to participate in Tunisia's public spaces in which he was able to take part.

---

[51] Interview in Tunis (38), 6 March 2012 and March 2013. [52] Ibid.

Nevertheless, he found one of the principal obstacles to democratisation and a critical element responsible for exacerbating social divisions in post-uprising Tunisia was the media. A significant proportion of the journalists operating during the Ben Ali regime were still in their posts following the revolution, and so there was a perception that many journalists were not independent and were continuing to encourage anti-Islamist attitudes. Najeeb contended, 'Objectively the principle of defending and protecting the liberty of the press is absolute but on the ground and in reality this is something else.'[53] He argued that many members of Ennahda, some of whom spent more than 15 years in prison, suffered enormously. However, now they believed that they are legitimate. His main concern was that despite mass support for the party, the media were only willing to show the contrary. This frustration with the media was also highlighted by Muammar, who founded an online media site after the revolution. He argued, 'The journalists' line during Ben Ali was "be afraid of the Islamists" and so far they are not covering the issues around the Salafis very objectively. This is a very biased press ... it borders on provocation.'[54]

Dr Faiqa also described the challenge of the media and its residue from the Ben Ali regime in post-revolution Tunisia. A full-time gynaecologist in Tunis, she has simultaneously to create an organisation to support a freer (more pluralist view) media whereby young people could become more involved. The activities would focus on media training and sensitisation. I was put in contact with Dr Faiqa as she was also in the process of establishing an association with a more religious ethos. She explained that under Ben Ali Tunisia did not have a free media, and now they have the opportunity to transform the media into an independent agent that 'reflects the image of the revolution'.[55] Arguing that the media had not changed since the revolution, she also believed the content of the various sources of media did not reflect the ethics of Islam or humanitarian values. She stated:

Islam should be in direct relation to the individual and guide him on the path to citizen engagement (*muwatana*) ... The Qur'an should be a part of life and through *rahman* (compassion) everyone should find their place in society so that people do not suffer and there is this equality, economic equality. Islam came to hold the hands of the poor and to help them live in dignity.[56]

[53] Ibid.   [54] Interview in Tunis (27), 30 January 2012.
[55] Interview in Tunis (51), 2 April 2012.   [56] Ibid.

Dr Faiqa also expressed a drive to embrace her *citoyenneté* and to participate in civil society, something she argued she could never have done before the revolution. She explained:

Now we are free to act, totally free and have no constraints as before we could not act. Before the revolution there were so few associations and even if we wanted to act we could not ... If you were not in the party [RCD], you were considered the enemy ... We were like animals, we worked, we ate, we slept, that is all. But now we are on the horizon of liberty, to act, to say what we think, without fear of going to prison.

The Islamist associations quickly moved to participate in Tunisia's expanding public spaces. They were able to implement an approach alongside on-the-ground programmes based on morality and piety with deprived communities – a formal participation denied to many under the former regimes. And while this space was open for a range of different activities, a sharp social delineation could soon be perceived between the secular organisations and their religiously oriented counterparts. The secular-religious divisions within civil society in post-revolution Tunisia were aggravated due to a myriad of factors, with two noted herein. The first was the efforts by both the Bourguiba and Ben Ali regimes to erase political opposition through targeted campaigns of repression, marginalisation and violence at the political and sociocultural levels. The second was the role of the media, which arguably played a part in reinforcing social divisions during the Ben Ali presidency, and which, following the uprising, continued to feed a secular moral panic concerning the ramifications of an 'Islamist revolution' as perceived in neighbouring Iran. Rather than exclusively a domain of expanding opportunities and solidarity, civil society was becoming characterised by growing social divisions alongside conflicting views regarding the transformation of Tunisian national identity.

A Plurality of Competing Publics

Some secular organisations actively sided with the Ben Ali regime in its efforts to deny a proportion of the population the opportunity to engage in the political or sociocultural landscape of Tunisia, such as through the formal establishment of a civil society organisation. Therefore, one must ask who the organisations considered as civil society represent and in whose interest they are working. Abdelrahman and

Fraser both echo and engage in untangling the aims of civil society. Both writers distinctly recognise the inherent conflictual nature of civil society as well as the pervasive tensions between 'bourgeois' publics and 'other'.[57] Abdelrahman writes, 'Civil society has become an arena for political conflict and its organisations have been seized by representatives of contending political programmes that often resort to violence and repression to suppress other groups within civil society.'[58] Similarly, Fraser argues, 'Thus, not only were there always a plurality of competing publics but the relations between the bourgeois publics and the other publics were always conflictual ... The public sphere was always constituted by conflict.'[59] Abdelrahman emphasises in particular, in her examination of the evolving notion of civil society in the Egyptian context, that competition among these actors continues to be polarised between the Islamists and the secular intellectuals.[60] She contends, 'The rivalry between Islamists and secularists has increasingly been expressed in the space provided by the newly expanded organisations of civil society, for example, professional syndicates and NGOs.'[61]

Arguing in a similar vein as Jane Mansbridge, Fraser asserted, 'Subordinate groups sometimes cannot find the right voice or words to express their thoughts, and when they do, they discover they are not heard. [They] are silenced, encouraged to keep their wants inchoate, and heard to say "yes" when what they have said is "no".'[62] In discussions with secular (self-identified) organisations and multilateral donors as well Islamist associations, there was a prominent dual discourse significantly centred around an 'us' versus 'them' perception. Fraser muses:

We should question whether it is possible even in principle for interlocutors to deliberate as if they were social peers in specially designated discursive

---

[57] See Abdelrahman, 'The Politics of "Uncivil" Society in Egypt', *Review of African Political Economy*, vol. 29, no. 91 (March 2002), pp. 21–35; Abdelrahman, *Civil Society Exposed*; and Fraser, 'Rethinking the Public Sphere'.
[58] Abdelrahman, 'The Politics of "Uncivil" Society in Egypt', p. 21.
[59] Fraser, 'Rethinking the Public Sphere', p. 61.
[60] Abdelrahman, 'The Politics of "Uncivil" Society in Egypt', p. 25.
[61] Ibid., p. 26.
[62] J. Mansbridge, 'Feminism and Democracy', *The American Prospect*, no. 1 (Spring 1990), p. 127 in Fraser, 'Rethinking the Public Sphere'.

arenas, when these discursive arenas are situated in a larger societal context that is pervaded by structural relations of dominance and subordination.[63]

Despite the conflicts and contentions between civil society actors and groups, Fraser underscores the value of these ongoing contestations, namely that multiple counter-publics actually allow for the eventual expansion of discursive spaces. She stipulates, 'In principle, assumptions that were previously exempt from contestation will now have to be publicly argued out. In general, the proliferation of subaltern counter-publics means a widening of discursive contestation, and that is a good thing in stratified societies.'[64] Fraser perceives this polarisation as one of the few effective means to expand the discursive arena – a relatively isolated and uncontested space in Tunisia up until now.

Contestation from the Periphery: Growing Cleavages among Civil Society

From 2011 to 2013, the interactions between civil society actors could be characterised with instances of respectful tolerance as well as discursive dominance and hostility with regard to perceptions of difference. As Tunisia's public space grew into more and more of a contested space, conflicts, competition and contentions emerged between not only the historic and newer actors within civil society but also among secular and Islamist associations (which cannot be homogenised into definitive factions). Through an examination of the discursive content of some of the print media and participant interviews, it is possible to observe how the language individuals adopted as they reasoned together favoured one discourse and discouraged others.[65] This section looks more closely to the polarised language of the different civil society actors in the two years following the revolution to further underscore the tensions and conflicts unfolding across this terrain. It analyses the words of the secular organisations that at times were found to contain reactionary sentiments and intolerance; it also looks to some of the Islamic associations, which, while adopting a similar 'us' versus 'them' discourse, arguably considered themselves vital members of civil society.

---

[63] Fraser, 'Rethinking the Public Sphere', p. 65.   [64] Ibid., p. 67.
[65] Ibid., p. 64.

The Compatibility between Civil Society and Islam

In Abdelrahman's research into further understanding the concept and application of civil society within the Egyptian context, she exposes the degrees of violence and repression that have been used to suppress other groups within civil society. Moreover, she underscores the tendency in academic literature as well as the media to portray Islamist groups as the only groups demonstrating intolerance for other political and sociocultural missions.[66] She argues that 'members of secular "liberal" associations have also shown extreme intolerance to individuals and groups, usually Islamists, who do not conform to their political project'.[67] Most poignantly, she advocates for a more precise empirical examination of the problems within civil society itself and recognition of the 'inherent contradictions' of this concept.[68] As in the case of Egypt, by observing the interactions between these groups before and after the 2010–2011 events in Tunisia, it is possible to discern a similar intolerance among the disparate actors manoeuvring in Tunisia's expanding public spaces. Moreover, the post-revolution period itself highlights the intensity of these conflicts in the drive towards democratisation.

Soon after the elections to the National Constituent Assembly whereby Ennahda governed through the 'Troika', a moral panic quickly set into a significant proportion of the secular-liberal factions of the population, particularly in Tunis. This moral panic was reflected in some of the print and television media and was manifested in the nature and aims of the public demonstrations that took place from this period. The moral panic fed on the perception that 'radical' Islamic ideology and practice would soon acquire a much more politicised role in Tunisian society.[69] Ambiguous political statements on behalf of Ennahda, accompanied by a visibly changing sociocultural street environment, aggravated these mounting fears among secular-liberal populations. This anxiety equally transferred across to civil society where many of the historic organisations and newer organisations encountered uncertain terrain and unanswered questions. Organisations that considered themselves members of civil

---

[66] Abdelrahman, 'The Politics of "Uncivil" Society in Egypt', p. 29.   [67] Ibid.
[68] Ibid., p. 23.
[69] Ajmi, 'More Than 4,000 People Descend' and L. Noueihed, 'Tunisian Protesters Demand Islamic State', AlArabiya.net, 17 March 2012.

society were asking just how 'civil' were the newer, Islamist associations that legally could acquire the associational visa. Historic and newer organisations would come to share not only a widening and ambiguous discursive space but also a very physical space (for example, both secular and Islamist demonstrations were being organised on the same day in the same place on a number of occasions). Moreover, some of the historic and the newer secular organisations perceived actual danger of violence from Salafi factions that also emerged to participate in this public space – some expressed feeling threatened, having been harassed, and having faced uncomfortable confrontations.[70] Finally, the secular organisations questioned the autonomy of the Islamist associations, namely from where and how they acquired their funding to operate.

There is often the argument that Islam and democracy are incompatible, and that as such, civil society and Islam therefore are equally incompatible. This perception has relied over time on often unquestioned binaries including modern versus traditional, West versus East and liberal versus illiberal. For example, Michaelle Browers explores in great depth the inherent challenge of exporting the concept of civil society to Islamic societies, noting, for example, 'The path of the contemporary re-emergence of civil society alongside democracy is fraught with the talk of the "clash of civilizations".'[71] Furthermore, she highlights over time conceptual manipulation of the term to represent that which is against Islamist society. She attempts to situate more precisely from where this moral panic is derived by stating:

The fear is that this Islam, once legitimated as the source of political and social norms, will prove repressive for individual liberties, especially for non-Muslims, non-practicing Muslims, Muslim minority groups, and Muslims with new or different interpretations of their religion. Women from all of those categories also express a particular concern about Islamic rule.[72]

---

[70] See: International Crisis Group, 'Tunisie: Violences et Défi Salafiste', p. 2.
[71] Referring to Huntington (1996) in M. Browers, *Democracy and Civil Society in Arab Political Thought: Transcultural Possibilities* (Syracuse: Syracuse University Press, 2006), p. 6.
[72] Browers, *Democracy and Civil Society*, p. 147.

Distrust and Division

In speaking to individuals working with secular organisations (historic and newer) and different Islamic associations as well as some multilateral donors (either based in Tunis or regional offices in Cairo), it became increasingly clear that distrust in the public space began to mirror the divergences manifesting in the political space in Tunisia at the time. A number of the interviewees spoke of a perceived growing secular-religious divide and the consequences this could have on Tunisia's efforts towards democratisation. For example, I spoke with Kader, an activist and outreach worker with key populations affected by HIV/AIDS in Tunis. He expressed his concern as to how civil these newly created organisations would be:

Do they have these civil and community-based objectives? Some of the associations are very open about promoting good morals with Islamic objectives, and many have strong influences from Saudi Arabia. So just because we have this explosion in associational activity, this does not necessarily mean it is civil; it could be just the opposite. Anyone now can create an association, but it is important to ask what are they doing and how they are working – perhaps they are working to restrict liberty and human rights?[73]

Moreover, Wail, a former human rights activist, also highlighted disbelief among some civil society actors that Islamists, in particular those perceived as Salafis, could have civil aims. He argued, 'The Salafis are active in the charity organisations and they actually do not believe in the work of the other associations, nor do they believe in liberty.'[74]

These expressions of distrust among some of the secular organisations also resonated in their discomfort in having to share the expanding discursive, as well as very physical space, with Islamists whose views and methods of civic activism were not always perceived as respectful. These actors referred to the 'space' in which multiple factions currently must co-exist. Muammar, a co-founder of an English-language online news journal created immediately after the Tunisia uprising, expressed how quickly the nature of this discursive and physical public space was being transformed. He observed, 'Now there is this freedom of expression and Tunisians are seeing just how truly conservative this society is. There is a very different kind of public

---

[73] Interview in Tunis (26), 30 January 2012.
[74] Interview in Tunis (41), 13 March 2012.

space now opening up and not everyone is happy about it; but it is a public space after all.'[75] Some also expressed uneasiness with regard to the range of issues currently featuring in the widening discursive space as well as the debates unfolding in the National Constituent Assembly. Radi, a sociologist and lead researcher on many of the HIV/AIDS-related bio-behavioural surveillance surveys conducted in Tunisia, expressed his concern that the post-revolution discursive arena was so immense. He elaborated:

Everything is permitted; however, the risks for me are the Salafis and violence. For years we have not had some of the debates we are having now – everything is open somehow for discussion – but what is interesting is that these are not discussions we want to revisit, such as polygamy, abortion, or the death penalty – but all discussions are being had now out in the open. It is necessary to pass through this phase.[76]

While the actual number of incidences of violence, in particular attributed to the Salafis, was small, it was argued that their capacity to cause a 'nuisance' was worrying, as was the past *jihadi* association of some of its members. In May 2012, the president of the Tunisian League of Human Rights (LTDH), Abdessatar Ben Moussa, issued a statement on the 35th anniversary of the organisation, stating that these groups (Salafis) propagate terror, 'aggress physically and morally women, intellectuals and journalists ... politicians and even human rights activists'.[77] This sentiment was also shared by Naeema, a women's rights activist, who expressed her frustration that the site of contestation for her activism has now shifted from the former authoritarian regime to Salafis. She spoke of how after the revolution her association organised an event to speak to and offer support to the victims of violence who died during the revolution; she reported that 'Ennahda' came to harass them so they would leave. She expressed frustration, asserting:

We can in effect do all the activities we want which is great ... but now we are not alone, there are the Salafis. Now it is not the government, now it is the Salafis who are trying to censure us – Ennahda and the Salafis, who are against our association. Their strategy is to largely discredit the associations

---

[75] Interview in Tunis (27), 30 January 2012.
[76] Interview in Tunis (30), 7 February 2012.
[77] *Associated French Press*, 'Tunisie: Les Salafistes Multiplient les Coups d'Eclat', JeuneAfrique.com, 27 May 2012.

working in women's rights through working through the media such as Facebook where they have set up campaigns to defame and pass misinformation on our work.[78]

Finally, there is an underlying suspicion of the aims and autonomy of some of the emerging religiously oriented associations, in particular an assumption that they have either been created by Ennahda as populist arms throughout the more deprived regions of Tunisia, or that their aims are inherently political in nature.[79] In addition, despite some Islamist associations admitting they were struggling to find the resources to implement their activities, some secular groups suggested that not only did these associations have funding from the wealthier Gulf Cooperation Council (GCC) countries, but also ample resources to affect/influence popular opinion, especially in vulnerable communities. For example, Soli and Merone argued, 'This new scenario of associations started a debate on the nature of influence coming from outside Tunisia ... Should the country really accept funding from other countries such as Qatar – hardly known for respecting human rights or transparent criteria of funding?'[80] While Islamic Relief and Qatar Charity were two principal donors in post-revolution Tunisia, alongside a range of Kuwaiti organisations and the International Islamic Charity Organisation, these Islamic funding networks also span across the West such as the United Kingdom (Manchester is home to the headquarters of two of the wealthiest and influential Islamic associations), Turkey and Germany.[81]

The concept and composition of civil society is often under-scrutinised by actors who consider themselves members of civil society. In my attempts to further discern the understanding of this concept from some of the organisations, my question was often met with indeterminate statements, such as from Soraya and her sister. They each exclaimed, 'Civil society is composed of citizens and associations, and not political parties with political aims. They have to be independent from political parties. This cannot be a means for an end for political parties to acquire more supporters.'[82] I not only observed

---

[78] Interview in Tunis (40), 12 March 2012.
[79] See Soli and Merone, 'Tunisia: The Islamic Associative System'; International Crisis Group, 'Tunisie: Violences et Défi Salafiste'; and Gray, 'Tunisia after the Uprising', p. 289.
[80] Soli and Merone, 'Tunisia: The Islamic Associative System', p. 2.
[81] Ibid., pp. 3–4.   [82] Interview in Tunis (47), 22 March 2012.

different assumptions concerning the definition of civil society among the associations but equally from international NGOs working in Tunisia and multilateral organisations such as the UN. Some of these actors were also not conscious that in their explanations of the definition or composition of civil society they would exclude the Islamist associations in their descriptions. For example, Dr Saqib, the director of one of the newly established UN organisations based in Tunis, stated:

> In a way some of the newer civil society organisations are trying to present a different vision than the Islamists, in a way resisting this participation. There is a high mobilisation towards a new political vision and this is a goal of the organisations. Ennahda won with this strong social network and the distribution of aid to poorer areas. Civil society is, however, focusing on the laicism of the state.[83]

However, Dr Dema, who established her own Islamist association to support vulnerable families, said that she believed that she and the work of her association indeed formed part of civil society, stating:

> We are a part of civil society as our country is going through a very difficult period and so therefore all associations need to be mobilised ... We lived for years thinking these things do not concern us and now we are trying to change this idea; our country concerns all of us, one has to believe in what one can do for his country.[84]

Conclusion

For many Tunisians unaccustomed to visible forms of politically motivated violence, the assassinations of Belaid and Brahmi in 2013 came as a shock. Critics of Ennahda felt their suspicions were being confirmed, that a new authoritarian regime was in the process of consolidating its power. This distrust directed at the new transition government was also reflected onto the new actors, namely social and political Islam, emerging in Tunisia's public spaces where they would interact with a range of groups and organisations. Social Islam carved a space for itself in post-uprising Tunisia's widening discursive arenas. Moreover, a host of religiously oriented actors established legal civil

---

[83] Interview in Tunis (34), 15 February 2012.
[84] Interview in Tunis (49), 28 March 2012.

Conclusion 161

society organisations to support deprived communities and participate in the changing national landscape. Nevertheless, growing social divisions could be perceived among the different civil society actors and groups in the two years following the downfall of the Ben Ali regime. As such, following the Tunisia uprising, it is not surprising that civil society became more conflictual between its different actors and groups as a result of a number of factors. Historically both the Bourguiba and Ben Ali regimes worked over several decades to remove political as well as social Islam from the national imagination. This was carried out as an ambitious drive to 'modernise' the country based on principles of secularism and political liberalisation as well as a mechanism to consolidate state legitimacy through the elimination of opposition and contestation to authoritarian rule. The promotion of the secular ideology also allowed for the propagation of 'Islamophobia' at both the political and social levels thereby leaving limited room in the national imagination for Islamist actors in the public domain. Ultimately, decades of repression and exclusion served as both a motivating factor for Islamists to participate in Tunisia's public spaces following the 2010–2011 uprising but also as a delimiting factor given ongoing contestations to this participation by some secular-left civil society actors and groups.

A multitude of Islamists movements (re)-emerged as some of the primary voices promoting alternative visions for Tunisia's national identity. This was a result of the vigour with which both previous regimes pursued secularisation, the extreme impiety and corruption associated with the Ben Ali regime and also the dissatisfaction among some Salafist factions with the transformation of Ennahda's political platform/project envisioned for Tunisia. And while Islamist movements were not the main force behind the events that began in December 2010, their potential to mobilise mass proportions of the population and to offer support to marginalised and deprived communities across Tunisia in part allowed them to visibly occupy a new public space opening in Tunisia. Moreover, with the rise of political Islam, there was also the concurrent rise in associative Islam where new, and often unfamiliar, actors filled new spaces offered up in the expanding post-revolution landscape. Effectively, the denial of participation in civil society prior to 2011, accompanied by the implementation of widespread liberalisation measures shortly after 2011, eventually helped to create the spaces for Islamist actors to establish associations and opportunities to embrace their own sense of *muwatana* or *citoyenneté* subsequent to the downfall of the former regime. The result of this participation was the materialisation of a multitude of unstable and reversible hegemonies giving rise to a host of visible as well as invisible emerging counter-publics in Tunisia's public spaces. For example, Al-Usra al-Amina and similar Islamist organisations working in humanitarianism were able to use their participation in civil society as a means to exercise their own sense of *muwatana* and national belonging in post-uprising Tunisia.

This chapter analysed the second core theme of the book concerning the emerging sociocultural and socio-religious divisions, including the rise of associational or social Islam, following the downfall of the Ben Ali regime in 2011. In particular it examined the growing conflicts and cleavages among civil society, specifically between the secular and religious actors. Following the downfall of the Ben Ali regime, both the secular and the Islamist civil society actors worked to repress contestation; at times these actors aggravated distrust through exclusion and intimidation. Moreover, as this had previously been a relatively uncontested space composed of mainly secular organisations, the consequence was a perceptible resistance, described here as well as in Chapter 4, to expanding this space to include disparate and unfamiliar views. A restricted sociocultural imagination often excluded associative Islam; this permeated across the historic civil society actors as well as the newer organisations and equally across some bilateral and multilateral donors providing support to these different organisations. This allowed for the increasing emergence of a dual discourse in which civil society was discussed in contrast to Islam. In the two years after the revolution, there were no clear winners or losers in Tunisia's public spaces, only what was considered by some Tunisians as the further exacerbation of social divisions tempered by conflicting worldviews and agendas for post-uprising Tunisia.

Alongside Chapter 4, this chapter also emphasises the dual understandings of civil society underpinning the actions and responses of the different actors. The secular civil society organisations that were established during the Ben Ali regime emerged within the ideology of neoliberalism – operating within a more or less homogenous field of actors enshrined in the 'liberal' secular ideology. The actors who emerged to become members of civil society following the 2010–2011 uprising more closely reflected a Gramscian understanding of the concept and field of actors. Through the cultural, education and religious institutions, civil society was able not only to restore its sense of agency through self-determination and self-management but also to contest state power; at times these actors, such as the emerging Salafi movement, even seemed capable of subverting this power. The Gramscian contemporary understanding of the concept that emphasises agency, instability and the reversible nature of hegemony stands in sharp opposition to the neoliberal understanding in which the role ascribed for these actors is largely functionalist. I argue that at the root of these social divisions and cleavages are also two simultaneously operating but incompatible concepts of civil society influenced by the ideology of Communism on the one hand and the ideology of neoliberalism on the other.

6 | Consensus and Marginalisation
The Mapping of Priorities in Post-Uprising Tunisia

Before Ben Ali and after, I am not afraid to say what I think.
– LGBT activist, Tunis[1]

Transitions from authoritarian rule often nourish expectations among a range of stakeholders for an expansion of space for political liberalisation, redistribution and, perhaps most importantly, recognition. Therefore, it is often easy to overlook the groups and actors that find spaces contracting around them as the priorities for democratisation are outlined and the hierarchy of concerns push certain groups and issues to the periphery. This narrowing of spaces also underscores the complex and unstable nature of democratisation itself. In the drive for consensus, one of the core principles of democracy, issues perceived as contentious are often excluded in favour of less controversial or more 'acceptable' imaginings of a country's national identity. In *Agonistics: Thinking the World Politically*, Chantal Mouffe poignantly writes, 'Every order is predicated upon the exclusion of other possibilities.'[2]

More recently, the issue of homosexuality has come to represent a benchmark for 'democratic' societies globally. The topic regularly rouses contention and sparks fierce debate internationally on the role of identity politics, religion and sexuality, and the international human rights agenda(s) tied to globalisation. In the Middle East and North Africa, homosexuality is a touchstone subject that continues to be the object of extreme taboo in Arab societies. Throughout the region, gay, bisexual and transgender communities continue to experience substantial levels of discrimination and violence, often related to criminalising policies situated at the political level or stigmatising sociocultural attitudes. However, a transition from authoritarian rule can also signal

---

[1] Interview in Tunis (25), 27 January 2012, November 2012 and 14 March 2013.
[2] Mouffe, *Agonistics*, p. 2.

new opportunities for sociopolitical transformation – for sexual minorities to openly advocate for legal measures to support freedom from violence and discrimination and for equal rights.

The concerns of gay, bisexual and transgender populations in many countries in the Middle East and North Africa are often overshadowed when not made discernible enough, and the groups acting for/on behalf of these different communities, such as HIV/AIDS organisations that work with marginalised populations, are routinely persecuted when the line between discretion and visibility is crossed. Vulnerable groups, in particular gay, bisexual and transgender men, perceived and also experienced increased degrees of marginalisation after the 2010–2011 Tunisia uprising. As a specific case study, I follow the experiences of a group of individuals in Tunisia who established the organisation Damj ('reintegration') to more effectively defend human rights and the rights of minorities, including lesbian, gay, bisexual and transgender (LGBT) populations. Through this case study, I further examine the different ways conflict manifests among civil society by looking to both the areas of these conflicts as well as the consequences of these contestations. Here I address the third core theme of the book, namely the exclusionary (and undemocratic) nature of consensus in 'liberal' democracies. The previous two chapters illustrate Tunisia's public spaces at their widest following the downfall of the Ben Ali regime, with the manifestation of a multiplicity of visions and priorities for post-uprising Tunisia. In the further mapping of democratic priorities, it is possible to observe in this chapter how these discursive spaces are at their most expansive point following political liberalisation measures, and then are gradually narrowed down. I argue that this discursive narrowing is a consequence of a fundamental democratic practice: consensus. Following a transition from authoritarian rule, consensus becomes a key mechanism to enforce hegemony as the post-revolution hierarchy of priorities is redefined and 'other' is pushed to the periphery or negated entirely – or rather, the notion of the hegemony of consensus.

Abandoning Consensus

At the core of deliberations on the nature of conflict among civil society actors is an underlying normative supposition that conflict is inherently destructive; more importantly, that it can fundamentally obstruct efforts towards creating more democratic and representative institutions. This normative frame is also inherent in neoliberal policies that support civil society organisations as critical agents for good governance. The preference for consensus over conflict among these different actors is implicit as democracy requires consensus on leadership, national priorities and identity. Conflicts among actors often characterised by solidarity, goodwill and cooperation are perceived as a negative consequence. However, in *Agonistics,* Mouffe advocates for a permanent role and space for conflict. Mouffe's aim is to re-position conflict within democratic society while concurrently accepting the hegemonic nature of 'every form of consensus'.[3] Although she concentrates her argument on democracy and liberal theory, her main contribution is to underscore the genuine limits of pluralism while scrutinising the two dimensions she considers fundamental to politics: antagonism and hegemony.[4] She writes:

What characterises democratic politics is the confrontation between conflicting hegemonic projects, a confrontation with no possibility of final reconciliation ... This is what can be called 'the moment of the political', the recognition of constitutive character of social division and the ineradicability of antagonism.[5]

Mouffe differentiates between agonistic and antagonistic forms of political confrontation in which there can exist (or should be allowed to exist) a permanent 'conflictual consensus' between adversaries. This can be achieved through conceptualising 'radical negativity', which refers to the recognition that indeed there are a multiplicity of publics but that they are also divided – and moreover, that one should abandon the notion that these divisions can (or should) be overcome.[6] At the core of the argument against a predilection for consensus is Mouffe's conviction in the democratic framework despite her dissatisfaction with the neoliberal architecture itself. It is in fact neoliberal discourses that have re-institutionalised the preference for consensus in political and public spaces above all else in order to promote the virtues of democratic processes. Mouffe contends that this overemphasis on popular consensus, to the contrary, actually exacerbates the exclusion of marginalised views and 'other'. In the *Democratic Paradox*, she argues, 'Under the pretence of rethinking and updating democratic

---

[3] Ibid., pp. xi, 11.   [4] Ibid., p. 14.   [5] Ibid., pp. 17–18.
[6] Ibid., pp. xii, xiv.

demands, their calls for "modernization", "flexibility" and "responsibility" disguise their refusal to consider the demands of the popular sectors which are excluded from their political and societal priorities. Worse even, they are rejected as "anti-democratic", "retrograde" ...'[7] She underscores the negative consequences of realising 'rational consensus' and questions the underlying objectives of unanimity and homogeneity inherent in democracy and liberalism. Mouffe also criticises the Habermasian model of the 'public sphere', arguing not only in favour of pluralism but for the constitutive potential it has. She writes:

> Pluralism is not merely a fact, something that we must bear grudgingly or try to reduce, but an axiological principle. It is taken to be constitutive at the conceptual level of the very nature of modern democracy and considered as something that we should celebrate and enhance.[8]

Mouffe underscores not only the necessity to abandon the overall aspiration for consensus without exclusion in the public space but to also embrace the virtues of dissent, conflict and a plurality of hegemonies. She writes, 'The search for a consensus without exclusion and the hope for a perfectly reconciled and harmonious society have to be abandoned.'[9] And while her contention is situated within the inner workings of neoliberalism, Mouffe is articulating something much grander on the nature of democratisation: that democracy (and the institutions that are inherently linked to it) requires conflict. She contends, 'Conflict in liberal democratic societies cannot and should not be eradicated, since the specificity of pluralist democracy is precisely the recognition and the legitimation of conflict.'[10] Hence, by understanding the desire for consensus as a negative consequence of hegemony, it is possible to see much more clearly the nature of the various conflicts and contentions that emerge between different civil society actors, in particular during periods where there are perceived opportunities to reshape national identity. In mapping national priorities, exclusion and marginalisation become accepted practice in both symbolic and physical public spaces. This is in contrast to practices that safeguard discursive arenas where conflicts and differences can be constructively confronted.

Finally, Mouffe engages with democratic theory and the tenets of liberalism in order to advocate for the move away from aspirations

---

[7] C. Mouffe, *The Democratic Paradox* (London: Verso, 2013), pp. 6–7.
[8] Ibid., p. 19.   [9] Mouffe, *Agonistics*, p. xi.   [10] Ibid., p. 7.

for reconciliation towards an 'uncertain something else' where relations of power are more fundamentally and explicitly acknowledged – whereby it is possible to move towards something that is unstable, messy, even at times troubling and chaotic, but which may also ultimately provide the institutions associated with 'liberal' democracy – including civil society, the most prolific opportunity for the expression of genuine political pluralism. The next section examines how and why issues related to sexual identity and sexual minorities often manifest in public debates during key moments of sociopolitical transformation. This concerns the simultaneous emergence of movements seeking recognition and human rights in public spaces alongside populist reactions, or moral panics, among both secular and religious actors within and outside these spaces. The principal question is whether there is a place within civil society during transitions from authoritarian rule for the views and voices of marginalised communities to materialise.

Whose Voice Matters: The Recovery of Personal Dignity

After the Tunisia 2010–2011 uprising, the designation of the hierarchy of concerns for the transition from authoritarian rule was articulated and re-articulated regularly in the drive for consensus on national priorities. A principal feature of transitions is that the 'rules of the game' are no longer defined and therefore transitions from authoritarian rule can be highly uncertain, if not volatile processes.[11] Although one has the impression of 'disorder' during such periods, according to O'Donnell and Schmitter there is also 'a context of expanding (if uncertain) choices, of widespread (if often exaggerated) hopes, of innumerable experiments towards the expansion of the political arena, and of manifold levels of social participation ... the exultant feeling that the future is open'.[12] In relation to post-revolution Tunisia, the expansion of space provided by the transition was also accompanied by a generalised perception of the recovery of personal dignity as leaders long considered morally bankrupt were ousted and new possibilities to rectify the residue of corruption were on the horizon. An

---

[11] O'Donnell and Schmitter (eds.), *Transitions from Authoritarian Rule: Tentative Conclusions*, p. 6.
[12] Ibid., pp. 4, 19.

example of this is the Tunisian revolutionary slogan calling for 'work, freedom and dignity' as seen branded alongside posters featuring '*irhal*' ('leave/get out') and 'the people want the fall of the regime!'[13]

Populist issues and rumour, however, can often obscure the ordering of priorities subsequent to the downfall of an authoritarian regime. Such rumours and even myth-making can serve to exacerbate moral panics and scapegoat individuals and groups. The choices that civil society makes, in particular for marginalised groups, are often predicated upon debates unfolding in the sociopolitical realm. In choosing strategies that involve publicity and visibility versus strategies that require discretion and invisibility, vulnerable groups and the organisations working with them are often required to gauge the terrain upon which they are operating. During political transitions, for example, it is not uncommon prior to national elections to find issues concerning sex and the rights of sexual minorities high on the agenda. Issues such as abortion and rights for gay, bisexual and transgender communities regularly feature in pre-election debates as they arouse emotions concerning family and the imaginings of national identity, issues that are also accessible to constituents. As such, activists who are looking to advocate for recognition, such as for greater rights and freedom from discrimination, must routinely contend with populist reactions.

For example, following the 2010–2011 Tunisia uprising there was a rise in public 'conservative' discourse(s) at the political and sociocultural levels. Perhaps for the first time, Tunisians participated in a range of debates as all issues for contestation were open; some of them were debates that many thought had been resolved following independence in 1956 – such as temporary marriage, polygamy, the 'problem' of single mothers, abortion and even female excision.[14] Sex in particular was back on the agenda. Michel Foucault situated the intermanipulation of sex and power – and in particular the multiplication of discourses on sex – at the beginning of the eighteenth century in France, when there 'emerged a political, economic and technical incitement to talk about sex ... in the form of analysis, stocktaking,

---

[13] N. Marzouki, 'From People to Citizens in Tunisia', *Middle East Research and Information Project* MER 259, vol. 41, no. 259 (Summer 2011).

[14] See: N. Borsali, 'Tunisie: 8 Mars 2012 ou le Défi Egalitaire', *La Presse de Tunisie*, 12 March 2012; Meziou-Dourai, 'A Propos du Mariage Coutumier'; and Khalsi, 'Excision ... ou les Prédictions d'un Psychopathe'.

classification and specification'.[15] Historically within the French context, Foucault endeavoured to understand, 'Why has sexuality been so widely discussed and what has been said about it? What were the effects of power generated by what was said?'[16] So in effect, what was gained from new and emerging discourses on sexuality following the downfall of the Ben Ali regime in Tunisia? And, who gained from speaking about them?

Nowhere can these mechanisms of power and control be better observed than in the emergence of the global HIV/AIDS epidemic in the early 1980s, which afforded scientists and government institutions great licence to monitor, map, and code sexuality throughout the world. Referring to these multiple apparatuses of power as the 'politics of AIDS', Denis Altman, along with Richard Parker, argues that HIV/AIDS has significantly changed our understanding of human sexuality.[17] And while he posits that HIV/AIDS has provided a global arena for more open discussions on sex and sexuality, it has also, according to Altman, 'required new ways of thinking about the links between "private" behaviour and public health, and the often huge discrepancies between actual behaviour and official ideology'.[18] Perhaps it is the conflation between the increasing identification and categorisation of multiple sexualities (as well as the systems and institutions to analyse and police them) and political discourses on disease, the spread of infection and death that have in part led to 'moral panics' at the sociocultural level and the growing practice of what Altman considers the 'scapegoating' of human sexualities.[19]

Moral panics historically have often led to the adoption and justification of a number of measures to halt the spread of disease and/or individuals identified as threats to society. Altman argues, '"Moral panics" can be understood as both specific populist reactions, and as calculated appeals by political and economic elites to these reactions as ways of winning popular support for other political shifts.'[20] In post-revolution Tunisia, one is able to distinguish two facets of moral panics – the moral panic concerning the secular population's response

---

[15] M. Foucault, *The History of Sexuality 1: The Will to Knowledge*, trans. by R. Hurley (London: Penguin, 1990), p. 24.
[16] Ibid., p. 11.
[17] R. Parker, 'Sexual Cultures, HIV Transmission, and AIDS Prevention', *AIDS*, vol. 8, supp. 1 (1994), p. 68.
[18] Altman, *Global Sex*, pp. 75, 83.   [19] Ibid., p. 142.   [20] Ibid., p. 143.

to the growing emergence of Salafist ideology and its physical presence in Tunisia's new public spaces (as explored in the previous chapter) – and specific to this case, the increasing conservative backlash against 'liberal' behaviour and identity associated with the immorality and corruption of the former regime.

Space for Identity Movements?

Similar to the concept of civil society and its underlying relationship to modernisation trajectories implicit within discourses on neoliberalism, the issue of homosexual identity and 'liberation' also shares this linkage to modernisation projects. A country is increasingly deemed as modern or democratic depending upon the policies and laws it has in place to combat inequality and discrimination against LGBT communities.[21] This trend can be seen in the international condemnation of Uganda and Russia in 2014 for their legal positions on same-sex acts. Furthermore, it seems gay, bisexual and transgender groups/organisations themselves are bestowed the recognition of modernity depending upon their chosen degree of visibility in public spaces – as activists calling for universal human rights, freedom from discrimination, and violence, or liberation. In 'How Do You Say "Come Out of the Closet" in Arabic?', Jason Ritchie argues that for several LGBT activist organisations in the Middle East and North Africa, such as for the organisation HaAguda, 'Visibility . . . is both a tactic and a goal, the means and the end of gay activism.'[22] However, he questions whether gay, bisexual and transgender communities 'need or want to come out and attain visibility'.[23] In considering the nature of the conflicts that emerged among civil society following the uprising (and over which issues), it is necessary to ascertain whether or not, and to what degree, these groups were seeking political recognition or freedom from discrimination and violence.

---

[21] See Altman, *Global Sex*, p. 91 and E. Saner, 'Gay Rights Around the World: The Best and the Worst Countries for Equality', TheGuardian.com, 30 July 2013.

[22] Quoting the Chair of *HaAguda*, J. Ritchie, 'How Do You Say "Come Out of the Closet in Arabic?": Queer Activism and the Politics of Visibility in Israel-Palestine', *GLQ: A Journal of Gay and Lesbian Studies*, vol. 16, no. 4 (2010), p. 563.

[23] Ritchie, 'How Do You Say "Come Out of the Closet" in Arabic?', p. 563.

Recognition could be related to identity, rights or simply the freedom from discrimination and violence. Fraser identifies a shift in the post-socialist terrain in which groups of actors are no longer simply 'economically defined classes' seeking an end to exploitation and means to greater distribution. Rather, these actors are also 'culturally defined' groups and 'communities of value' seeking to preserve their identities and to attain recognition.[24] However, Fraser also underscores the difficult choices subaltern and marginalised groups must routinely make between strategies of publicity and visibility and the protection that invisibility and discretion offer. She argues, 'It is not correct to view publicity as always and unambiguously an instrument of empowerment and emancipation. For members of subordinate groups it will always be a matter of balancing the potential uses of publicity against the dangers of the loss of privacy.'[25] Furthermore, in supporting the creation and safeguarding of spaces to allow room and the opportunity for a multiplicity of views and counter-publics to emerge through discursive contestation, 'communities of value', such as gay, bisexual and transgender communities could encounter greater space to manoeuvre for recognition. She contends, 'What will count as a matter of common concern will be decided precisely through discursive contestation. It follows that no topics should be ruled off limits in advance of such contestation. Democratic publicity requires positive guarantees of opportunities for minorities to convince others that what in the past was not public ... should now become so.'[26]

The question remains as to whether there was in fact space in post-revolution Tunisia for issues concerning gay, bisexual and transgender populations to emerge as public issues. Issues concerning sex regularly featured in the media; however, they were manipulated by both liberal and conservative factions as a means to underscore the other's own illegitimacy to rule following the downfall of the Ben Ali regime. Sex was being used by the secular elements of the population to highlight the more extreme or 'conservative' tendencies of Ennahda, for example, and by the more conservative (religiously-oriented) factions to demonstrate the immorality associated with the Ben Ali regime (or secular regimes in general). So for both of these sides issues

[24] N. Fraser, *Justice Interruptus: Critical Reflections on the 'Postsocialist' Condition* (New York: Routledge, 1997), p. 2.
[25] Ibid., p. 116.   [26] Fraser, 'Rethinking the Public Sphere', p. 71.

concerning sexual minorities were being debated within a non-neutral and heavily charged terrain. It is this conservative backlash against 'liberal' behaviour that dictated the strategies LGBT communities would employ to bring issues of sexual identity and human rights to the discursive arena following the 2010–2011 Tunisia uprising.

The Expansion of Space for Marginalised Communities?

At present it is illegal to engage in same-sex conduct in 78 countries, and in five countries – Mauritania, Saudi Arabia, Sudan, United Arab Emirates and Yemen – the death penalty can be invoked for homosexual activity.[27] The countries that have retained the death penalty all justify this punishment based on the foundations of Islamic law.[28] For other countries in the region, the penalty for sodomy in Bahrain is 10 years' imprisonment; 7 years in Kuwait; 5 years in Libya and Qatar; 3 years in Algeria, Morocco, Oman, Somalia and Tunisia; and 1 year in Lebanon and Syria.[29] The number of individuals prosecuted or arrested for same-sex offenses in the Middle East and North Africa remains impossible to determine.[30]

Alongside formal legal codes that persecute same-sex behaviour throughout the region, there is also discrimination, harassment and violence committed by state security forces as well as by individuals and groups at the community-level acting on their own sense of moral authority. There are examples across the Middle East and North Africa of the flagrant abuse of authority against gay, bisexual and transgender populations and equally homophobic acts committed by individuals that consequently, through non-response, can indicate sanctioning by state entities. For example, in May 2001, the police raided a Cairo discothèque known as 'Queen Boat'; of the 52 men eventually sent to trial, 23 were convicted and sentenced to prison terms of one to five

---

[27] Speech by the RT. Hon. John Bercow, MP, Speaker of the British House of Commons to the Kaleidoscope Trust IDAHO event (16 May 2012, www.kaleidoscopetrust.com/features-bercow-speech-5-12.php). It is important to note that some activists and academics (such as the International Gay and Lesbian Association) cite 81 countries as outlawing same-sex acts and Iran is also reported to invoke the death penalty for sodomy; this also does not include the more recent passing of the Uganda Anti-Homosexuality Act in February 2014 that criminalises same-sex acts; see B. Whitaker, *Unspeakable Love: Gay and Lesbian Life in the Middle East* (London: Saqi, 2006), pp. 112, 123.
[28] Whitaker, *Unspeakable Love*, p. 112.   [29] Ibid., p. 123.   [30] Ibid., p. 139.

years for 'immoral behaviour and contempt of religion'.[31] From early 2001 until 2004 (when the report was published), Human Rights Watch reported that it was aware of more than 170 men whose cases under the Egyptian law of 'debauchery' were brought before prosecutors.[32] Furthermore, in March 2012 international human rights groups urged Iraqi authorities to investigate targeted killings against approximately 15 teenagers perceived to be gay. Young people with 'emo-like' features such as tight-fitting clothes and 'alternative' hairstyles were brutally stoned, beaten or shot. The Iraqi minister of interior denied any homophobic or 'anti-emo' killings took place.[33] Finally, 36 men were arrested in Beirut in July 2012 in an adult cinema. The men were subjected to anal examinations to determine whether or not they were homosexual.[34] These events at a minimum reflect the degree of stigmatisation and violence against sexual minorities throughout the Middle East and North Africa.

In part, this discrimination stems from discourses that situate homosexuality within the context of an imported phenomenon, or 'western borrowing', as well as firmly within colonial discourses. These discourses allow intermittent moral panics to (re)surface at peculiar times, resulting in targeted discrimination and, in some cases, brutality. Brian Whitaker attributes these crackdowns against gay, bisexual and transgender communities on the part of the government as serving enough to 'appease moral outrage and make an example of a few people, but not so many as to cast doubt on the public fiction that there is little or no homosexuality in the country'.[35] Since the uprising, LGBT communities in Tunisia have experienced noteworthy advances and have advocated for greater rights for marginalised citizens and freedom from violence. However, they have also simultaneously faced considerable contractions in the space to manoeuvre at the political as well as sociocultural levels. The following two sections examine in more detail

---

[31] Human Rights Watch, 'In a Time of Torture: The Assault on Justice in Egypt's Crackdown on Homosexual Conduct' (2004), p. 2 and D. Crary, 'Gays in Egypt, Tunisia Worry about Post-Revolt Era', TheGuardian.com, 21 May 2011.
[32] Human Rights Watch, 'In a Time of Torture', p. 1.
[33] *Associated French Press*, 'Rights Groups Urge Iraq to Investigate "Emo" Killings', AlArabiya.net, 16 March 2012.
[34] See Human Rights Watch, 'Lebanon: Stop "Tests of Shame"', 10 August 2012 and S. Assir, 'Lebanon's Gay Community Despite Liberal Mideast Reputation', HuffingtonPost.com, 5 August 2013.
[35] Whitaker, *Unspeakable Love*, p. 140.

the conflicts and contentions that arose both within and outside civil society as gay, bisexual and transgender communities attempted to put issues of identity, human rights and freedom from discrimination on the post-revolution agenda.

Some Openings, in Some Places

In 1996, post-apartheid South Africa became the first country in the world to explicitly integrate protections for the rights of gays and lesbians into its constitution.[36] Since 1996, South African courts have decriminalised sodomy, ruled in favour of gay employees seeking benefits for their partners and supported immigration appeals for foreign partners of homosexual South Africans. In 'South Africa's Democratisation and the Politics of Gay Liberation', Sheila Croucher observes, 'These gains are remarkable given the previously weak gay movement and the country's already crowded political and economic agenda in the wake of apartheid.'[37] She adds, 'In South Africa, the availability of an anti-apartheid master frame, rooted in respect for human rights and equality for all, helped galvanise gays and lesbians and to legitimate their demands in the eyes of politicians and society as a whole.'[38] Given the historical precedent for increased opportunities and indeed success in putting greater rights for sexual minorities high on the agenda in other countries that passed through extreme periods of sociopolitical transition, it should come as no surprise that soon after the 2010–2011 uprising different actors mobilised to take maximum advantage of these new spaces opening up in Tunisia. Tunisia's LGBT communities perceived post-revolution opportunities for the expansion of freedoms – such as freedom from discrimination and violence. They worked to quickly maximise what was perceived as a definitive window of opportunity following the fall of the Ben Ali regime in January and elections to the National Constituent Assembly in October 2011.

In one of the first instances, gay, bisexual and transgender communities participated in the Atakni rally in October 2011 in protest of the significant conservative backlash against the broadcasting of the

---

[36] S. Croucher, 'South Africa's Democratisation and the Politics of Gay Liberation', *Journal of Southern African Studies*, vol. 28, no. 2 (2002), pp. 315–330.
[37] Ibid.   [38] Ibid., p. 324.

film *Persepolis*[39] and to counter threats to the principle of freedom of expression. It is reported that several dozen youths carried a large rainbow flag marked with the word 'PEACE'.[40] Moreover, there were articles in the Tunisian press – Arabic, French and English-speaking – on the issue of homosexuality that many observers agreed would not have happened during the Ben Ali era. There was also an online magazine *GayDay*, which was founded just after January 2011 by a group of 'like-minded individuals' and maintained by Editor-in-Chief Fadi Krouj.[41] In addition, the year 2012 marked the first year in Tunisia in which LGBT communities publicly celebrated the International Day Against Homophobia and Transphobia, including by launching a declaration on behalf of this community. The statement reaffirmed LGBT rights by claiming, 'Stunned by the wind of revolt blowing over Tunisia, they no longer hid themselves, they fought for the right to employment and for dignity, as well as for sexual liberties.'[42]

Not long after the revolution, a group of three LGBT activists worked to establish the non-profit charity L'Association Tunisienne pour la Justice et l'Egalite (The Tunisian Association for Justice and Equality), which was known as Damj ('reintegration') in Arabic.[43] The activists, Moazzam, Nasser and Kader, each began their advocacy training in HIV/AIDS, starting out as volunteers while students in university. Moazzam explained that he began his training as a peer educator in 2008 with one of the HIV/AIDS organisations with programmes in Sousse while undertaking his studies. Nasser served as a volunteer in Tunis from the age of 18, working with organisations such as the Red Crescent and Greenpeace. Nasser heard about the work of an HIV/AIDS organisation in Tunis early in 2004; however, initially he was afraid to volunteer with the group. However, in 2007 Nasser was

---

[39] Chawki, 'Vidéo-Manifestation Contre La Violence et Pour La Liberté d'Expression sous le Signe "A3ta9ni"', Tunisienumerique.com, 6 October 2011.
[40] R. Collins, 'Effemines, Gigolos, and MSMs in the Cyber Networks, Coffeehouses and "Secret Gardens" of Contemporary Tunis', *Journal of Middle East Women's Studies*, vol. 8, no. 3 (Fall 2012), p. 105.
[41] http://gaydaymagazine.com/.
[42] Déclaration du 17 mai de la communauté LGBT Tunisienne, Mai 2012, featured in F. Krouj, 'Editor-In-Chief of Gayday Magazine Fadi Krouj Comments on International Day Against Homophobia', Tunisia-Live.net, 18 May 2012.
[43] Homosexual women also eventually became involved in the development of the organisation *Damj* soon after its official establishment in Tunisia.

the target of a physical assault. He went to the police, who initially worked with him, but eventually the case was dropped. No longer feeling safe in Tunis, Nasser moved to Sousse where Moazzam and Kader were living. His friends encouraged him to volunteer with the organisation, especially given the association's anti-stigma programme. He eventually moved back to Tunis, where he acquired a paid position with the HIV/AIDS organisation as a supervisor of volunteers and outreach workers.[44] Kader, meanwhile, began to volunteer with the HIV/AIDS organisation with its programme in Sousse, along with Moazzam and eventually Nasser. He made the decision to volunteer with the organisation after attending one of its HIV/AIDS awareness-raising sessions. He explained that at the time he was anxious about working with an organisation that engaged so outwardly in work with men who have sex with men. In 2009 he became a full-time employee with the organisation in Tunis to oversee outreach work with key populations affected by HIV.

The newly formed organisation Damj acquired its formal associational visa in October 2011 under the rubric of work in 'stigma and discrimination and human rights'. The word Damj was chosen by the founders because it signified 'integration' and alluded to the continued exclusion of minorities and other vulnerable groups at the time. Kader explained:

We labelled the application as 'the fight against stigma and human rights' because we felt it needed to be as general as possible in order for it to be accepted. [Members of] the LGBT [community] were some of the first groups to come out and speak about human rights before the revolution and we are the Tunisians who have been outwardly demonstrating against these injustices. On our marches and participation in the demonstrations, before and now, we bring the two flags – the LGBT flag and the Tunisian flag![45]

Kader stated that as a new civil society organisation, Damj 'wants to continue to mobilise young people to take this fight forward and to be strong advocates'. On its Facebook page (added in summer 2013), the organisation outlined its goal to participate in spreading the culture of universal human rights while specifically anchoring the principles of *citoyenneté* and equality among Tunisian citizens; highlighting the factors that exacerbate marginalisation and vulnerability; combating

---

[44] Interview in Tunis (25), 27 January 2012, November 2012 and 14 March 2013.
[45] Interview in Tunis (26), 30 January 2012.

all forms of stigma and discrimination; developing partnerships and networks of mutual aims and understanding as they pertain to the fight against stigma and discrimination; and promoting human rights. Finally, the organisation advocates that it aims to support individuals in precarious situations, such as those who are victims of injustices, to help them to attain greater physical and moral integrity. In a later conversation with Nasser, who was also involved in the high-profile Tunisian graffiti urban art group Zwela,[46] he said that his organisation worked to advocate for the National Constituent Assembly to include issues of equality and justice for minorities in the constitution, acknowledging, however, that a majority of the Assembly's members were 'conservative'. He hoped that Damj would be able to strengthen the rights of minority groups, including members of LGBT communities, and to document human rights abuses as a stronger advocacy tool for rights reform.[47]

In addition to the establishment of Damj after January 2011, different groups such as the Human Rights Observatory and the Tunisian Association for Minorities also came forward to engage more in the protection of individual human rights, including the rigorous documentation of human rights abuses against gay, bisexual and transgender communities – abuses, some would argue, that had increased since the revolution.[48] Moazzam asserted that there was significant violence and aggression – including homicide – against men engaging in same-sex acts, adding, 'And of course we never see this information in the media, our friends tell us. There is no protection, there is not as much security, and this creates many problems. The law does not favour MSM [men who have sex with men].'[49] In response to this perception of increasing violence, a group of human rights lawyers came together to form the Human Rights Observatory. This organisation aimed to document and collect information related to HIV and human rights violations, including incidents of abuse. The information would be used to advocate greater attention to universal human rights. Walid, one of the principal proponents of the Observatory, stressed

---

[46] See L. Ben Mhenni, 'Le Graffiti n'a pas Bonne Presse dans La Révolution Tunisienne...', Opinion-Internationale.com, 12 September 2013.
[47] Interview in Tunis (25), 27 January 2012, November 2012, and 14 March 2013.
[48] See S. Mersch, 'No Gay Rights Revolution in Tunisia', *Deutsche Welle*, 7 November 2012.
[49] Interview in Tunis (23), 24 January 2012.

that regionally the issue of human rights was a very serious challenge. 'We will have to act now or we will lose this space,' he said. 'We have to adopt our discourse now so that this is not eventually turned against us. The rise in conservative discourse is worrying, and so we can no longer work as we did before.'[50]

There was also a host of regional initiatives that arose following the Arab uprisings to specifically address how the revolutions across the Middle East and North Africa would impact upon LGBT communities. Shereen El Feki cites the example of the establishment in 2010 of Mantiqitna Kamb ('our region's camp'). The regional network provides the opportunity for individuals working in LGBT communities to participate in clandestine workshops on issues such as sexuality, gender and activism, as well as training on life skills. The network stipulates that its key aim is to connect less through gay identity and more through Arab identity.[51] Through the regional network, Kader and Nasser were able to attend a meeting organised in Turkey shortly after January 2011 of more than 70 members of LGBT communities throughout the region. Nasser explained, 'We wanted to make sure that everyone at this meeting was from this region as we felt this was our problem and we need to come up with our own solutions. So we tried to exchange experiences of this (the Arab uprisings) and learn from each other.'[52] Nasser later remarked, 'We felt we needed to be prepared because we were afraid of the worst ... There were many ideas but there were also so many different priorities among these [LGBT] groups.'[53]

Finally, activists and academics working in HIV/AIDS, in particular with gay, bisexual and transgender populations, used the finalisation of the 2012–2016 National Strategic Plan (NSP) to Fight AIDS in Tunisia as a primary example of the advances that could be made in the post-revolution window of opportunity. Bio-behavioural surveys conducted in 2009 and again in 2011 indicated HIV prevalence of 4.9 and 13 per cent, respectively, in men who have sex with men (MSM).[54] The UNAIDS UNGASS Report (Tunisia 2012) underscored the significant impact of the revolution in Tunisia and the subsequent effects of

[50] Interview in Tunis (36), 16 February 2012.
[51] El Feki, *Sex and the Citadel*, p. 270. For additional information, see: www.mantiqitna.org.
[52] Interview in Tunis (25), 27 January 2012, November 2012 and 14 March 2013.
[53] Ibid.   [54] Le Programme National de Lutte Contre le Sida, p. 8.

sociopolitical turmoil on the overall health system.[55] It indicated that administrative and key management functions were practically paralysed during the majority of 2011.[56] Given these higher levels of prevalence, the 2012–2016 NSP not only highlighted strategic objectives to intensify targeted prevention and education work with sexual minorities but also underscored the need to conduct advocacy regarding the current legal and juridical frameworks in Tunisia – Article 230 of the penal code[57] – which criminalises same-sex behaviour and specifies penalties of up to three years in prison.[58] Radi, an academic and activist who worked on many of the HIV/AIDS bio-behavioural studies conducted among youth and key populations at higher risk in Tunisia, argued that he and his colleagues would not have had the courage to produce a similar NSP before January 2011. He stated:

> The NSP went through without exceptions ... Each time different actors are saying, 'now is not the time to be doing work on MSM', but we now have very real and worrying data so now is in fact the time to push these boundaries and now is the time to act ... But this can go against our objectives if we are not careful.[59]

Following the 2010–2011 uprising, the founders of Damj chose to operate increasingly in Tunisia's expanding public spaces as many perceived greater opportunities to advocate for more peripheral issues. The members of the organisation engaged in strategies of publicity and visibility through a range of mechanisms that reflected the experience they gained in working with one of the larger HIV/AIDS associations prior to the revolution. Through the organisation they gained skills in advocacy, mentoring, campaigning, mobilising against stigma and discrimination and perhaps most importantly, the ability to manoeuvre through and between disparate networks at the national and regional levels. Damj initially perceived the new openings with the formal

---

[55] The United Nations General Assembly Special Session (UNGASS) on HIV/AIDS took place in 2001 and produced a declaration of commitment on HIV/AIDS, setting out national targets and global actions to reverse the HIV epidemic. See: www.unaids.org.ua/un_support/strategies/UNGASS.
[56] Le Programme National de Lutte Contre le Sida, p. 33.
[57] See: www.jurisitetunisie.com/tunisie/codes/cp/cp1200.htm.
[58] Minister of Public Health and the National Programme to Fight HIV and STIs, p. 45.
[59] Interview in Tunis (30), 7 February 2012.

changes to the laws of association as a key opportunity to establish their own organisation. This provided them a platform to work with other organisations such as human rights organisations and regional LGBT networks to advocate further for the rights of sexual minorities in Tunisia. They engaged in public advocacy with the National Constituent Assembly to advocate for the inclusion of freedom from discrimination in the new constitution. They also increasingly came to rely on social media such as Facebook to demonstrate the objectives of their organisation as well as to participate in international commemorative days such as the International Day Against Homophobia and Transphobia. These bold strategies to engage more fully in the national political terrain were intended as tools to expand the discursive arena and to contest what was perceived as repression against gay, bisexual and transgender populations. However, given what could be characterised as an often violent ordering and re-ordering of post-revolution priorities following a transition from authoritarian rule, sexual minorities also faced the challenge of a rising 'conservative' backlash against the 'immorality' associated with the former regime.

Contracting Spaces for Discursive Contestation: 'Now Is Not the Time'

During the two years following the 2010–2011 uprising, spaces for political expression and for democratic liberalisation in the political realm expanded; however, sociocultural spaces regarding what was acceptable in the post-revolution era simultaneously contracted. Often individuals would remark that 'now is the right time to talk about everything in Tunisia', but that in reality it seems that 'everything' had its limits. Same-sex acts in Tunisia, for example, are virtually forbidden at three principal levels. At the political level, Article 230 of the Tunisian penal code criminalises same-sex relations for up to three years in prison, and at the time of this writing the law still applied.[60] At the religious level, in a country that is approximately 98 per cent Muslim, same-sex behaviour, while not being officially *haram* in the Qur'an, is forbidden in Sharia, and the punishments vary according to

---

[60] More recent evidence of the application of the law; see: *Agence France-Presse*, 'Tunisia Jails Six Students for Homosexuality', TheGuardian.com, 14 December 2015.

the school of *fiqh* (Islamic jurisprudence). Finally, at the sociocultural level, men who have sex with men are highly stigmatised in the media (including online, print and television) and at the community level, in families and in the workplace. Kader observed, 'Our society is schizophrenic, people say one thing and do the complete opposite.' He used the example of alcohol consumption, referring to men in bars drinking alcohol who at the same time insist that homosexuality is *haram*. In Kader's analysis, 'The act of homosexuality is one thing, speaking about it is another. It is not the act that is forbidden here it seems. It is saying you are "homosexual". When you want to express yourself, it is here where the problems begin.'[61]

LGBT activists in the Middle East and North Africa are well read in the specific legal verses of the Qur'an, as this is an essential strategy and tool in their advocacy arsenal. Radi, a sociologist interviewed for the research, felt that increasingly to reach his audience he could not simply rely on his scientific audience – he also had to refer back to Arab–Muslim culture to reach what he perceived as a more religious audience to make his point and to win his arguments.[62] For example, some would argue quite vociferously that nowhere in the Qur'an is homosexuality *haram*, or forbidden. Whitaker, for example, contends, 'While Islamic teaching often provides a rationale for anti-homosexual laws the law in practice is shaped mainly by the prevailing attitudes in each country, and particularly by the extent to which government seeks to police personal morality.'[63] Whitaker cites Scott al-Haqq Kugle's challenge to more traditionalist views as he asserts that the issue of homosexuality is not addressed anywhere in the Qur'an, nor is there any evidence that the Prophet [Muhammad] ever punished people for same-sex acts.[64] The experience of Nasser also underscored the necessity for activists to understand the Sources in order to effectively engage in debates as they relate to homosexuality in Islamic contexts. He remarked:

People here are also saying 'this homosexuality' is something new, brought after the revolution by westerns and occidentals. However there is no sanction against homosexuality in the Qur'an, all sins in the Qur'an have a punishment or sanction but not homosexuality ... We try to convince people

---

[61] Interview in Tunis (26), 30 January 2012.
[62] Interview in Tunis (30), 7 February 2012.
[63] Whitaker, *Unspeakable Love*, p. 113.   [64] Ibid., p. 119.

that our behaviour is not *haram* but they now block and become violent. The sources of Islam – the Qur'an and the *hadith*s – are silent on the issue of homosexuality.[65]

Nevertheless, prevailing conservative attitudes in Tunisia perceive homosexuality to be not only an illegal act but also as something 'permitted' under the 'corrupt' and 'impious' Ben Ali regime. Nasser remarked that LGBT communities in Tunisia became afraid shortly after the 2010–2011 uprising; eventually it was reported that hundreds of sexual minorities left Tunisia. Nasser and Kader had both been subject to physical violence after 14 January 2011 through attacks on the street or in known safe spaces for gay, bisexual and transgender populations. According to Nasser, 'Before the 14th, the gay community in Tunisia did not necessarily live freely, but at least we lived in security . . . Since the 14th, homophobic acts are clear and direct. Now everyone gives himself the right to criticize our way of dressing, to stare or to physically assault us.'[66] Trespassers physically beat Kader as he tried to protect one of the known gay safe spaces in Tunis. His friend Nasser said that these events were rare before the revolution. As to whether this was a traumatic experience for him, Kader shrugged his shoulders and said, 'Je reste et je résiste encore.' ('I am staying and I am still resisting.')[67]

Some would argue that during the Ben Ali regime, gay, bisexual and transgender communities were not singled out because repression was targeted at political dissent in the form of opposition. However, after the Tunisia uprising, as one self-identified gay male in Tunisia remarked in a press interview, 'Don't forget the Islamist parties who are trying to play the role of judge right now, and who view homosexuality and the gay community as a product of the former regime.' He added, 'They call it "rot" that must be cleaned away.'[68] Some also argued that while there was indeed a specific article of the penal code that penalised same-sex acts, it was not applied in practice. However, members of gay, bisexual and transgender communities reported having direct experience of the law being applied in practice as well as in theory, even following the revolution. Nasser referred to a friend who was reportedly robbed and beaten. The police caught the two

---

[65] Interview in Tunis (25), 27 January 2012, November 2012 and 14 March 2013.
[66] Ibid.   [67] Interview in Tunis (26), 30 January 2012.
[68] As cited in Crary, 'Gays in Egypt, Tunisia Worry'.

perpetrators, who then argued to the police that the victim was homosexual. Soon the victim himself was threatened with 11 months incarceration under Article 230 of the penal code. Eventually he received a jail sentence of two months and was forced to sign a confession that he was homosexual and had broken the law; similar arrests were made under the offense of 'atteinte a la pudeur' – for being at risk of offending the moral sensibilities of the population.[69]

There was (and most likely continues to be) a blurred conflation between the legal, the religious and the moral in the post-uprising government, media and society in Tunisia. For example, in February 2012, newly appointed Minister for Human Rights Samir Dilou was quoted in a television interview speaking of homosexuality as 'a perversion to be medically treated' and that 'freedom of expression has its limits'.[70] Of concern for human rights activists in Tunisia was the contradiction of 'pas les droits de l'homme, mais les droits de certains hommes' ('not of human rights but of rights only for some').[71] Furthermore, in response to the demonstration organised on 28 January 2012 for liberty (and against violence), during which a rainbow flag was again featured, a Tunisian talk-show host (who also interviewed the human rights minister during which the aforementioned comments were made) condemned the protesters on his Facebook page, writing, 'Do we need further strife because a very small minority expresses its perversion ... not caring about the feelings and the sacred beliefs of a majority?'[72]

Before the Tunisia uprising, the former regime supported interventions to engage in outreach work with men who have sex with men and permitted the United Nations Development Programme (UNDP) and the Joint United Nations Programme on HIV/AIDS (UNAIDS) to conduct in-depth bio-behavioural research on multiple categories of same-sex practice across the different regions of Tunisia. Ouroub, an employee of one of the United Nations country offices based in Tunis, explained, 'In a way they [men who have sex with men] were a bit protected by the former system, but now this is perhaps the population which is the most stigmatised by the government, by the police and the larger society. They have suffered a lot of violence and unfortunately

---

[69] Interview in Tunis (25), 27 January 2012, November 2012 and 14 March 2013.
[70] Baeder, 'Tunisian Human Rights Minister's Remarks'.
[71] Interview in Tunis (36), 16 February 2012.
[72] Baeder, 'Tunisian Human Rights Minister's Remarks'.

with this population they also have the highest HIV prevalence.' Moreover, she remarked, 'So in a sense you have this enormous new opening but also very high and somewhat new stigma that was not there before.'[73] The experience of the LGBT activist Moazzam also underscored the more 'conservative' backlash against sexual minorities following the revolution. He stated, 'They (Ennahda) played on their words, on God and on religion, this is what I see at this time. Nothing is sure for the rights of homosexuals, personally I do not feel safe, I even have friends who have left the country out of fear.' He added, 'Actuellement, je ne veux pas vivre ici.' ('These days, I do not want to live here.')[74]

Reports of discrimination and violence against gay, bisexual and transgender communities in Tunisia, both before and after the Tunisia uprising, spurred members to advocate for the addition of freedom from stigma and violence to the democratic reform agenda. However, greater advocacy for the expansion of the post-revolution liberalisation terrain was met with voices encouraging caution at home and abroad as even civil society actors themselves warned that 'now is not the time'. I met with a group of journalists from a newly established Tunisian news English-language website who had recently published an article on homosexuality in Tunisia, just less than one year after the uprising.[75] Despite warnings from the website's lawyers not to publish the article, the piece drew a range of responses from both within and outside gay, bisexual and transgender communities (including many reactionary blog commentaries). Muammar, one of the founders of the website and a former public health professional working in HIV/AIDS, remarked, 'In 2011 there was so much opportunity to take that space and LGBTs and most liberals did not act or were afraid to act. We were very disappointed as the NGOs in general have taken a very hands-off approach with the media.'[76]

According to the journalists, when the article was being developed they asked a number of members of LGBT communities if the transition government should prioritise issues for gay, bisexual and transgender populations. They reported that most, if not all, responded in

---

[73] Interview in Tunis (20), 16 January 2012 and 13 March 2013.
[74] Interview in Tunis (23), 24 January 2012.
[75] F. Samti and J. Belkhiria, 'Gay Tunisia: A "Don't Ask, Don't Tell" Situation', Tunisia-Live.Net, 27 January 2012.
[76] Interview in Tunis (27), 30 January 2012.

the negative, arguing that 'this was not the time'; furthermore, several consulted felt it would never be a good time. In discussing Fedi's viewpoints and opinions, the article states that 'despite his strong conviction about the need for legally guaranteed rights for the homosexual community, [he] thinks that it is still too soon to officially demand them from the government'. Fedi was quoted as saying, 'Such a move would only destabilize the situation in which we are living, and cause more violence and more insecurity.'[77]

Voices of caution also came from secular civil society actors and groups that filtered and re-ordered the reform agenda within Tunisia's expanding public spaces. For example, following the comments made against homosexuality by the human rights minister in February 2012, a number of individuals from LGBT communities signed a petition advocating for the homophobic comments made by the minister to be addressed by the Tunisian League of Human Rights (LTDH) as an illustration of the need to tackle homophobia in the new constitution. Despite the petition and open confrontation during one of the meetings of the organisation, the human rights association concluded that 'now is not the time to address these issues in Tunisia'. Even when one looks outside the country across the Middle East and North Africa in the post-Arab uprising era, members of LGBT organisations themselves advise against engaging in overt advocacy for greater rights for gay, bisexual and transgender communities, such as establishing new LGBT associations. El Feki describes a member of a well-known LGBT organisation in Lebanon advising caution to gay, bisexual and transgender communities in Egypt, for example stating, 'Now is not the time to say in Egypt, "I want to establish an LGBT organisation." There are foundational things that need to be laid first. You're talking about a society in a huge sway of transition, and the building blocks of a more open and democratic society need to be laid down first.'[78]

Perhaps it should come as no surprise that even actors from within gay, bisexual and transgender communities (both nationally and in the broader region) did not have consensus on whether or not freedom from violence and discrimination should feature as a critical post-revolution priority. During a transition from authoritarian rule the

---

[77] As quoted in Samti and Belkhiria, 'Gay Tunisia: A "Don't Ask, Don't Tell" Situation'.
[78] El Feki, *Sex and the Citadel*, p. 269.

space available for 'other', in particular minority groups, shrinks as civil society actors and groups attempt to make as many 'wins' as possible without thwarting or reversing other gains made. Voices are regularly marginalised in the name of democracy and consensus as different groups and issues emerging within civil society are often sidelined in favour of what is 'acceptable' and what features understandings of Tunisia's new national identity. Consequently one observes a minority that could move with relative freedom under the former system finding itself excluded from the new imaginings of the Tunisian state. During my return visit to Tunisia in March 2013, I learned that all three of the men who established Damj to defend greater human rights at the national level had left Tunis because they felt unsafe as gay men in post-revolution Tunisia. Moazzam and Kader were given asylum in Europe and the United States, respectively, and Nasser moved outside of Tunis to an environment where he could find more like-minded peers. I spoke to Nasser later about these changes. He said that he thought Kader never recovered after the violence he experienced soon after the end of the uprising in January 2011 (when he was robbed and beaten). He remarked that many of his own friends had left Tunisia following the uprisings and that this has been a difficult time for him and his peers. He concluded by saying that homophobic attacks were regular and that individuals were even killed.[79] The way the violence is explained, he remarked, is that it never relates to homosexuality (but rather to random untargeted acts of crime or violence), so these instances of violence continue to be impossible to prove.[80]

Conclusion

Following the 2010–2011 Tunisia uprising, a variety of shifting priorities were fiercely contested within a multiplicity of discursive arenas where dominant publics sought to marginalise and enforce the hegemony of consensus. This marginalisation was facilitated through moral panics produced at both the political and sociocultural level seeking manifold forms of transitional justice associated with the impiety and

---

[79] See: S. Ben Ammar, 'Les Islamistes Tuent des Gays de Peur de se Regarder dans leur Propre Miroir', TunisieNews.Com, 5 August 2012.
[80] Interview in Tunis (25), 27 January 2012, November 2012 and 14 March 2013.

corruption of the former regime. These moral panics also heavily featured sex as a topic for national debate. Multiple discourses on sex eventually permitted both the 'liberal' and the 'conservative' factions to emphasise the other's unsuitability to govern post-revolution Tunisia. Each side could gain as these discourses scapegoated minorities and marginalised new voices attempting to be heard in Tunisia's public spaces. Some members of vulnerable groups perceived a post-revolution environment where they would likely continue to encounter marginalisation at multiple levels and in which their own personal sense of security and well-being would remain uncertain. Actors who were hoping to maximise opportunities to widen the discursive arena, such as through the touchstone issue of homosexuality, ultimately had to weigh the benefits of visibility to advocate for greater inclusion and freedom from discrimination against the risks of further violence and personal insecurity.

Some members of gay, bisexual and transgender communities were able to make remarkable advances within post-revolution Tunisia by adopting different mechanisms to contest the hegemonic transition discourse(s). These actors explicitly chose to engage in a range of strategies to advocate recognition and freedom from discrimination alongside the numerous priorities tabled for discursive contestation. Actors working within these communities participated in Tunisia's public spaces through combined strategies of publicity and visibility, such as participating in public demonstrations articulating the need for recognition through symbols such as the rainbow flag; appropriating social media such as Facebook to demonstrate solidarity to the International Day Against Homophobia and Transphobia; establishing a formal civil society organisation to combat stigma and discrimination against minorities; publicly countering homophobic statements in the media through mass petitions; and working through a range of national and regional networks such as human rights groups to articulate solutions to challenges for sexual minorities in Tunisia. They even altered their typical advocacy discourse to feature more Islamist language to engage with more 'conservative' communities at the sociocultural level.

Nevertheless, these actors also believed they encountered increased marginalisation at the individual/personal level as an outcome of this growing visibility at the political and sociocultural levels – even from actors within civil society cautioning that 'now is not the time'.

Conclusion 189

This was also exacerbated by a series of public homophobic statements made by the newly appointed human rights minister and media figures shortly after the uprising. Even in 2015, the issue of freedom from discrimination and violence for gay, bisexual and transgender populations continued to spark controversy and contention in Tunisia as several Tunisian students were imprisoned on official charges of same-sex acts (Article 230 of the penal code).[81] The justice minister under the new secular government, Salah Ben Aissa, subsequently called for the removal of Article 230; he was dismissed from his post the following month, in October 2015.[82] In one case, six students were given the maximum sentence of three years. Moreover, Human Rights Watch reported that from 2010 to 2011, 10 homosexual men in Tunisia had been killed in hate crimes.[83]

This chapter examined the third and final theme of the book, specifically the exclusionary nature of consensus in 'liberal' democracies. In continuing to analyse the different ways conflict manifests among civil society actors and groups, it traced the areas of these contestations and the consequences for these actors. Rather than critical conflicts and contestations emerging between secular and religious groups, as demonstrated in the previous chapter, the areas of contestation herein were over key touchstone issues such as sex and homosexuality. Issues concerning sexual minorities often spark intense debates on identity politics, socio-religious norms and the influence of Western understandings of liberalism as they relate to human rights and equality. As many Tunisians felt 'now is not the time' to highlight human rights abuses against gay, bisexual and transgender communities or to advocate for changing criminalising penal codes, the consequence was an effective discursive narrowing following earlier political liberalisation measures to expand these spaces. This discursive narrowing is a consequence of a fundamental democratic practice, consensus. The ideal of consensus allows a host of actors to exclude and negate alternative views through the hegemony of consensus. Moreover, through discourses on neoliberalism, the preference for consensus has been

---

[81] See: *Agence France-Presse*, 'Tunisia Jails Six Students for Homosexuality', TheGuardian.com, 14 December 2015 and C. McCormick-Cavanagh, 'Tunisia LGBT Group Battles for Justice in Case of Imprisoned Gay Man', *Middle East Eye*, October 2015.
[82] See: *Agence France-Presse*, 'Tunisia Jails Six Students for Homosexuality'.
[83] McCormick-Cavanagh, 'Tunisia LGBT Group Battles for Justice'.

re-institutionalised to promote the virtues of democratisation. Following a transition from authoritarian rule, consensus effectively becomes a key means to enforce hegemonies as the post-revolution hierarchy of priorities is redefined, and 'other' is pushed to the periphery or negated entirely. As such, consensus becomes a critical mechanism through which conflicts are muted and discursive arenas are squeezed. In the absence of these conflicts, the consequence is that there remains little evidence as to whether genuine discursive contestation is taking place.

7 Conclusion

Imagining Change – Determining the Parameters of Pluralism

The image I keep thinking of is a mother giving birth to her child, with cries of pain. Out of this, I think we can grow into a Tunisia that's more modern, open, and tolerant.

– Tunisian activist[1]

The year 2014 marked a milestone in Tunisia's evolution and in the post-'Arab Spring' era when the country ratified a new Constitution and elected a new president. In January of that year, the National Constituent Assembly adopted the new Constitution based on the consensus of the majority, thereby putting an end to the political stalemate between secular and Islamist factions in which the country had been mired for more than two years.[2] Moreover, in October 2014, Beji Caid Essebsi, who briefly served as a transitional prime minister in 2011 immediately following the downfall of the Ben Ali regime, won 55 per cent of votes cast as the candidate of the secular Nidaa Tounes party. Essebsi, a former three-time minister under Bourguiba, was confirmed as the winner of Tunisia's 'first free presidential election' since independence from France in 1956.[3] Nevertheless, it is estimated that more than half of the new 86 Nidaa Tounes parliamentary members are former members of the RCD party, reflecting both change and continuity in the years following the 2010–2011 Tunisia uprising.

Tunisia, a country of approximately 11 million inhabitants wedged between Algeria and Libya in North Africa, has claimed a number of firsts since the Arab uprisings began in early 2011, including being the first country to bring down a repressive dictator and the first to hold peaceful democratic elections. The small country nourished

---

[1] As cited in Crary, 'Gays in Egypt, Tunisia Worry'.
[2] R. Grote, 'The New 2014 Tunisian Constitution', *Oxford Constitutions of the World* (Oxford: Oxford University Press, 2014).
[3] E. Byrne, 'Tunisia Elections: Veteran Politician Beji Caid Essebsi Wins Run-Off Vote', TheGuardian.com, 22 December 2014.

expectations globally that a higher standard of democracy was being put forward, cultivated and led by the will of the people. In effect, every move in Tunisia's political and public spaces was intensely monitored by both those within and outside the country. Moreover, the 'resurrection of civil society' captured the attention of activists, associations, academics, decision makers and international donors, who once again attempted to determine the role for civil society during a transition from authoritarian rule. On 10 October 2015, almost five years after the Tunisia uprising, a handful of civil society organisations known as the Tunisian National Dialogue Quartet were awarded the Nobel Peace Prize for their 'decisive contribution to the building of a pluralist democracy in Tunisia' following the 2010–2011 uprising.[4] These four organisations were the Tunisian General Labour Union (UGTT), the Tunisian Confederation of Industry, Trade and Handicrafts (UTICA), the Tunisian Human Rights League (LTDH) and the Tunisian Order of Lawyers. While praising the Tunisian groups' specific work, the Norwegian Nobel Committee indicated that the honour also reflected on civil society actors more broadly. The press release on the committee's official website stated that 'the transition in Tunisia shows that civil society institutions and organisations can play a crucial role in a country's democratisation, and that such a process, even under difficult circumstances, can lead to free elections and the peaceful transfer of power'.[5] As observed in the social movements of Eastern Europe and Latin America in the 1980s, and across discourses on neoliberalism today, civil society has come to serve as a torchbearer for democracy and simultaneously as the antithesis to authoritarianism.

I undertook both a conceptual and an empirical analysis of civil society in Tunisia by focusing on a collection of the sector's actors during a two-year period of critical sociopolitical disruption and transformation following the downfall of the Ben Ali regime. I analysed how and where different conflicts and cleavages emerged among civil society actors and groups after the Tunisia uprising. As an initial point of departure I recognised that just as there are areas of consensus and solidarity among these actors, there are also matters over which there is

---

[4] See: 'The Nobel Peace Prize for 2015', available at: www.nobelprize.org/nobel_prizes/peace/laureates/2015/press.html.
[5] Ibid.

intense disagreement and divergence. Therefore, just as there is harmony and inclusion, there is also conflict and exclusion. Within the context of a transition from authoritarian rule and a national drive towards democratisation, the aim of this book was to determine the consequences of civil society's splits, shifts and divergences and to further explore what could be discerned from these different sites of contestation – ultimately, to determine the function of conflict in civil society. I conducted this research within the post-uprising context to first, shed further light on these conflicts as they emerged in the country's expanding symbolic and physical discursive arenas, and second, to determine whether these conflicts served as productive forces to maintain discursive contestation as Tunisia pursued a pluralist democracy. The actions and motivations of civil society actors and groups took on vital importance in Tunisia's post-revolution climate at a time when touchstone issues such as the status of women, human rights, the freedom of the press, legalised prostitution and homosexuality became critical matters of contestation. Across the book I argue that conflict among these actors is indeed consequential and worthy of further scrutiny as conflict is in fact essential to pluralism and dialogism.

As the principal context for this book is grounded in the events that occurred during the two years subsequent to the 2010–2011 uprising, I identified and explored three principal themes: the 'illiberal' effects of the opening of the public space(s), the emerging sociocultural and socio-religious divisions (including the rise of associational or social Islam) and finally the exclusionary (and undemocratic) nature of consensus in 'liberal' democracies. Effectively, these three themes bring into sharp relief the different divergences and sites of contestation that can arise as a country embarks on the pursuit of democratisation. They illustrate simultaneously the dynamism of a host of actors and groups collectively mobilised to shape the priorities of Tunisia and also illuminate the genuine constraints for actors limited by the political residue they inherited. As such, each core theme reveals a gradual narrowing down over two years of various contests and counter-contests in public spaces, demonstrating the enduring impact of decades of authoritarian rule on all actors at both the political and social levels.

A range of actors emerged to fill Tunisia's public spaces following the implementation of political liberalisation measures in the immediate months following the departure of the Ben Ali regime. These groups not only included social welfare provision organisations but also organisations working with marginalised populations who often found themselves on the periphery, excluded from mainstream public discourses. Specifically, I analysed human rights organisations established before and after the downfall of the regime, humanitarian development organisations (including Islamic associations) created after 2011, and organisations working with communities living with and affected by HIV/AIDS and sexual minorities established before and after the uprising in Tunisia. Finally, I advocated the importance of researching marginalised communities who experienced the brunt of sociopolitical turmoil and who often struggled to participate in mainstream discursive arenas. What happens at the periphery sheds light on populations who are routinely stigmatised and criminalised and, more importantly, who often find their human rights eroded as a result of populist decisions and moral panics associated with political transitions.

Expansions and Contractions: Tracking the Movement of National Priorities in Post-Uprising Tunisia

In January 2011 a space opened. The moments of solidarity and national unity of having brought down a dictator created a momentum whereby the popular masses forced the field open for political liberalisation. As a result, a range of both secular and religious political parties were able to register, and the laws of association were amended, two developments that allowed thousands of new organisations to find their voices and strive to openly influence the shaping of a new Tunisia. However, one also witnessed the disruption and transformation wrought by a country in the pursuit of a higher or different standard of democracy. These moments of sociopolitical unrest carried with them a host of emerging conflicts and contestations within political as well as public spaces as critical decisions were made regarding political leaders and national priorities. Moreover, previously marginalised actors and groups sought recognition and dignity as the country defined its new national identity. The three core themes of this book underscore the specific areas and consequences of these conflicts, in particular among civil society actors and groups as they move to participate in Tunisia's new and expanding symbolic and physical public spaces following the 2010–2011 uprising. They also illuminate the nature of these conflicts, stemming from both the practices of the pre-revolution regimes of Bourguiba and Ben Ali as well as the new and uncertain sociopolitical terrain that materialised after 2011.

Both the Bourguiba and Ben Ali regimes manipulated the spaces for civil society to manoeuvre from the period of independence in 1956. The origins, initial structures and leadership of the Tunisian state shaped the way it engaged with these actors. Through Ben Romdhane's description of the 'authoritarian spiral', it becomes clear that specific crisis moments in the transformation of the state represent critical watersheds in Tunisia's sociopolitical development. For example, although Bourguiba inherited a highly centralised and efficient state apparatus following independence from French colonial rule in 1956, he was required to repeatedly prevent and manage the conflicts that emerged prior to and following his rise to leadership. He encountered contestations to his legitimacy both within the Neo-Destour Party (PSD) and throughout his drive to implement controversial policies such as the Code of Personal Status and austere socio-economic reforms. Over the three decades in which Bourguiba governed Tunisia, the overall project and prioritisation of national construction inevitably supplanted measures to foster political pluralism and liberalism. As this 'authoritarian spiral' intensified, the response to perceived opposition became increasingly severe. As a result, the institutions of civil society became weak or non-existent and were gradually co-opted into the broader Tunisian state and PSD.

The residue of authoritarianism eventually carried over into the Ben Ali regime despite initial optimism for democratic reform and a more pluralist society. After Ben Ali succeeded Bourguiba, the new president was keen to demonstrate a commitment to neoliberal economic reform both at home and abroad; he was equally committed to demonstrating his outward conviction in liberal political reform. As early as the 1990s, Ben Ali created perceptible openings for political liberalisation. What accompanied these measures was an international enthusiasm for the democratic potential these new opportunities could offer Tunisian political society. Nevertheless, the regime's preoccupation with the implementation of neoliberal economic reform and political stability and security eventually necessitated harsh crackdowns on perceived unrest and opposition. Following an initial loosening of the laws of association, for example, these laws were then amended to bring civil society organisations under the further control of the state and the RCD party. Moreover, the threat of Islamist extremism as perceived more broadly in the Middle East and North Africa during the 1990s allowed the Ben Ali regime to repress significant sections of the population as well as many forms of collective activism understood as potential opposition. In addition to the targeting of secular organisations, the regime gradually closed down spaces for religiously oriented groups to manoeuvre. Over time, the vigorous targeting of the Islamists by the government had a direct impact on the nature of Tunisian society as some secular organisations also began to distance themselves from Islamist organisations. Eventually, this resulted in a more or less homogenous field of civil society actors and groups interacting within relatively uncontested, albeit constrained, public spaces. Moreover, as many of these organisations emerged during a period of the implementation of neoliberal policies, many were largely restricted to the provision of social welfare services. The limited nature of the work civil society organisations could engage in, the repressive conditions under which they operated and the homogeneity of the field in which they manoeuvred all had direct implications for the conflicts and cleavages that manifested among these different actors following the 2010–2011 uprising. However, the force of the state security apparatus and the RCD party applied against these actors also unwittingly provided the conditions and momentum for independent social action to arise following decades of authoritarian rule.

The opening up of Tunisia's public spaces came about as a result of the critical and sustained pressure from the popular masses on the High Authority for political liberalisation following the downfall of the regime in January 2011. Chapter 4 examined the first core theme of the book, specifically the 'illiberal' effects of the opening of the public space(s). This and the remaining chapters reflect the analogy of a reverse pyramid in order to conceptualise the transformation of the discursive arena during the transition from authoritarian rule in Tunisia. Chapters 4 and 5 illustrate this pyramid at its widest point as Tunisia's public spaces rapidly expanded to accommodate a host of new actors, priorities, ideologies and contests and counter-contests; Chapter 6, however, reflects this discursive pyramid at its narrowest point as conflicts and contestations are gradually muted and the practice of consensus filters down national priorities in the subsequent years following the uprising. For example, during the initial months following the downfall of the Ben Ali regime, the discursive arena was at its widest as not only were thousands of new organisations legally established but also a host of new priorities, visions, and ideologies filled this expansive space. These expanding spaces were also shared with the organisations formerly established under the Ben Ali regime. The newer and historic organisations effectively encountered opportunities and challenges as they endeavoured to participate in Tunisia's post-uprising public spaces. As a consequence of a multitude of actors emerging to the forefront, a range of issues were tabled, including the issue of freedom of the press and media (or the limits of); issues regarding the status of women; support to and recognition of vulnerable but also criminalised populations such as people affected by HIV/AIDS, including sex workers and men who have sex with men; and finally, a key symbol of national identity, the Tunisian flag. These issues became critical areas of conflict among civil society actors and groups in the months that followed the Tunisia uprising. In addition to navigating these debates, many civil society actors also found themselves operating on uncertain terrain as they were required to cultivate relationships with new political leaders and donors as well as to rearticulate their post-revolution mandates. During this time, the landscape of Tunisia's public spaces was characterised by an unfolding sense of *citoyenneté* and dynamism as well as by competition, uncertainty and at times, distrust.

There are two specific and yet incompatible understandings of civil society that are evident in much of the transitology literature and which, as such, are highlighted across the book. The first is the Gramscian understanding in which civil society is a dynamic set of actors capable of subverting the hegemony of the state, an approach revived and rearticulated during the social movements in Eastern Europe and Latin America in the 1980s and which has come to recognise civil society as antithetical to authoritarianism. The second is the neoliberal understanding applied and upheld during the Ben Ali regime during which many of these actors served as providers of social welfare services to supplement the social contract between the Tunisian state and its citizens. Both of these understandings, and the ideologies underpinning them – Communism and neoliberalism – manifested in Tunisia's public spaces following the uprisings, arguably exacerbating conflicts and cleavages among civil society actors.

The opening of space following the downfall of an authoritarian regime can create new opportunities for participation in sociopolitical processes as well as establish fresh priorities as the state transitions to an uncertain something else. Conflict is manifested within civil society when the public space suddenly widens to accommodate a vast range of new actors and disparate, often competing, ideologies. In the case of

Tunisia, this space opened following the amendments to the laws of association in early 2011. However, the residue of authoritarian rule, and the residue it left upon the different webs of relationships forged in Tunisian society throughout the former regime, significantly influenced how these actors responded to change – the disruption and transformation brought by the transition. I demonstrate that there is a tumultuous but definitive period following the downfall of an authoritarian regime that is intensified by the implementation of political liberalisation measures during which actors can take maximum advantage of these expanding spaces and where the field for discursive contestation grows to its widest point. The consequence of the opening up of these new and vast public spaces, and the multiplicity of different conflicts that emerge, can result in an uncivil and illiberal jostling of views, visions and ideologies. These sites of contestation reveal a crowded terrain of actors yet also give evidence that discursive contestation is indeed taking place.

Disruption, Change, and Transformation: Situating Conflict

In late 2010 and early 2011 Tunisians mobilised in solidarity to bring down a dictator with the critical revolutionary slogan 'Ash-sh'ab yurid isqat al-nizam' ('The people want the overthrow of the regime'). The slogan eventually spread across the Middle East and North Africa to Bahrain, Egypt, Libya, Syria and Yemen, igniting in all these places popular protest in the face of authoritarian regimes. Tunisians demonstrated together, calling for dignity, employment and freedom, and through sustained popular mobilisations they advocated for the institutionalisation of political liberalism. In the months following the departure of the Ben Ali regime, Tunisian activists succeeded in making a number of key gains, including the widening of the terrain for the emergence of new political actors and parties to participate in the National Constituent Assembly and the expansion of Tunisia's public spaces to harness a multitude of old and new actors seeking to put into practice their own conception of *citoyenneté*. Given the national and regional momentum behind the moments leading up to and following the downfall of the regime, the stakes for choosing political leaders, alliances and national priorities were high, resulting in what could be perceived as an uncivil jostling among actors as these critical battles unfolded in Tunisia's vast discursive arenas.

Nevertheless, civil society became more conflictual and contested among its diverse elements during the two years following the Tunisia 2010–2011 uprising than previously under authoritarian rule. However, over time, as consensus was eventually taken on a number of critical national priorities, these conflicts and contentions gradually waned. In fact, conflict manifests among civil society actors and groups as a result of four specific factors. These four factors are prominent across each of the three thematic areas in each of the three core chapters concerning the 'illiberal' effects of the opening of the public space(s), the emerging sociocultural and socio-religious divisions (including the rise of associational or social Islam) and the exclusionary (and undemocratic) nature of consensus in 'liberal' democracies. The first factor is the residue of authoritarian rule, in particular the cleavages that materialised and were perpetuated by the former regime. In the case of Tunisia, both the Bourguiba and Ben Ali regimes exacerbated tensions and divergences between secular and Islamist actors in an overall effort to sustain their legitimacy to rule. The divisions that were established and maintained in the five decades following independence from French colonial rule in 1956 carried over into post-uprising Tunisia and influenced how civil society actors responded to diversity and conflict.

The second factor affecting the conflicts that emerge within civil society is the rapid expansion of a space with the simultaneous emergence of a multiplicity of views, priorities and ideologies. Under the direction of the High Authority, the transition government implemented measures for political liberalisation in March and April 2011 to expand the opportunities for political representatives and parties to register and amended the former laws of association to allow new civil society organisations to be legally created. As a result of the concurrent quantitative and qualitative expansion of these spaces in a relatively short amount of time, thousands of new organisations were created and many older organisations dissolved. Moreover, a range of touchstone issues featured across Tunisia's public spaces – issues that often ignited contention and sparked intense national debate.

The third factor that affected the contestations that manifested among civil society actors is the political mirroring that occurs as a consequence of the debates unfolding at the political level, within the Ennahda party, inside the National Constituent Assembly and in the media. These debates in Tunisia's political spaces reflect back onto the country's symbolic and physical public spaces; the conflicts that emerged at the political level – for example, on the status of women and sexual minorities – were reproduced and re-enacted in the discursive arenas where civil society actors encountered one another.

Finally, the fourth factor that impacts the nature of the conflicts that emerge among civil society actors relates back to the conceptual understandings of civil society considered in Chapter 2. This chapter underscored the Gramscian understanding of civil society in which its actors are attributed a more dynamic sense of agency and are capable of self-management and self-organisation. This understanding was eventually resurrected during the social movements in Eastern Europe and Latin America in the 1980s. As many of the actors during this period re-appropriated the concept of civil society in seeking defence and freedom from the state, this concept was also rearticulated to subvert the power of the state. The active understanding of the concept was later co-opted, however, by neoliberalism to celebrate the role of civil society actors in the transition to and consolidation of democracy through good governance agendas. Over time a concept that emphasised the dynamic nature of conflict was gradually eroded by conceptual understandings that de-emphasised these divisions. Underpinning the conflicts that manifest among these actors today are two simultaneously active but incompatible concepts of civil society defined and upheld by disparate ideologies – Communism on the one hand and neoliberalism on the other. At the root of the conflicts within civil society are these irreconcilable ideologies. This also brings the book back to Pearce, who in Chapter 2 observed a fundamental shift in the spirit of civil society organisations as agents formerly organised to contest hegemony to actors who now are often considered to consolidate and maintain hegemonies in authoritarian contexts. This follows on from the premise that the concept of civil society and the role of these immeasurably different organisations have gained greater prominence in the neoliberal architecture over the last three and a half decades. This change has resulted in criticisms by some actors in the academic and international development sectors based on their scepticism as to whether these organisations can effectively put forward alternatives to social change or can realistically contest hegemonic international development discourses. Because civil society organisations are expected to fill both a role of public service contractor for the provision of social welfare services and act as agents to uphold democratic values and good governance, many of them have instead gradually become instruments to maintain and consolidate authoritarianism. This practice can be observed in the jostling over priorities and worldviews between both the historic and newer civil society actors and groups in Tunisia's post-uprising public spaces. And while I underscore here, and across the book, the constraints of the structure of neoliberalism on the agency of civil society actors, I also acknowledge that which is indeterminate in the deliberate acts of many civil society organisations who choose to engage in challenging contexts despite the often personal risk they assume – the manifold acts of hypervisibility and invisibility to both reach marginalised populations and to influence sociopolitical change. Within the constraints of this structure, are there spaces to pursue such alternatives, a question that necessitates further reflection on areas where there has been change and upon areas where there is continuity in Tunisia's discursive arenas today.

The implications of this research on civil society are three-fold. First, academics, international development practitioners, donors and perhaps most importantly, civil society actors and groups themselves must give further scrutiny as to whether the two roles afforded to civil society in neoliberal policies – as providers of social welfare services and as key actors in holding states accountable and in democratisation – are compatible. Does civil society have the tools and the capacity to do both? Does one necessarily relate to the other? Given these two incompatible mandates, it comes as no surprise that there is conflict among actors that on the one hand are defined by their apolitical nature of delivering services to deprived communities, and yet on the other hand are driven by a mandate to engage in the political by holding states accountable. Moreover, perhaps it is this dual role articulated for these actors that prevents civil society as a field of disparate actors from being genuinely politically transformative, from offering real alternatives particularly within authoritarian contexts. As such, this has implications for the promotion and design of donor-driven 'civil society strengthening', 'capacity building' and 'democracy promotion' initiatives in countries with a heavy authoritarian inheritance. Has the 'demand-side' approach with an implicit focus on strengthening civil society in relation to the state to instigate democratisation and good governance run its course, and can we continue to promote this as a principle and viable strategy following the downfall of authoritarian regimes?

Second, this research elucidates the destructive nature of democratisation and its associated principles, namely consensus. International development practitioners and donors regularly give weight to the importance of consensus among civil society actors and groups on key matters of concerns, whereby conflict among these actors is perceived as unproductive and destructive. Conflicts are muted in favour of a predilection for these actors to 'speak with one voice'. One returns to Mouffe, who underscores the inherent problematic with a preference for 'rational consensus' in which conflicting views are negated. Her premise, that you cannot have consensus without exclusion, should serve as a reminder that democracy requires conflict, and hence its associated institutions such as civil society require the practice of dissent. I advocate and urge practitioners, donors and civil society stakeholders and groups to consider which actors and which critical matters of concern are being excluded when consensus is achieved. Moreover, democratisation is both violent and dynamic, with regularly shifting power relations between actors at the political and social levels. Durac and Cavatorta's notion that liberalism is easily reversible points to the notion that there are no certainties in transitions from authoritarian rule, nor is there a formula for political transformation.[6]

Finally, at the heart of deliberations on the nature and function of conflict in civil society is an underlying normative supposition that conflict is inherently negative and therefore destructive – and, more importantly, that it can fundamentally obstruct efforts towards creating more democratic and representative institutions. This normative frame is also inherent in neoliberal policies that support civil society organisations as critical agents for good governance and democratisation. The eventual preference for consensus over conflict among these different actors is implicit as democracy requires consensus on a range of issues and priorities. Conflicts among actors whose relations are often characterised by solidarity, goodwill and cooperation are perceived as a negative consequence. Together, the different chapters and three core themes featured across the book demonstrate that during periods of sociopolitical turmoil, such as seen through the lens of the Arab uprisings, contestations among civic actors are in fact productive as they enable disputation and counter contests; we should in fact be worried when there is an absence of conflict as this indicates that

---

[6] Durac and Cavatorta, *Politics and Governance in the Middle East*, p. 12.

discursive spaces are contracting and pluralism is narrowing. I reason that conflict is in fact proof of pluralism and dialogism.

The dynamic of the three themes reveals, in effect, the complexity and volatility of democratisation as observed through the lens of civil society. Following the downfall of an authoritarian regime or any significant sociopolitical transformation, time often becomes seemingly chaotic and non-linear as a range of different ideas, priorities and visions effectively rush into the public space. Static concepts are reborn as multiple actors emerge to stamp their ideological claim onto the present. Transitions from authoritarian rule can be characterised by a jostling between state and society whereby relations of power are both macro and micro, horizontal and vertical, repressive and emancipatory whereby the parameters of pluralism are habitually tested. These moments of disruption, change and transformation are also remarkable periods that can offer a renewed dynamism to these concepts and actors. It is a period of expansions and contractions across many levels simultaneously, fluid change and micro-practices that reveal, in their temporariness, the plurality of humanity itself.

APPENDIX:

List of Interviewees

Annex 1 *Qualitative Interview Database and Organisational Typology Oct. 2011–Mar. 2013*

	Name	Type	Entity	Title/Position	Location	Date of Interview
1	Fatiha	Health/HIV	Multi-lateral	HIV/AIDS Technical Adviser	Cairo, Egypt	Oct. 2011
2	Nadje	Human Rights	Association	Health and Discrimination Project Officer	Cairo, Egypt	11 Oct. 2011
3	Lamia	HIV/Health	Multi-lateral	Country Officer	Cairo, Egypt	11 Oct. 2011 and 1 May 2012
4	Said	HIV/Health	Association	Programme Director	Cairo, Egypt	18 Oct. 2011
5	Richard	Development/HIV	Multi-lateral	Programme Adviser	Cairo, Egypt	17 Oct. 2011 and 30 Apr. 2012
6	Dr Mehdi	HIV and Harm Reduction	Association	Executive Director	Cairo, Egypt	17 Oct. 2011
7	Dr Tariq	Association of People living with HIV (PLHIV)	Association	Board Member	Alexandria, Egypt	20 Oct. 2011
8	Sonia	Development	Association	President	Cairo, Egypt	20 Oct. 2011
9	Rita	Association of PLHIV	Association	President	Alexandria, Egypt	20 Oct. 2011
10	Ahmed	Association of PLHIV	Association	Programme Officer	Alexandria, Egypt	20 Oct. 2011
11	Amal	Health/HIV	Multi-lateral	Executive Director	Cairo, Egypt	23 Oct. 2011
12	Dr. Arsalan	HIV	Association	Executive Director	Alexandria, Egypt	24 Oct. 2011
13	Dr. Mohammed	HIV	Association	Consultant in Harm Reduction Program	Alexandria, Egypt	24 Oct. 2011

Annex 1 (*cont.*)

	Name	Type	Entity	Title/Position	Location	Date of Interview
14	Dr. Senim	HIV	Association	Project Coordinator Home-Based Care	Alexandria, Egypt	24 Oct. 2011
15	Hamida	HIV/Technical Support	Association	Coordinator MENA	Marrakesh, Morocco	Oct. 2011
16	Fatima	HIV/Civil Society	Consultant	Public Health and Social Development Consultant	Cairo, Egypt	8 May 2012
17	Catherine Jenkins	HIV/Health	Bi-lateral	Health Advisor, MENA	Washington, USA	15 May 2012
18	Dr Malik	HIV	Association	Executive Director	Tunis, Tunisia	13 Jan. 2012 and 5 Mar. 2013
19	Dr Zied	HIV/Health	INGO	Associate Director	Brighton, England	20 Dec. 2011
20	Ouroub	Development and HIV	Multi-lateral	Country Officer	Tunis, Tunisia	16 Jan. 2012 and 13 Mar. 2013
21	Amir	HIV	Association	Executive Coordinator	Tunis, Tunisia	18 Jan. 2012
22	Amina	Human Rights	Lawyer	Attorney at Law Partner	Tunis, Tunisia	18 Jan. 2012
23	Moazzam	HIV	Association	Outreach worker with sex workers; founder of Damj	Tunis, Tunisia	24 Jan. 2012
24	Mohid	HIV	Association	PLHIV Representative and person living with HIV	Tunis, Tunisia	24 Jan. 2012 and 7 Mar. 2013
25	Nasser	HIV	Association	Supervisor of Peer educators and Outreach Work; founder of Damj	Tunis, Tunisia	27 Jan. 2012, call Nov. 2012, and 14 Mar. 2013

26	Kader	HIV	Association	Supervisor of Key Populations and Outreach Worker; founder of Damj	Tunis, Tunisia	30 Jan. 2012
27	Muammar, Jason and Maha	English News website	Media	Co-Founder and 2 Journalists	Tunis, Tunisia	30 Jan. 2012
28	Kareem	Development	Multi-lateral	Project Coordinator	Tunis, Tunisia	1 Feb. 2012
29	Dr Raahil	HIV	Association	Executive Director	Tunis, Tunisia	5 Feb. 2012
30	Radi	HIV/Gender	Academic	Sociologist, Faculty of Human and Social Sciences	Tunis, Tunisia	7 Feb. 2012
31	Tawfiq	HIV/Harm reduction	Association	Programme Manager/ Medical Doctor	Sfax, Tunisia	9 Feb. 2012
32	Fajr	Democracy/ Civil Society Capacity Building	Association	Programme Officer (former employee of HIV association)	Tunis, Tunisia	10 Feb. 2012
33	Uday	Development	Association	Co-Director	Nabeul, Tunisia	13 Feb. 2012
34	Saqib and Mohammed	Human Rights	Multi-lateral	Director and Policy Adviser	Tunis, Tunisia	15 Feb. 2012
35	Shafiq	Human Rights	Association	Communication Officer	Tunis, Tunisia	15 Feb. 2012
36	Walid	Human Rights	Association	Founder and Lawyer	Tunis, Tunisia	16 Feb. 2012
37	Dr Faiza	Women and Human Rights	Association	President	Tunis, Tunisia	6 Mar. 2012

Annex 1 (*cont.*)

	Name	Type	Entity	Title/Position	Location	Date of Interview
38	Najeeb	Development/ Environment	Bi-Lateral And Associational	Senior Expert Environment; associational member	Tunis, Tunisia	6 Mar. 2012 and 12 March 2013
39	Dr Nadiyah	HIV/ Reproductive Health	Medical Professional and former government employee	Public Health Specialist	Tunis, Tunisia	9 Mar. 2012
40	Naeema	Women and Human Rights	Association	Director	Tunis, Tunisia	12 Mar. 2012
41	Wail	Human Rights	Association	Secretary General	Tunis, Tunisia	13 Mar. 2012
42	Naila	Women and Human Rights	Association	Founder and Secretary	Tunis, Tunisia	16 Mar. 2012
43	Shiyam	Urbanism/ Development	Association	Treasurer and former Programme Coordinator	Tunis, Tunisia	16 Mar. 2012
44	Siham	HIV	Association	Programme Coordinator and Head of Testing	Sfax, Tunisia	21 Mar. 2012
45	Dr Waseem	HIV	Association	Executive Director	Sfax, Tunisia	21 Mar. 2012
46	Yasir	HIV and Harm Reduction	Association	Outreach worker and program assistant	Sfax, Tunisia	21 Mar. 2012
47	Soraya	Women and Human Rights	Association	Programme Coordinator	Kef, Tunisia	22 Mar. 2012

48	Busrah	HIV	Association	President and Founder; person living with HIV	Tunis, Tunisia	23 Mar. 2012
49	Dema	Development/ Education	Association	Founder and President	Tunis, Tunisia	28 Mar. 2012
50	Dr Youssef	Family Planning/ Reproductive Health	Government	Director of Communication	Tunis, Tunisia	29 Mar. 2012
51	Dr Faiqa	Media	Association	Co-Founder	Tunis, Tunisia	2 Apr. 2012
52	Elizabeth Lewis	HIV	Bi-lateral	Policy Adviser (Former)	Washington, USA	2 Apr. 2012
53	Ghilzlan	Democracy and Human Rights	Association	Secretary General	Tunis, Tunisia	3 Apr. 2012
54	Dr Zahir	HIV/Family Planning/ Reproductive Health	Government	Head Coordinator of Global Fund Programmes	Tunis, Tunisia	3 May 2012
55	Dr Haajar	Development and HIV/AIDS	Multi-lateral	Former Director of Regional HIV/AIDS Programme	Cairo, Egypt	10 May 2012
56	Charles Taylor	HIV/AIDS, TB, Malaria	Multi-lateral/ international org.	Manager, Country Partnerships	Geneva, Switzerland	16 May 2012
57	Dr Abdul	HIV/AIDS	Government	Former Manager of National HIV Programme	Tunis, Tunisia	18 May 2012
58	Wajid	HIV/AIDS and Reproductive Health	Foundation/ Donor	Senior Programme Officer, MENA Office	Cairo, Egypt	21 May 2012

Bibliography

Aarts, P. and F. Cavatorta, *Civil Society in Syria and Iran: Activism in Authoritarian Contexts* (London: Lynne Rienner, 2013).

Abdelrahman, M., *Civil Society Exposed: The Politics of NGOs in Egypt* (London: Tauris Academic Studies, 2004).

'The Politics of "UnCivil" Society in Egypt', *Review of African Political Economy*, vol. 29, no. 91 (March 2002), pp. 21–35.

Achcar, G., *The People Want: A Radical Exploration of the Arab Uprising* (London: Saqi, 2013).

Agence France-Presse, 'Tunisia Jails Six Students for Homosexuality', TheGuardian.com, 14 December 2015.

Ajmi, S., 'More than 4,000 People Descend on Constituent Assembly to Call for Sharia Law', Tunisia-Live.net, 16 March 2012.

'Tunisian Women Question Future and Role of Personal Status Code', Tunisia-Live.net, 7 March 2012.

Al-Azm, S., 'Orientalism and Orientalism in Reverse', *Khamsin*, vol. 8 (1981), pp. 5–26.

Al-Azmeh, A., 'Populism Contre Democracy: Recent Democratist Discourse in the Arab World' in G. Salame (ed.), *Democracy without Democrats: The Renewal of Politics in the Muslim World* (New York: I. B. Tauris, 1994).

Al-Sayyid, M., 'Civil Society Activism in Authoritarian Regimes' in P. Aarts and F. Cavatorta (eds.), *Civil Society in Syria and Iran: Activism in Authoritarian Contexts* (London: Lynne Rienner, 2013).

Albrecht, H., 'The Nature of Political Participation' in E. Lust-Okar and S. Zerhouni (eds.), *Political Participation in the Middle East* (Boulder: Lynne Rienner, 2008).

Alexander, C., 'Back from the Democratic Brink: Authoritarianism and Civil Society in Tunisia', *Middle East Report*, no. 205 (October–December 1997), pp. 34–38.

Tunisia (London: Routledge, 2010).

Alhamad, L., 'Formal and Informal Venues of Engagement' in E. Lust-Okar and S. Zerhouni (eds.), *Political Participation in the Middle East* (Boulder: Lynne Rienner, 2008).

Altman, D., *Global Sex* (Chicago: University of Chicago Press, 2001).
 'Rupture or Continuity? The Internationalization of Gay Identities', *Social Text*, vol. 14, no. 48 (Autumn 1996), pp. 77–94.
Amara, T., 'Tunisian Protesters Reject Calls for Islamic State', AlArabiya.net, 20 March 2012.
'Analysis: Tough Post-Revolution Reality for NGOs in Egypt', IRINnews.org, 25 October 2011.
Anderson, L., *The State and Social Transformation in Tunisia and Libya* (Princeton: Princeton University Press, 1986).
Anheier, H., M. Kaldor, and M. Glasius, 'The Global Civil Society Yearbook, Lessons and Insights 2001–2011' in M. Kaldor, H. Moore and S. Selchow (eds.), *Global Civil Society 2012: Ten Years of Critical Reflection* (Hampshire: Palgrave Macmillan, 2012).
Arce, A., M. Villarreal and P. de Vries, 'The Social Construction of Rural Development: Discourses, Practices and Power' in D. Booth (ed.), *Rethinking Social Development: Theory, Research and Practice* (Essex: Addison Wesley Longman Ltd, 1994).
Arendt, H., *On Revolution* (London: Penguin Books, 2006).
The Human Condition (Chicago: Chicago University Press, 1958).
Assir, S., 'Lebanon's Gay Community Despite Liberal Mideast Reputation', HuffingtonPost.com, 5 August 2013.
Associated French Press, 'Rights Groups Urge Iraq to Investigate "Emo" Killings', AlArabiya.net, 16 March 2012.
 'Tunisie: Les Salafistes Multiplient les Coups d'Eclat', JeuneAfrique.com, 27 May 2012.
 'TV Boss Goes on Trial for Showing "Persepolis"', France24.com, 17 November 2011.
Associated Press, 'Ansar al-Sharia Blamed for Tunisia Killings', AlJazeera.com, 27 August 2013.
 'Islamist, Leftist Students Clash in Tunisia over Right to Wear the Veil', Haaretz.com, 7 March 2012.
Auffray, E., 'Ces Ligues qui Protegent La Revolution Tunisienne', Liberation.fr, 14 January 2013.
Ayeb, H., 'Understanding the Rise of Tunisia's Islamists', *Egypt Independent*, 1 February 2012.
Ayubi, N., *Over-Stating the Arab State: Politics and Society in the Middle East* (London: I. B. Tauris, 1995).
Badie, B. and P. Birnbaum, *The Sociology of the State* (Chicago: University of Chicago Press, 1983).
Baeder, C., 'Controversial Cleric, Advocate of Female Genital Mutilation, Challenges Tunisian Critics', Tunisia-Live.net, 15 February 2012.

'Release of Unauthenticated Prison-Sex Video Denounced in Defence of Tunisian Interior Minister', Tunisia-Live.net, 19 January 2012.

'Tunisian Human Rights Minister's Remarks Spark Debate on Homophobia', Tunisia-Live.net, 9 February 2012.

Baker, G., *Civil Society and Democratic Theory: Alternative Voices* (London: Routledge, 2002).

Barnett, M. and T. Weiss, 'Humanitarianism: A Brief History of the Present' in M. Barnett and T. Weiss (eds.), *Humanitarianism in Question: Politics, Power, Ethics* (Ithaca: Cornell University Press, 2008).

Bastin, J., 'La Révolution Militante', *Transversal*, no. 58 (May–June 2011), pp. 9–11.

Bayat, A., *Life as Politics: How Ordinary People Change the Middle East* (Stanford: Stanford University Press, 2010).

BBC News, 'Tunisia Votes in Historic Free Election', 23 October 2011.

'Tunisian Politician Mohamed Brahmi Assassinated', 25 July 2013.

Bebbington, J., S. Hickey and D. Mitlin, 'Introduction: Can NGOs Make a Difference? The Challenge of Development Alternatives' in J. Bebbington, S. Hickey and D. Mitlin (eds.), *Can NGOs Make a Difference?: The Challenge of Development Alternatives* (London: Zed Books, 2008).

Beinin, J. and F. Vairel, 'Afterword: Popular Uprisings in Tunisia and Egypt' in J. Beinin and F. Vairel (eds.), *Social Movements, Mobilization, and Contestation in the Middle East and North Africa* (Stanford: Stanford University Press, 2011).

Social Movements, Mobilization, and Contestation in the Middle East and North Africa (Stanford: Stanford University Press, 2011).

Belaid, F., 'Tunisia: Persepolis Trial Verdict Signals "Erosion" of Free Speech', Amnesty International, 3 May 2012.

Bellin, E., 'Civil Society in Formation: Tunisia' in A. Norton (ed.), *Civil Society in the Middle East: Volume I* (Leiden: E. J. Brill, 1995).

Ben Ammar, S., 'Les Islamistes Tuent des Gays de Peur de se Regarder dans leur Propre Miroir', Tunisie-News.Com, 5 August 2012.

Ben Mhenni, L., 'Le Graffiti n'a pas Bonne Presse dans La Révolution Tunisienne...', Opinion-Internationale.com, 12 September 2013.

Ben Romdhane, M., *Tunisie: Etat, Economie et Société : Ressources Politiques Légitimation Regulations Sociales* (Tunis: Sud Editions, 2011).

Ben Salem, D., 'Flagrant Deficit au Niveau des Capacités', *La Presse de Tunisie*, 26 March 2013.

Bendana, K., *Chronique d'une Transition* (Tunis: Les Editions Script, 2011).

Bensaied, I., 'Les Islamistes s'Attaquent aux Maisons Closes', France24.com, 18 March 2011.

'Le Gouvernement Progresse et l'Opposition Sort-Elle de l'Impasse?', La Presse de Tunisie, 26 March 2012.
Biehl, J., 'Technologies of Invisibility: Politics of Life and Social Inequality' in J. Inda (ed.), *Anthropologies of Modernity: Foucault, Governmentality and Life* (Oxford: Blackwell, 2005).
Blair, H., 'Donors, Democratisation and Civil Society: Relating Theory to Practice' in D. Hulme and M. Edwards (eds.), *NGOs, States and Donors: Too Close for Comfort?* (London: Macmillan Press Ltd, 1997).
Blaney, D. and M. Pasha, 'Civil Society and Democracy in the Third World: Ambiguities and Historical Possibilities', *Studies in Comparative International Development*, vol. 28, no. 1 (Spring 1993), pp. 3–24.
Blibech, F., A. Driss and P. Longo, 'Citizenship in Post-Awakening Tunisia: Power Shifts and Conflicting Perceptions', *Euspring* (February 2014).
Borsali, N., 'Tunisie: 8 Mars 2012 ou le Défi Egalitaire', *La Presse de Tunisie*, 12 March 2012.
Bouandel, Y., 'Human Rights in the Maghreb' in Y. Zoubir (ed.), *North Africa in Transition: State, Society, and Economic Transformation in the 1990s* (Gainesville: University Press of Florida, 1999).
Bozarslan, H., 'Réflexions sur les Configurations Révolutionnaires Tunisienne et Égyptienne', *Mouvements des Idées et des Luttes*, no. 66 (Summer 2011), pp. 12–21.
Bromley, S., *Rethinking Middle East Politics* (Austin: University of Texas Press, 1994).
Browers, M., *Democracy and Civil Society in Arab Political Thought: Transcultural Possibilities* (Syracuse: Syracuse University Press, 2006).
Byrne, E., 'Tunisia Elections: Veteran Politician Beji Caid Essebsi Wins Run-Off Vote', The Guardian.com, 22 December 2014.
Calhoun, C., *Habermas and the Public Sphere* (Cambridge: MIT Press, 1992).
Camau, M., 'La Disgrace du Chef: Mobilisations Populaires Arabes et Crise du Leadership', *Mouvements des Idees et des Luttes*, no. 66 (Summer 2011), pp. 22–29.
Cavallo, D., 'Trade Unions in Tunisia' in E. Lust-Okar and S. Zerhouni (eds.), *Political Participation in the Middle East* (Boulder: Lynne Rienner, 2008).
Cavatorta, F., 'No Democratic Change ... and Yet No Authoritarian Continuity: The Inter-Paradigm Debate and North Africa after the Uprisings', *British Journal of Middle Eastern Studies*, vol. 42, no. 1 (2015), pp. 135–145.
Cavatorta, F. and F. Merone, *Salafism after the Arab Awakening Contending with People's Power* (London: Hurst and Company, 2017).
Chabot, S. and J. Duyvendak, 'Globalisation and Transnational Diffusion between Social Movements: Reconceptualising the Dissemination of the

Gandhian Repertoire and the "Coming Out" Routine', *Theory and Society*, vol. 31, no. 6 (2002), pp. 697–740.

Challand, B., *Palestinian Civil Society: Foreign Donors and the Power to Promote or Exclude* (London: Routledge, 2009).

Chandhoke, N., 'Civil Society', *Development in Practice*, vol. 17, no. 4–5 (2007), pp. 607–614.

State and Civil Society: Explorations in Political Theory (New Delhi: Sage Publications, 2005).

Charnovitz, S., 'Two Centuries of Participation: NGOs and International Governance', *Michigan Journal of International Law*, vol. 18, no. 183 (1996–1997), pp. 183–286.

Chawki, 'Video-Manifestation Contre La Violence et Pour La Liberté d'Expression sous le Signe "A3ta9ni"', Tunisienumerique.com, 6 October 2011.

Chazan, M., 'Surviving Politics and the Politics of Surviving: Understanding Community Mobilisation in South Africa' in M. Foller and H. Thorn (eds.), *The Politics of AIDS: Globalisation, the State and Civil Society* (New York: Palgrave Macmillan, 2008).

Cheffi, S., 'Les Droits de la Femme Sont une Ligne Rouge', *La Presse de Tunisie*, 12 March 2012

Cock, J., 'Engendering Gay and Lesbian Rights: The Equality Clause in the South African Constitution', *Women's Studies International Forum*, vol. 26, no. 1 (2002), pp. 35–45.

Collins, R., 'Effemines, Gigolos, and MSMs in the Cyber Networks, Coffeehouses and "Secret Gardens" of Contemporary Tunis', *Journal of Middle East Women's Studies*, vol. 8, no. 3 (Fall 2012), pp. 89–112.

Connolly, K., 'Egypt's New Face in Swap for Israeli "Spy" Ilan Grapel', *BBC News*, 27 October 2011.

Crary, D., 'Gays in Egypt, Tunisia Worry about Post-Revolt Era', TheGuardian.com, 21 May 2011.

Croucher, S., 'South Africa's Democratisation and the Politics of Gay Liberation', *Journal of Southern African Studies*, vol. 28, no. 2 (2002), pp. 315–330.

D'Emilio, J., 'Capitalism and Gay Identity' in A. Snitow, C. Stansell and S. Thompson (eds.), *Powers of Desire: The Politics of Sexuality* (New York: Monthly Review Press, 1983).

De Waal, A., *AIDS and Power: Why There Is No Political Crisis Yet* (London: Zed Books, 2006).

Deboulet, A. and D. Nicolaidis, 'Les Hirondelles Font-Elles le Printemps?', *Mouvements des Idées et des Luttes*, no. 66 (Summer 2011).

Denoeux, G., 'Promoting Democracy and Governance in Arab Countries' in S. Ben Nefissa, N. Al-Fattah, S. Hanafi and C. Milani (eds.), *NGOs and*

Governance in the Arab World (Cairo: American University in Cairo Press, 2005).
Dewalt, K. and B. Dewalt, *Participant Observation: A Guide for Fieldworkers* (Walnut Creek: Altamira Press, 2002).
Diamond, L., *Political Culture and Democracy in Developing Countries* (Boulder: Lynne Rienner, 1993).
  'Toward Democratic Consolidation', *Journal of Democracy*, vol. 5, no. 3 (July 1994), pp. 4–17.
Dridi, J., 'Pourquoi Ennahdha Rencontre un Succès Populaire en Tunisie?', Kapitalis.com, 18 October 2011.
Durac, V. and F. Cavatorta, *Politics and Governance in the Middle East* (London: Palgrave, 2015).
Durham, K., 'Fertilizing the Grassroots', *Egypt Today Magazine* (19 September 2013; originally published 10 July 2011).
Edwards, M., *Civil Society* (Oxford: Polity Press, 2004), pp. 961–973.
Edwards, M. and D. Hulme, 'Too Close for Comfort? The Impact of Official Aid on Nongovernmental Organisations', *World Development*, vol. 24, no. 6 (1996).
El Amrani, I. and U. Lindsey, 'Tunisia Moves to the Next Stage', *Middle East Research and Information Project* (8 November 2011).
El Feki, S., *Sex and the Citadel: Intimate Life in a Changing Arab World* (London: Random House, 2013).
Entelis, J., *Islam, Democracy, and the State in North Africa* (Bloomington: Indiana University Press, 1997).
  'Political Islam in the Maghreb: The Nonviolent Dimension' in J. Entelis (ed.), *Islam, Democracy, and the State in North Africa* (Bloomington: Indiana University Press, 1997).
Euro-Mediterranean Human Rights Network. 'Freedom of Association in the Euro-Mediterranean Region' (2007).
Evans, P., D. Rueschemeyer and T. Skocpol, *Bringing the State Back in* (Cambridge: Cambridge University Press, 1985).
Ferguson, J. and A. Gupta, 'Spatializing States: Toward an Ethnography of Neoliberal Governmentality' in J. Inda (ed.), *Anthropologies of Modernity: Foucault, Governmentality and Life Politics* (Oxford: Blackwell, 2005).
Foucault, M., *The History of Sexuality 1: The Will to Knowledge*, trans. by R. Hurley (London: Penguin, 1990).
  Power/Knowledge: Selected Interviews and Other Writings 1972–1977, ed. by C. Gordon (New York: Vintage Books, 1972).
Fox, J., 'How Does Civil Society Thicken? The Political Construction of Social Capital in Rural Mexico', *World Development*, vol. 24, no. 6 (1996), pp. 1089–1103.

Fraser, N., 'Foucault on Modern Power: Empirical Insights and Normative Confusions', *Praxis International*, no. 3 (1981): pp. 272–287.

Justice Interruptus: Critical Reflections on the 'Postsocialist' Condition (New York: Routledge, 1997).

'Rethinking the Public Sphere: A Contribution to the Critique of Actually Existing Democracy', *Social Text*, no. 25/26 (1990), pp. 56–80.

Geyer, G., *Tunisia: A Journey through a Country That Works* (London: Stacey International, 2003).

Ghorbal, S., *Orphelins de Bourguiba et Héritiers du Prophète* (Tunis: Ceres Editions, 2012).

Ghribi, A., 'Tunisians Erupt in Anger Over Desecration of Flag', Tunisia-Live.net, 9 March 2012.

'Tunisian Journalists Subject to Recent Wave of Violence', Tunisia-Live.net, 24 January 2012.

Giddens, A., 'From Marx to Nietzsche? Neo-Conservatism, Foucault and Problems in Contemporary Political Theory' in A. Giddens (ed.), *Profiles and Critiques in Social Theory* (Berkeley: University of California Press, 1982).

Giner, S., 'Civil Society and Its Future' in J. Hall (ed.), *Civil Society: Theory, History, Comparison* (Cambridge: Polity Press, 1995).

Goldberg, E., R. Kasaba and J. Migdal, *Rules and Rights in the Middle East: Democracy, Law and Society* (Seattle : University of Washington Press, 1993).

Gordenker, L. and T. Weiss, 'Pluralising Global Governance: Analytical Approaches and Dimensions' in *NGOs, the UN and Global Governance* (Boulder: Lynne Rienner, 1996).

Goueset, C., 'Les Droits des Femmes en Tunisie "Ce n'est pas Qu'un Affaire de Jupe ou de Voile"', Express.fr, 8 March 2012.

Gramsci, A., *Selections from the Prison Notebooks*, ed. and trans. by Q. Hoare and G. Smith (London: Lawrence and Wishart, 1971).

Gray, D., 'Tunisia after the Uprising: Islamist and Secular Quests for Women's Rights', *Mediterranean Politics*, vol. 17, no. 3 (November 2012), pp. 285–302.

Grote, R., 'The New 2014 Tunisian Constitution', *Oxford Constitutions of the World* (Oxford: Oxford University Press, 2014).

Guellali, A., 'Pathways and Pitfalls for Tunisia's New Constituent Assembly', ThinkAfricaPress.com (14 October 2011).

Gunning, J. and I. Baron, *Why Occupy a Square: People, Protests and Movements in the Egyptian Revolution* (London: Hurst and Company, 2013).

Habermas, J., *The Structural Transformation of the Public Sphere: An Inquiry into a Category of Bourgeois Society*, trans. by T. Burger and F. Lawrence (Cambridge: Polity Press, 1989).

Hallaq, W., 'On the Origins of the Controversy about the Existence of Mujtahids and the Gate of Ijtihad', *Studia Islamica*, no. 63 (1986), pp. 129–141.
Hamdi, M., *The Politicisation of Islam: A Case Study of Tunisia* (Boulder: Westview Press, 1998).
Harik, I., 'Pluralism in the Arab World', *Journal of Democracy*, vol. 5, no. 3 (July 1994), pp. 43–56.
Harris, P. and P. Siplon, *The Global Politics of AIDS* (Boulder: Lynne Rienner, 2007).
Haugbolle, R. and F. Cavatorta, 'Beyond Ghannouchi: Islamism and Social Change in Tunisia', Haugbølle, Rikke Hostrup; Cavatorta, Francesco. In: Middle East Report, vol. 262, no. Spring 2012, 15.03.2012, pp. 20–25.
Havel, V., S. Lukes and J. Keane, *The Power of the Powerless: Citizens against the State in Central-Eastern Europe* (New York: M. E. Sharpe, 1985).
Hegel, G., *Elements of the Philosophy of Right* (Cambridge: Cambridge University Press, 1991).
Heller, K., 'Power, Subjectification and Resistance in Foucault', *SubStance*, vol. 25, no. 1 (1996), pp. 78–110.
Hennessey, R., *Profit and Pleasure: Sexual Identities in Late Capitalism* (New York: Routledge, 2000).
Henry, C., 'Postcolonial Dialectics of Civil Society' in Y. Zoubir (ed.), *North Africa in Transition: State, Society, and Economic Transformation in the 1990s* (Gainesville: University Press of Florida, 1999).
Heydemann, S., 'Upgrading Authoritarianism in the Arab World', Brookings Institution, Analysis Paper no. 13 (October 2007) in V. Durac and F. Cavatorta (eds.), *Politics and Governance in the Middle East* (London: Palgrave, 2015).
Hibou, B., *The Force of Obedience: The Political Economy of Repression In Tunisia* (Cambridge: Polity Press, 2011).
Hibou, B., H. Meddeb and M. Hamdi, 'Tunisia after 14 January and its Social and Political Economy: The Issues at Stake in a Reconfiguration of European Policy', Euro-Mediterranean Human Rights Network (2011).
Hinnebusch, R., 'Change and Continuity after the Arab Uprising: The Consequences of State Formation in Arab North African States', *British Journal of Middle Eastern Studies*, vol. 42, no. 1 (2015), pp. 12–30.
Human Rights Watch, 'In a Time of Torture: The Assault on Justice in Egypt's Crackdown on Homosexual Conduct', 2004.
  'Lebanon: Stop "Tests of Shame"', 10 August 2012.
  'Tunisia: Drop Criminal Investigation of TV Station for Airing Persepolis' (13 October 2011).

Huntington, S., *The Third Wave: Democratization in the Late Twentieth Century* (Norman: University of Oklahoma Press, 1991).

International Crisis Group. 'Tunisie : Violences et Défi Salafiste', *Rapport Moyen-Orient/Afrique du Nord*, Crisisgroup.org, no. 137 (13 February 2013).

Ismael, T., *Middle East Politics Today: Government and Civil Society* (Gainesville: University Press of Florida, 2001).

Jacquard, A., 'Les Turbulences d'un Cyclone', *Le Temps* (Tunis), 21 March 2012

Jamal, A., *Barriers to Democracy: The Other Side of Social Capital in Palestine and the Arab World* (Princeton: Princeton University Press, 2007).

Jebnoun, N., 'Salafi Trouble in Tunisia's Transition', Jadaliyya.com, 13 July 2012.

Jennings, M., 'Do Not Turn Away a Poor Man: Faith-Based Organisations and Development'. ed. by M. Clarke *in Handbook of Research on Religion and Development* (2013), pp. 359–375.

Surrogates of the State: NGOs, Development and Ujama in Tanzania (Bloomfield: Kumarian Press, 2008).

Joffe, G., 'The Arab Spring in North Africa: Origins and Prospects', *The Journal of North African Studies*, vol. 16, no. 4 (2011), pp. 507–535.

Kabeer, N. and H. Kabir, 'Quantifying the Impact of Social Mobilisation in Rural Bangladesh: Donors, Civil Society and 'The Road Not Taken'', *Institute for Development Studies Working Paper*, no. 333 (2009), pp. 1–54.

Kabeer, N., S. Mahmud and J. Castro, 'NGOs' Strategies and the Challenge of Development and Democracy in Bangladesh', *Institute for Development Studies Working Paper*, no. 343 (2010).

Kaldor, M., *Global Civil Society: An Answer to War* (Cambridge: Polity Press, 2003).

Kaldor, M. and S. Selchow, 'The "Bubbling Up" of Subterranean Politics in Europe', *Journal of Civil Society*, vol. 9, no. 1 (2013), pp. 78–99.

Kausch, K., '"Foreign Funding" in Post-Revolution Tunisia', AFA, Fride and Hivos, 2013.

Keane, J., *Civil Society and the State: New European Perspectives* (London: Verso, 1988).

Kennard, M., 'Neoliberals, Not Islamists, Are the Real Threat to Tunisia', TheGuardian.com, 31 March 2012.

Khalfi, S., 'A Celles qui s'Obstinent Encore a Porter La Burqa', *Le Temps* (Tunis), 29 March 2012.

Khalsi, R., 'Excision ... ou les Prédictions d'un Psychopathe', *Le Temps* (Tunis), 14 February 2012.

'Islamisme: Le Bouc Emissaire "Providentiel"', *Le Temps* (Tunis), 23 March 2012.
Khatib, L., 'Syria's Civil Society as a Tool for Regime Legitimacy' in P. Aarts and F. Cavatorta (eds.), *Civil Society in Syria and Iran: Activism in Authoritarian Contexts* (London: Lynne Rienner, 2013).
Khazbak, R., 'NGOs Face Smear Campaign Ahead of Elections', EgyptIndependent.com, 17 October 2011.
Khefifi, W., 'L'Expression "Système des Valeurs Islamiques" Remplace la Chariaa: C'est Ambigüe', Le Temps (Tunis), 9 March 2012.
Kidd, A., 'Civil Society or the State: Recent Approaches to the History of Voluntary Welfare', *Journal of Historical Sociology*, vol. 15, no. 3 (September 2002), pp. 328–342.
King, R., 'Regime Type, Economic Reform, and Political Change in Tunisia' in Y. Zoubir (ed.), *North Africa in Transition: State, Society, and Economic Transformation in the 1990s* (Gainesville: University Press of Florida, 1999).
Kinninmont, J., 'The Next Fight Will Be among the Islamists', *The World Today* (February and March 2012).
Korany, B., R. Brynen and P. Noble, *Political Liberalization and Democratization in the Arab World: Volume I Theoretical Perspectives* (Boulder: Lynne Rienner, 1995).
Krasner, S., 'Approaches to the State: Alternative Conceptions and Historical Dynamics', *Comparative Politics*, vol. 16, no. 2 (January 1984), pp. 223–246.
Krouj, F., 'Editor-in-Chief of Gayday Magazine Fadi Krouj Comments on International Day Against Homophobia', Tunisia-Live.net, 18 May 2012.
Lajili, T., 'Visite et Prêche Prévus de Wajdi Ghonaim: Levée de Boucliers de la Société Civile', *Le Temps* (Tunis), 17 February 2012.
'La Menace Terroriste n'est pas Très Elevée en Tunisie, mais ...', interview with Alaya Allani, *Le Temps* (Tunis), 4 February 2012.
Largueche, A. and D. Largueche, *Marginales en Terre Terre d'Islam* (Tunis: Cérès Editions, 1992).
'Le Prédicateur Wajdi Ghonaiem Annonce: La Tunisie Appliquera Prochainement la Chariaa', *Le Temps* (Tunis), 18 February 2012.
Le Programme National de Lutte Contre le Sida et les Maladies Sexuellement Transmissibles, UNAIDS. 'Rapport d'Activité sur La Riposte au SIDA—Tunisie', *UNGASS Report,* République Tunisienne Ministre de la Sante Publique, Programme Nationale de Lutte Contre le SIDA et les MST, March 2012.
Le Réseau Euro-méditerranéen des Droits de l'Homme. 'Contribution de la Mission du Réseau Euro-méditerranéen des Droits de l'Homme en

Tunisie a la Description du Nouveau Paysage Associatif Tunisien', October 2011.
'Libya and Tunisia: Two Faces of the Arab Spring', TheGuardian.com, 22 October 2011.
Ltifi, A., 'Salafists Burn Down Bars, Liquor Stores while Police Are Passive in Sidi Bouzid', Tunisia-Live.net, 20 May 2012.
Luciani, G., *The Arab State* (London: Routledge, 1990).
Luengo-Cabrera, J., 'How Europe's Deteriorating Peace Is Facilitating the Rise of Populism', LSE-EUROPP Blog, 10 July 2018.
Lust-Okar, E. and S. Zerhouni, *Political Participation in the Middle East* (Boulder: Lynne Rienner, 2008).
Lust-Okar, E. 'Taking Political Participation Seriously' in E. Lust-Okar and S. Zerhouni (eds.), *Political Participation in the Middle East* (Boulder: Lynne Rienner, 2008).
Maarouf, Y., 'Quelle Perception de la Sexualité par les Salafistes?', *Le Temps* (Tunis), 21 March 2012.
Majoub, M., 'La Gouvernance Environnementale Démocratique: Rôle et Place de la Société Civile', *Rapport National sur l'Etat de l'Environnement*, Edition Spéciale 2011.
Manhire, T., *The Arab Spring: Rebellion, Revolution and a New World Order* (London, Guardian Books, 2002).
Manji, F., 'Collaboration with the South: Agents of Aid or Solidarity?', *Development in Practice*, vol. 7, no. 2 (May 1997), pp. 175–178.
Manji, F. and C. O'Coill, 'The Missionary Position: NGOs and Development in Africa', *International Affairs*, vol. 78, no. 3 (2002), pp. 567–583.
Mansbridge, J., 'Feminism and Democracy', *The American Prospect*, no. 1 (Spring 1990).
Marzouki, N., 'From People to Citizens in Tunisia', *Middle East Research and Information Project* MER 259, Vol. 41, no. 259 (Summer 2011).
Massad, J., 'Re-Orienting Desire: The Gay International and the Arab World', *Public Culture*, vol. 14, no. 2 (Spring 2002), pp. 361–385.
McCormick-Cavanagh, C., 'Tunisia LGBT Group Battles for Justice in Case of Imprisoned Gay Man', *Middle East Eye* (5 October 2015).
McFarland, W., L. Abu-Raddad and Z. Mahfoud, 'Progress in HIV Research in MENA: New Study Methods, Results, and Implications for Prevention and Care', *AIDS*, vol. 24, supp. 2 (July 2010).
Merone, F., 'Enduring Class Struggle in Tunisia: The Fight for Identity beyond Political Islam', *British Journal of Middle Eastern Studies*, vol. 42, no. 1 (2015).
Mersch, S., 'No Gay Rights Revolution in Tunisia', *Deutsche Welle*, 7 November 2012.

Meziou-Dourai, K., 'A Propos du Mariage Coutumier: Attaque Frontale Contre le Code du Statut Personnel', *Le Temps* (Tunis), 4 February 2012.

Migdal, J., *State in Society: Studying How States and Societies Transform and Constitute One Another* (Cambridge: Cambridge University Press, 2001).

Strong Societies and Weak States: State-Society Relations and State Capabilities in the Third World (Princeton: Princeton University Press, 1988).

Mikdashi, M., 'The Uprisings Will Be Gendered', Jadaliyya.com, 28 February 2012.

Minister of Public Health and the National Program to Fight HIV and STIs, 'National Strategic Plan to Respond to HIV and STIs in Tunisia 2012-2016' (Tunis, 2012).

Miszlivetz, F., '"Lost in Transformation": The Crisis of Democracy and Civil Society' in M. Kaldor, H. Moore and S. Selchow (eds.), *Global Civil Society 2012: Ten Years of Critical Reflection* (Hampshire: Palgrave Macmillan, 2012).

Morton, A., *Unravelling Gramsci: Hegemony and Passive Revolution in the Global Political Economy* (London: Pluto Press, 2007).

Mouffe, C., *Agonistics: Thinking the World Politically* (London: Verso, 2013).

The Democratic Paradox (London: Verso, 2013).

Najjar, Y., 'Drug Use Climbs among Tunisian Students', Magharebia.com, 24 July 2013.

National Democratic Institute. 'Final Report of the Tunisian National Constituent Assembly Elections', 23 October 2011.

Nefissa, S., N. Al-Fattah, S. Hanafi and C. Milani, *NGOs and Governance in the Arab World* (Cairo: American University in Cairo Press, 2005).

Nemlaghi, A., 'Associations et Embrigadement', *Le Temps* (Tunis), 21 March 2012.

'Que Mijote Ennahdha?', *Le Temps* (Tunis), 4 February 2012.

Norton, A., *Civil Society in the Middle East: Volume I* (Leiden : E. J. Brill, 1995).

Civil Society in the Middle East, Volume II (Leiden : E. J. Brill, 1995).

'The Future of Civil Society in the Middle East', *Middle East Journal*, vol. 47, no. 2 (Spring 1993), pp. 205–216.

Noueihed, L., 'Tunisian Protestors Demand Islamic State', AlArabiya.net, 17 March 2012.

O'Donnell, G. and P. Schmitter, *Transitions from Authoritarian Rule: Tentative Conclusions about Uncertain Democracies* (Baltimore: Johns Hopkins University Press, 1986).

O'Donnell, G., P. Schmitter and L. Whitehead, *Transitions from Authoritarian Rule: Comparative Perspectives* (Baltimore: Johns Hopkins University Press, 1986).

Organisation for Economic Co-Operation and Development (OECD), 'Aid for CSOs: Flows of Official Development Assistance to and through Civil Society Organisations in 2011', October 2013.

Ouannes, M., *Le Phénomène Associatif au Maghreb* (Tunis : Les Editions Altier International, 1997).

Owen, R., *State, Power and Politics in the Making of the Modern Middle East* (London: Routledge, 2000).

Parker, R. 'Sexual Cultures, HIV Transmission, and AIDS Prevention', *AIDS*, vol. 8, supp. 1 (1994).

Pearce, J., 'Development NGOs and Civil Society: The Debate and Its Future' in D. Fade (ed.), *Development, NGOs and Civil Society* (Oxford: Oxfam, 2000).

'Is Social Change Fundable? NGOs and Theories and Practices of Social Change', *Development in Practice*, vol. 20, no. 6 (2010), pp. 621–635.

Perez-Diaz, V., 'The Possibility of Civil Society: Traditions, Character and Challenges' in J. Hall (ed.), *Civil Society: Theory, History, Comparison* (Cambridge: Polity Press, 1995).

Puar, J., *Terrorist Assemblages: Homonationalism in Queer Times* (Durham: Duke University Press, 2007).

Putnam, R., *Making Democracy Work: Civic Traditions in Modern Italy* (Princeton: Princeton University Press, 1993).

Rao, R., *Third World Protest: Between Home and the World* (Oxford: Oxford University Press, 2010).

Redissi, H., 'Tunisia: The Difficulties of the Coalition', Tunisia-Live.net, 3 March 2012.

Ritchie, J., 'How Do You Say "Come Out of the Closet in Arabic?": Queer Activism and the Politics of Visibility in Israel-Palestine', *GLQ: A Journal of Gay and Lesbian Studies*, vol. 16, no. 4 (2010), pp. 557–575.

Rivetti, P., 'Continuity and Change before and after the Uprisings in Tunisia: Regime Reconfiguration and Policymaking in North Africa', *British Journal of Middle Eastern Studies*, vol. 42, no. 1 (2015).

Robson, C., *Real World Research: A Resource for Social Scientists and Practitioner-Researchers* (Oxford: Blackwell, 2002).

Roca, J., 'Insiders and Outsiders: NGOs in International Relations' in S. Nefissa, N. Al-Fattah, S. Hanafi and C. Milani (eds.), *NGOs and Governance in the Arab World* (Cairo: American University in Cairo Press, 2005).

Rossi, B., 'Order and Disjuncture: Theoretical Shifts in the Anthropology of Aid and Development', *Current Anthropology*, vol. 45, no. 4 (August/October 2004), pp. 556–560.

'Revisiting Foucauldian Approaches: Power Dynamics in Development Projects', *The Journal of Development Studies*, vol. 40, no. 6 (August 2004), pp. 1–29.

Sadiki, L., 'Popular Uprisings and Arab Democratization', *International Journal of Middle East Studies*, vol. 32, no. 1 (February 2000), pp. 71–95.

Sadiki, L., H. Wimmen, and L. Al-Zubaidi, *Democratic Transition in the Middle East: Unmaking Power* (London: Routledge, 2012).

Sajoo, A., *Civil Society in the Muslim World: Contemporary Perspectives* (London: I. B. Tauris, 2002).

Salame, G., *Democracy without Democrats: The Renewal of Politics in the Muslim World* (New York: I. B. Tauris, 1994).

Samti, F. and J. Belkhiria, 'Gay Tunisia: "A Don't Ask, Don't Tell" Situation', Tunisia-Live.Net, 27 January 2012.

Saner, E., 'Gay Rights around the World: The Best and the Worst Countries for Equality', TheGuardian.com, 30 July 2013.

Santos, B., *Toward a New Legal Common Sense: Law, Globalization and Emancipation* (London : Butterworths, LexisNexis, 2002).

Sayah, J., 'Retour sur une Occupation pas Comme les Autres', *La Presse de Tunisie*, 12 January 2012.

Schwedler, J., *Toward Civil Society in the Middle East? A Primer* (Boulder : Lynne Rienner, 1995).

Shami, S., *Publics, Politics and Participation: Locating the Public Sphere in the Middle East and North Africa* (New York: Social Science Research Council, 2009).

Singerman, D., *Avenues of Participation: Families, Politics and Networks in Urban Quarters of Cairo* (Princeton: Princeton University Press, 1995).

Sivan, E., 'The Islamic Resurgence: Civil Society Strikes Back', *Journal of Contemporary History*, vol. 25, no. 2/3 (May–June 1990), pp. 353–364.

Soli, E. and F. Merone, 'Tunisia: The Islamic Associative System as a Social Counter-Power', OpenDemocracy.net, 22 October 2013.

Snoussi, M. 'La Prostitution en Tunisie au Temps de la Colonisation' in J. Alexandropolous and P. Cabanel (eds.), *Mosaique: Diasporas, Cosmopolitisme, Archeologies de l'Identite* (Toulouse: Presses Universitaires du Mirail, 2008), pp. 389–413.

Spade, D., *Normal Life: Administrative Violence, Critical Trans Politics, and the Limits of the Law* (Brooklyn: South End Press, 2011).

Stiglitz, Joseph E., 'The Post-Washington Consensus Consensus' (New York: The Initiative for Policy Dialogue, 2004).

Stychin, C., *A Nation by Rights: National Cultures, Sexual Identity Politics, and the Discourse of Rights* (Philadelphia: Temple University Press, 1998).

Suleiman, N., 'The Disintegrating Fabric of Tunisian Politics: The Niqab Ban and Tunisian Flag Desecration at Manouba University', Jadaliyya.com, 13 April 2012.

Tocqueville, A., *Democracy in America: Volume I*, edited by P. Bradley (New York: Vintage Books, 1945).

Torelli, S., 'The Multi-Faceted Dimensions of Tunisian Salafism' in F. Cavatorta and F. Merone (eds.), *Salafism after the Arab Awakening Contending with People's Power* (London: Hurst and Company, 2017).

'Tunisie: Marzouki S'Excuse pour Avoir Traite Wajdi Ghanim de "Microbe"', Kapitalis.com, 16 February 2012.

UNAIDS, 'AIDS in the Middle East and North Africa: Regional Compilation of 2010 UNGASS Reports', June 2010.

   'Investing in Universal Access: To HIV Prevention, Treatment, Care and Support in MENA', 2010.

   'Middle East and North Africa Regional Report on AIDS', 2011.

   'Morocco Launches New National AIDS Strategy', 4 April 2012.

   'Outlook Report 2010'.

   'Regional Factsheet for the Middle East and North Africa', 2016.

   'Regional Report for the Middle East and North Africa', 2013.

   'Report on the Global AIDS Epidemic 2010'.

   'Terminology Guidelines', October 2011.

Union Européenne, 'Rapport de Diagnostic sur la Société Civile Tunisienne', Mission de Formulation Programme d'Appui à la Société Civile en Tunisie, March 2012.

Voll, J., 'Sultans, Saints, and Presidents: The Islamic Community and the State in North Africa' in Entelis (ed.), *Islam, Democracy and the State in North Africa* (Bloomington: Indiana University Press, 1997).

Voorhoeve, M., '"Islam Is Tunisia's Religion": Continuity and Change in Article One of the Tunisian Constitution', *Journal for Politics and Religion* (2014), under review.

Wallerstein, I., 'The Contradictions of the Arab Spring', Aljazeera.net, 14 November 2011.

Waltz, S., 'Clientelism and Reform in Ben Ali's Tunisia' in W. Zartman (ed.), *Tunisia: The Political Economy of Reform* (Boulder: Lynne Rienner, 1991).

   Human Rights and Reform: Changing the Face of North African Politics (Berkeley: University of California Press, 1995).

   'The Politics of Human Rights in the Maghreb' in J. Entelis (ed.), *Islam, Democracy, and the State in North Africa* (Bloomington: Indiana University Press, 1997).

Warren, A., 'Tunisia Steps Out', ForeignPolicy.com (23 February 2012).
Waterbury, J., 'Democracy without Democrats? The Potential for Political Liberalization in the Middle East' in G. Salame (ed.), *Democracy without Democrats: The Renewal of Politics in the Muslim World* (New York: I. B. Tauris, 1994).
Wedeen, L., 'Concepts and Commitments in the Study of Democracy' in I. Shapiro, R. Smith and T. Masoud, *Problems and Methods in the Study of Politics* (Cambridge: Cambridge University Press, 2004), pp. 274–306.
Weffort, F., 'Why Democracy?' in A. Stephan (ed.), *Democratising Brazil* (Oxford: Oxford University Press, 1995), pp. 347–348.
Whitaker, B., *Unspeakable Love: Gay and Lesbian Life in the Middle East* (London: Saqi, 2006).
Wiktorowicz, Q. and S. Farouki, 'Islamic NGOs and Muslim Politics: A Case from Jordan', *Third World Quarterly*, vol. 21, no. 4 (August 2000), pp. 685–699.
Willis, M., *Politics and Power in the Maghreb: Algeria, Tunisia, and Morocco from Independence to the Arab Spring* (London: Hurst, 2012).
  'Tunisia: The Trailblazer and the Benchmark', Conservative Middle East Council, *The Arab Spring: Implications for British Policy* (24 October 2011).
The World Bank, 'Characterizing the HIV/AIDS Epidemic in the Middle East and North Africa', 2010.
  'Policy Note: Characterizing the HIV/AIDS Epidemic in the Middle East and North Africa Time for Strategic Action', 2010.
World Health Organization, 'Toward Universal Access: Scaling Up Priority HIV/AIDS Interventions in the Health Sector. Progress Report', 2009.
World Health Organization (Europe), 'Status Paper on Prisons, Drugs and Harm Reduction', May 2005.
Zartman, W., *Tunisia: The Political Economy of Reform* (Boulder: Lynne Rienner, 1991).
  'The Conduct of Political Reform: The Path toward Democracy' in W. Zartman (ed.), *Tunisia: The Political Economy of Reform* (Boulder: Lynne Rienner, 1991).
Zebais, H., 'Tunisia Sees Sharp Rise in Drug Use Following Revolution', AlMonitor.com, 3 February 2013.
Zemni, S., 'The Extraordinary Politics of the Tunisian Revolution: The Process of Constitution Making', *Mediterranean Politics* (2014), pp. 1–19.

Zghal, A., 'The New Strategy of the Movement of the Islamic Way: Manipulation or Expression of Political Culture?' in W. Zartman (ed.), *Tunisia: The Political Economy of Reform* (Boulder: Lynne Rienner, 1991).
Znazen, A., O. Frikha-Gargouri, L. Berrajah et al., 'Sexually Transmitted Infections among Female Sex Workers in Tunisia: High Prevalence of Chlamydia Trachomatis', *Sex Transm Infect*, vol. 86, no. 7 (2010), pp. 500–505.
Zoubir, Y., *North Africa in Transition: State, Society, and Economic Transformation in the 1990s* (Gainesville: University Press of Florida, 1999).

Index

Aarts, Paul, 20
Abdelrahman, Maha, xi–xii, 34–35, 152–153, 155
  on neoliberal paradigm, 44–45
Achcar, Gilbert, xi, 19, 140–141
Afghanistan, 144
agency, 35, 134, 162–163
Agonistics: Thinking the World Politically (Mouffe), 164, 166
Alexander, Christopher, 58, 61–62, 77
Algeria, 71, 116
Alhamad, Laila, 77–78, 80
Altman, Denis, 170–171
Amnesty International, 81–82
El Amrani, Issandr, 99, 113
Anheier, Helmut, 4–5, 31–32
Ansar al-Sharia, 107–108, 145
antagonism, 166
'anti-emo' killings, 174
anti-Islamic sentiments, x, 151
anti-poverty initiatives, 52
anti-terrorist law of 2003, 144
anti-war protests, 36
Arab Spring, ix–x
  domino effect of, 116
  neoliberalism and, 27–28
  post-Arab Spring era, 191
Arab–Muslim world, 63
ARDD. *See* L'Association de Recherches sur la Démocratie et le Développement
Article 1 of Tunisian Constitution, 1959, 63, 100
Article 230 of penal code, 179–181, 183–184, 189
assassinations, 107–108, 136, 147, 160
L'Association de Recherches sur la Démocratie et le Développement (ARDD), 123, 126–128
L'Association Tunisienne de la Prévention de la Toxicomanie (ATUPRET), 86, 90–91
L'Association Tunisienne de Lutte Contre les Maladies Sexuellement Transmissible et le SIDA (ATL MST/SIDA), 86
L'Association Tunisienne d'Information et d'Orientation sur le SIDA (ATIOS), 86
associational Islam, 148–152, 161–162
Atakni rally, 175–176
ATFD. *See* Tunisian Association of Democratic Women
ATIOS. *See* L'Association Tunisienne d'Information et d'Orientation sur le SIDA
ATL MST/SIDA. *See* L'Association Tunisienne de Lutte Contre les Maladies Sexuellement Transmissible et le SIDA
ATUPRET. *See* L'Association Tunisienne de la Prévention de la Toxicomanie
austerity measures, 43–44, 56
authoritarian regimes
  downfall of, 16
  events that transpire following downfall of, xi
  expectations for transitions from, 164
  genuine political liberalisation after life under, 122
  precise needs of transition from, 129
  strategies to manoeuvre under, 81
  transitions from, 8
authoritarian resilience, 13
authoritarian upgrading, 44, 70
authoritarianism, 4–5, 40, 55, 77, 80

authoritarianism (cont.)
  authoritarian spiral, 62, 195
  liberal, 68–73
  residue of, 195, 198
  solidarity against, 15–16
autonomous social action, 80
Ayeb, Habib, 99
Al-Azmeh, Aziz, 138

Bahrain, 3
Baker, Gideon, 38–39, 128
Bayat, Assef, 43
Bebbington, Anthony, 49–52
Belaid, Chokri, 12, 107–108, 136, 147, 160
Bellin, Eva, 57, 69–70
Ben Achour, Yadh, 98
Ben Aissa, Salah, 189
Ben Ali, Zine El Abidine, xi, 2, 57, 92–93, 161
  downfall of, 4, 6–7, 12, 192–193
  Islam and, 137, 139–140, 145, 152, 161–162, 182–183, 195–196
  journalists under, 151
  laws of association and, 75
  liberalisation policies of, 73
  rise of, 68–73
  in Saudi Arabia, 3–4, 113
  secular-religious divisions and, 199
  social contracts under, 118
  social divisions under, 152
  violence and repression of, 18
Ben Romdhane, Mahmoud, 58, 61–63, 65, 195
Ben Salah, Ahmed, 63–64
Ben Youssef, Salah, 61
Bendana, Kmar, 4
Bensaid, Mehrez, 142
bey (civil administrator), 59
bilateral organisations, 51
bloodless revolution, 39
Bouazizi, Mohamed, 3–4, 15–16
Bourguiba, Habib, 2, 57
  crackdowns by, 67–68
  feminist movements under, 82–83
  Islam and, 65, 161
  laws of association of, 73–74
  leadership of, 58, 61–65, 92
  medical coup against, 68
  secular-religious divisions and, 199

Bouthafi, Nesrine, 103–104
Bozarslan, Hamit, 3–4
Brahmi, Mohamed, 12, 107–108, 136, 147, 160
Brexit, ix–x
Browers, Michaelle, 156
burqa, 143

Caid Essebsi, Beji, 62–63
Can NGOs Make a Difference: The Challenge of Development Alternatives (Bebbington, Hickey, Mitlin), 49–50
capacity building, 8, 201
capitalism
  civil society and, 30–32, 35–36
  consolidation of, 34
  disruption of capitalist systems of production, 35, 54–55
  inequalities of, 38
Cavatorta, Francesco, 18, 20–21, 31–32, 53–54, 102, 119, 140, 202
centralisation of land, 59
Centre d'Information, de Formation d'Etudes et de Documentation sur les Associations (IFEDA), 111–112
Chandhoke, Neera, 7, 27–29, 34
  on civil society, 37, 46
  on hegemony, 36
Charnovitz, Steve, 49–50
Chronique d'une Transition (Bendana), 4
citizen engagement, 129
citoyenneté (citizenship), 5–6, 94, 96, 131, 152, 161–162, 177–178, 197–198
  materialisation of, 134
  in practice, 123
  re-birth of, 111–114
civic activism, 96
civic education, 115
civic engagement, 54
civil rights campaigns, 36
civil society, 159–160, 192–193, 201
  capitalism and, 30–32, 35–36
  Chandhoke on, 37, 46
  civil society utopia, 128, 134
  consolidation of, 73–74

Index

229

democratisation and, 45–48
in Eastern Europe, 36–40
emerging issues for newer
  associations, 128–132
hegemony within, 35
historic civil society organisations,
  133–134, 155–156, 197
institutionalisation of, 48–50
Islam and, 155–156
in Latin America, 36–40
neoliberal discourses and, 9, 22, 52
newer organisations, 134–135,
  155–156, 197
proliferation of, 50–52
public spaces and, 29–30
resurgence of, 3–8
resurrection of, 15, 17, 97, 109–110,
  132, 192
secular-religious divisions and,
  152–153
strengthening, 8, 47, 116–117, 123,
  129, 201
surveillance of, 77–80
voices of, 28
'Civil Society' (Chandhoke), 27
class divisions, 36, 43
class reductionism, 39
Clinton, Bill, 47
CNPR. *See* National Council for the
  Protection of the Revolution
Code of Personal Status (CPS), 63, 102,
  127, 195
Cold War, 50
collective action, 16–17
collective organisation, 17
colonialism, 138–139
Commissioner for Enlargement and
  European Neighbourhood Policy,
  116–117
Committee for Political Reform, 98
Communism, 56, 197, 200
  Communist reform, 37
  influence of, 163
communities of value, 172
community mobilisation, 6
conflict, 35–36, 58, 189, 197
  deliberations on nature of, 165–166
  pluralism and, 193
  public spaces and, 96–97
  situating, 198–203

conflictual consensus, 166
Congress for the Republic, 100
consensus, 192–193
  abandoning, 165–168
  conflictual, 166
  exclusionary nature of, 8, 165, 189,
    193
  neoliberal discourses and, 166–167,
    189–190
  transitions and, 165, 190
conservative attitudes, 119, 134,
  169–170
  toward homosexuality, 182–183
Constitutional Democratic Rally
  (RCD), 69–71, 78, 92–93, 113,
  195–196
corruption, 86–87, 168–169
cost of living, 43–44
counter-publics, 128, 136–138
Court of First Degree of Tunis, 104
CPS. *See* Code of Personal Status
criminalised populations, 132
Croucher, Sheila, 175
Czechoslovakia, 37

DAC. *See* Development Assistance
  Committee
Damj, 165, 176–181, 187
debt, 18–19, 42, 69
decentralisation, 20
Decree-law 88 of 24 September 2011,
  118
demand-side approaches, 47–48, 201
democracy
  desire for greater standard of, 27
  Islam and, 156
  liberal, 40–42
  Mouffe and, 166–168
democratic elections, 4–5, 69–70,
  98–100
Democratic Paradox (Mouffe),
  166–167
Democratic Patriot's Movement,
  107–108
democratisation, x, 8
  attacks on, 136
  civil society and, 45–48
  consolidation of, 28
  limits of, 12
  narratives, 8

democratisation (cont.)
  national drive toward, 193
  of neoliberalism, 51
  priorities for, 164
  secular-religious divisions and, 157
  third wave of, 18
  volatile nature of, 7, 155, 202–203
Denoeux, Guilain, 47
deregulation, 96
Destour party, 60
Development Assistance Committee (DAC), 49–51
dictatorships, ix, 2–8
dignity, 18, 111–112, 140, 168–171, 194
Dilou, Samir, 184
discretion, 81, 84–85, 88–89, 122
discrimination, 10
discursive contestation, 181–187, 198
discursive space, 7
domestic violence, 125–126
donors, 46, 51, 129, 201–202
  aspirations for Tunisia, 67–68
  bilateral, 162
  good governance in donor-led development, 97
  HIV-specific interventions and, 120
  international donor funding, 48–49
  Islamic, 159, 162
  multilateral, 153, 157, 162, 192
  official, 49
  organisations' ability to mobilise resources from, 134
  after revolution, 133
  in transition, 116–118
  uncertain donor commitment, 119
drug trafficking, 89–90
drug use, x, 10, 89–91
Durac, Vincent, 18, 31–32, 53–54, 202

Eastern Europe, 55–56, 128, 192
  citoyenneté and, 134
  civil society in, 36–40
  transitions in, 40–41
economic crisis, 146
economic policies, 41–43

Edwards, Michael, 41–42
Egypt, 3, 152–153, 155
Eid, 148
Eid al-Fitr, 125
empowerment, 48
Ennahda party, 71, 98–101, 131, 143–144
  ambiguous political statements on behalf of, 155
  assassinations of critics of, 136
  challenges for, 147
  debates within, 199–200
  Ghannouchi and, 66–67, 99
  homosexuality and, 185
  leadership of, 140
  majority in National Constituent Assembly, 141
  post-revolution political project of, 145
  reform agenda of, 141
  Salafis and, 141–142
Entelis, John, 72
Essebsi, Beji Caid, 191
Ettakatol, 100
European Commission, 116–117
European Union, 116–117, 129

faragh, 6
El Feki, Shereen, xii, 179, 186
fellow citizens/compatriot. *See muwatana*
feminist movements, 36, 82–83
Femmes et Citoyenneté, 123, 125–126
Ferguson, James, 45
FIS. *See* Islamic Salvation Front
Foucault, Michel, 169–170
Foundation for the Future, 110
Fox, Jonathan, 47
Fraser, Nancy, 30, 152–154, 172
free speech, 16–17
freedom of expression, 72
French colonial rule, 58–61, 195, 199
Front of January 14th, 97–98

GCC. *See* Gulf Cooperation Council
GDP. *See* gross domestic product
General Labour Union of Tunisia (UGTT), 21, 64–65, 70, 79, 143, 192

Index

Ghannouchi, Rachid, 70–71
  Ennahda party and, 66–67, 99
  MTI and, 70–71
Ghonaim, Wajdi (Imam), 142
Ghorbal, Samy, 63, 65
Glasius, Marlies, 4–5, 31–32
Global Civil Society 2012: Ten Years of Critical Reflection (Anheier, Kaldor and Glasius), 31–32
Global Fund to Fight AIDS, Tuberculosis and Malaria, 87
global health initiatives, 52
good governance, 9
  neoliberal policies and, 165–166
  neoliberalism and, 46–47, 54
graffiti, 178
Gramsci, Antonio, 22, 35–37, 39–40, 54–56, 134, 162–163, 197
gross domestic product (GDP), 19
Gulf Cooperation Council (GCC), 11, 159
Gupta, Akhil, 45

HaAguda, 171
Habermas, Jurgen, 29–30, 167
Hafsid dynasty, 58–59
Hamdi, Mohamed, 71, 116–117
harm reduction, 90
hate crimes, 189
Haugbolle, Rikke, 119, 140
Hegel, Georg W. F., 22, 35–36, 54–56, 134
hegemonic, 28, 137, 166
  contestations to existing hegemonic order, 57
  international development discourses, 52, 200
  transition discourse, 188
hegemony, 49, 109, 165, 197, 200
  of consensus, 27–28, 167, 187, 189
  Gramsci on, 34–36, 197
  Mouffe on, 166
  of poverty agenda in international aid, 51
  reversible nature of, 162–163
  self-rule and, 134
Hennessey, Rosemary, 42–43
Henry, Clement, 74–75
Hermassi, Abdelbaki, 139
Heydemann, Steven, 44, 70
Hibou, Beatrice, 78–79, 116–117
Hickey, Samuel, 49–52
High Authority for the Realisation of the Objectives of the Revolution, Political Reform and Democratic Transition, 97–98, 109, 132, 196, 199
Hinnebusch, Raymond, 54, 77
HIV/AIDS, x, xii, 10, 93–94
  access to services for, 11, 81
  advocacy training in, 176–177
  bio-behavioural studies on, 179–180
  epidemic, 85, 170
  exposure to, 85
  government support for HIV/AIDS organisations, 119–120
  historic organisations working in HIV/AIDS, 120–121, 124–125
  HIV-thematic, 86–87
  institutional brothels and, 88
  materialisation of HIV/AIDS organisations, 85–92
  Middle East and North Africa and, 11
  National Strategic Plan to Fight AIDS, 179–180
  sex work and, 2
Hizb Ennahda, 71, 139–140
Hizb Ettahrir, 103–104
homophobia, x, 173–174, 186
  attacks, 187
  hate crimes, 189
  homophobic acts, 183
  International Day Against Homophobia and Transphobia, 176, 181, 188
  publicly countering homophobic statements, 188
homosexuality, 3, 10, 174, 181–182, 184, 188
  conservative attitudes toward, 182–183
  Ennahda party and, 185
  legalised, 193
  in Middle East and North Africa, 164–165
  modernisation and, 171
  police and, 183–184
Hulme, David, 41–42, 51–52

human rights, 3, 69, 72–73, 93–94, 168, 177–178, 193
  abuses, 84, 140
  organisations, 82
Human Rights Observatory, 178
Human Rights Watch, 174
humanitarian initiatives, 123, 130, 194
Hungary, 37
hyper-visibility, 81, 84–85, 131–132, 201

ibadat (religious obligations), 149
identity movements, 171–173
IFEDA. *See* Centre d'Information, de Formation d'Etudes et de Documentation sur les Associations
illiteracy, 63–64
IMF. *See* International Monetary Fund
infitah (opening), 19, 63–64
institutional brothels (*maisons closes*), 1–2, 88, 107
  HIV/AIDS and, 88
institutional stigma, 10
institutionalisation, 40–41, 48–52, 198
intensification, 48, 50–52
international aid, 51
International Crisis Group, 148
International Day Against Homophobia and Transphobia, 176, 181, 188
international development aid, x, 54
international financial institutions, 44
International Islamic Charity Organisation, 159
International Monetary Fund (IMF), 9, 41–43, 64–65
International Women's Day, 103–104, 106
invisibility, 81, 88–89, 122, 201
Iranian revolution, 66–67, 104
Iraq, 70, 144
'Is Social Change Fundable?' (Pearce), 48–49
Islam, 63, 119, 127. *See also* political Islam; Salafis
  associational, 148–152, 161–162
  Ben Ali and, 137, 139–140, 145, 152, 161–162, 182–183, 195–196
  Bourguiba and, 65, 161
  civil society and, 155–156
  democracy and, 156
  future role of, 133
  interpretations of, 100–101
  Islamist women, 103
  moral value system of, 149
  'radical,' 139–140, 155
  Ramadan, 65–66
  restriction of, 122
  revival of, 138–142
  social, 147–148, 160–161
  'visible,' 143
Islamic associations, 10, 149, 154, 157, 159, 194
Islamic Relief, 159
Islamic Salvation Front (FIS), 70–71
Islamism. *See* political Islam

Jamal, Amaney, 53, 115
Al Jazeera, 140–141
Joffe, George, 80
Journal officiel de la République Tunisienne (*JORT*), 75–76
journalists, 151

Kabeer, Naila, 46
Kaldor, Mary, 4–5, 31–32
Karoui, Nabil, 104–105
Kausch, Kristina, 118
Keane, John, 31–33
Khatib, Line, 8–9
Kidd, Alan, 31
Kinninmont, Jane, 138
Krichen, Zied, 105
Krouj, Fadi, 176
Kugle, Scott al-Haqq, 182
Kuwait, 70

labour exploitation, 59
labour laws, 43–44
labour rights, 21
Larayedh, Ali, 107–108
Latin America, 55–56, 128, 192
  citoyenneté and, 134
  civil society in, 36–40
  Marxist theory and, 38–39
  progressive social change in, 48–49
  transitions in, 40–41
law of 7 November 1959, 75–76
laws of association, 6–7, 73–77, 92–93

Index

amendments to, 109–112, 118
deregulation of, 96
loosening of, 195–196
Lebanon, 83
lesbian, gay, bisexual and transgender (LGBT), 164–165, 169, 171–173
  activists in Middle East and North Africa, 182
  caution against overt advocacy for, 186
  clandestine workshops for, 179
  discrimination before and after the Tunisia uprising, 185
  International Day Against Homophobia and Transphobia, 176, 181, 188
  national identity and, 186–187
  in post-apartheid South Africa, 175
  post-revolution advances for, 174–175, 188
  rights of, 178
  transitions and LGBT issues, 185–186
liberalisation measures, 15–16, 73, 94. *See also* political liberalism
  implementation of, 193–194, 199
  socio-economic liberalisation, 20
liberalism, 92
Libya, 3, 16, 116
Lindsey, Ursula, 99, 113
lower-income communities, 124–125
LTDH. *See* Tunisian Human Rights League

macroeconomic instability, 15
macroeconomic stability, 18
Al Madanya, 123–125, 131
maisons closes. *See* institutional brothels
Majoub, Mounir, 114–115
Mansbridge, Jane, 153
Mantiqitna Kamb, 179
marginalisation, 43, 54–55, 165
marginalised communities, 8–12, 38, 168, 194
  conservative attitudes towards, 119
  expansion of space for, 173–175
market deregulation, 42–43
market fundamentalism, 45
market liberalisation, 42–43

Marx, Karl, 22, 35–39, 54–56
Marzouki, Moncef, 142
mass mobilisations, 15–16, 97
Meddeb, Hamza, 116–117
media, 151
men who have sex with men (MSM), 85–86, 91, 179–180
Merone, Fabio, 147, 159
methadone maintenance therapy, 89–90
Middle East and North Africa
  GDP per capita average annual growth rate in, 19
  HIV/AIDS and, 11
  homosexuality in, 164–165
  human development indicators in, 18–19
  LGBT activists in, 182
  neoliberal policies in, 8
  ongoing social movements in, 28
  in periods of transition, 27
  socio-cultural change in, 118–119
Mikdashi, Maya, 102–103
militias, 148
Ministry of Development, 124–125
Ministry of Health, 85–87
Ministry of the Interior, 75–76, 91
Mitlin, Diana, 49–52
modernisation, 61–66, 93–94, 139, 171
moral panics, xi, 72, 102–103, 152, 155–156, 168–171, 187–188, 194
Morocco, 53
Morton, Adam, 35
Mouffe, Chantal, 7, 30, 164, 166–168, 202
Le Mouvement de la Tendance Islamique (MTI), 66–67, 137, 139–140
  Ghannouchi and, 70–71
MSM. *See* men who have sex with men
MTI. *See* Le Mouvement de la Tendance Islamique
al-mujtama al-ahli, 28, 150
al-mujtama al-madani, 28
multilateral donors, 117, 157
multilateral organisations, 51
Muslim Brotherhood, 138–139
muwatana (fellow citizens/compatriot), 5–6, 94, 96, 111–112, 161–162

NAP. *See* National AIDS Programme
nation states, 32–33, 43, 128–132, 197
  erosion of legitimacy of, 44–45
  limited, 41, 55
  low-and middle-income countries, role of, 37
  overthrow of, 33–34, 36, 38, 55
  Tunisian state, 58–61
National AIDS Programme (NAP), 85–87
National Constituent Assembly, 97–98, 137, 146–147
  citizen monitoring of, 131–132
  Ennahda party majority in, 141
  national identity and, 100
  political debates of, 101–102
  widening discursive space in, 158
  women in, 98–99
National Council for the Defence of Public Liberties, 64–65
National Council for the Protection of the Revolution (CNPR), 98
National Democratic Institute, 98–99
national identity, 12, 140
  alternative visions for, 161
  conflicts over, 103–104
  LGBT and, 186–187
  National Constituent Assembly and, 100
  opportunities to reshape, 167
  stakes for shaping, 25
  symbols of, 24, 132, 197
  transformation of, 152
national priorities, post-uprising, 194–198
National Strategic Plan to Fight AIDS (NSP), 179–180
nationalism, 60
  pan-Arab nationalism, 61
negotiation, 81, 84–85, 89
Neo-Destour party, 60–61, 195
neoliberal discourses, 8
  civil society and, 9, 22, 52
  consensus and, 166–167, 189–190
neoliberal policies, 8, 40–42, 44, 50, 133, 196
  of economic reform, 77
  good governance and, 165–166
  mass mobilisations against, 56

neoliberalism, 8–9, 29, 40, 54, 162–163, 197, 200
  Arab Spring and, 27–28
  constraints of, 201
  democratisation of, 51
  emergence of, 50
  good governance and, 46–47, 54
  hegemony of, 109
  social and economic inequalities created under, 146
neopatrimonial relationships, 77
Nessma TV, 104–105
New Policy Agenda, 9, 41–42, 55–56
NGOs. *See* non-governmental organisations
Nidaa Tounes party, 191
niqab, 105–107, 143
Nobel Peace Prize, 192
non-governmental organisations (NGOs), 44–45, 49–50
  increase support to, 47–48
  institutionalisation of, 40–41
  'NGO boom,' 40, 50–51, 55–56
  proliferation of, 116
  scrutiny of international donors and contributions to, 86
  structural inexperience of, 129–130
non-traditional mobilisations, 20
non-violent collective action, 15
normative consent, 34
Norton, Augustus, 28
Norwegian Nobel Committee, 192
NSP. *See* National Strategic Plan to Fight AIDS

O'Donnell, Philippe, 14–18, 168
oil crisis of 1970s, 41–42
oil prices, 18–19
oil rents, 18–19
one-party systems, 37
organisational capacity, 129, 134
Ottoman control, 58–59
Ouannes, Moncef, 76–77

Palestinian Liberation Organisation (PLO), 83
pan-Arab nationalism, 61
Parker, Richard, 170

Parti Socialiste Destourien (PSD)
State–Party, 63–65
PDP. *See* Progressive Democratic Party
Pearce, Jenny, 48–49
peer education, 88
The People Want (Achcar), 19
People's Movement, 107–108
Persepolis (2007), 104–109, 175–176
personalism, 69–70, 72–73
pessimism for post-revolution Tunisia, 121
PLO. *See* Palestinian Liberation Organisation
pluralism, x, 54, 92, 202–203
  conflict and, 193
  genuine political, 167–168
  indications of, 12
  limitations of, 27–28, 166
  narrowing, 7
Poland, 37
police, 78–79, 91
  homosexuality and, 183–184
  lack of, 113–114
political barometer survey, 107
political Islam, 65–68, 72, 74–75, 122–133, 160–161
  contestation of, 138
  extremism, 195–196
  networks of Tunisian Islamist diaspora, 141
  prominent Islamist thinkers, 138–139
  in public spaces, 152
  repression of, 140, 196
  rise of, 161–162
  young Islamists, 145
political liberalism, 4–5, 69, 95–96, 139, 161, 189
  attacks on, 107–108
  genuine political liberalisation, 122
  institutionalisation of, 198
  measures for, 109, 132
  openings for political liberalisation, 195
  spaces for, 96–101
political participation, 80
political reform, 63
politically motivated violence, 160
Politics and Governance in the Middle East (Durac and Cavatorta), 53

polygamy, 63, 102
popular upsurge, 15–16
populism, ix, 159, 169
'Post-Washington Consensus Consensus' (Stiglitz), 45
poverty, 63, 147
privatisation, 19, 42–43, 59, 68–69
Profit and Pleasure: Sexual Identities in Late Capitalism (Hennessey), 42
Progressive Democratic Party (PDP), 106
PSD. *See* Parti Socialiste Destourien
public services, 43
public spaces, 5–6, 94, 105–106, 145–146, 168, 197
  civil society and, 29–30
  conflict and, 96–97
  constrained, 122–133
  contested, 154
  counter-publics, 128, 136–138
  opening up of, 16–17, 193, 196–199
  political Islam in, 152
  Sunnism and, 143
  terrain of uncertainty in, 108–109
public sphere, 30, 167
Putnam, Robert, 46–47, 53

Qatar Charity, 159
Qur'anic education, 147

racism, x
radical negativity, 166
Ramadan, 65–66, 148
Rassemblement Socialiste Progressiste (RSP), 74
RCD. *See* Constitutional Democratic Rally
recognition, 168–169, 172, 194
Red Crescent, 176–177
Redissi, Hamadi, 105, 146–147
'Reflections on NGOs and Development' (Hulme), 51–52
relations of power, 167–168, 198–203
religious obligations. *See ibadat*
religious piety, 149
representative governance institutions, 18
'The Return of an Occupation not like the Others' (Sayah), 143–144

revolution, 4, 111–113, 119–120, 123, 134
  bloodless, 39
  democratic elections post-revolution, 2, 104
  Ennahda party, post-revolution political project of, 145
  freedom of speech in post-revolution environment, 105
  national identity post-revolution, 100
  pessimism for post-revolution Tunisia, 121
  post-revolution euphoria, 12
  socio-political transformations of post-revolution Tunisia, 2
  women let down by, 103
right to association, 16–17
rights-based organisations, 81–85
riots, 43–44
Roca, Jean, 31
RSP. *See* Rassemblement Socialiste Progressiste
Russia, 171

Sadiki, Larbi, 6, 15–18
Saheb Ettabaa Association of Islamic Culture in Tunis, 147
Sajoo, Amyn, 31
Salafis, 66, 101, 104, 138–139, 157–158
  Ansar al-Sharia, 107–108
  danger of violence from, 155–156
  emergence of Salafism, 137, 142–147
  Ennahda party and, 141–142
  looting by, 107
  militias, 148
  student protest by, 106
Salafiyyah, 138–139
same-sex behaviour, 10, 171, 178
  bans on, 91
  criminalised, x, 173–174
  penal code on, 183, 189
  prohibition of, 181–182
Saudi Arabia, 3–4, 70, 113
Sayah, J., 143–144
Schmitter, Guillermo, 14–18, 168
School of Oriental and African Studies (SOAS), xi–xii
secularisation, 61–65, 139, 161

secular-liberal women, 102–104
secular-religious divisions, 137, 150–152, 199
  civil society and, 152–153
  democratisation and, 157
  rise of, 162
The Secure Family. *See* Al-Usra al-Amina
self-determination, 6, 39, 97, 134, 162–163
self-rule, 134
sensationalism, 21–22
sex work, x, 85–86
  bans on, 91
  clandestine, 88–89
  criminalisation of, 10
  HIV/AIDS and, 2
  institutional brothels, 1–2
  legalised, 3, 193
  sex tourism, 89
sexism, x
sexual health, x
sexual minorities, 10, 87, 164–165, 180–181, 189
  leaving Tunisia, 183
  transitions and, 169
sexually transmitted infection (STI), 88
Al-Shaab, 12
Sharia, 100–101, 181–182
Sidi Bouzid, 3–4
SOAS. *See* School of Oriental and African Studies
social capital, 53
social contracts, 43, 118, 128
social divisions, 152
social Islam, 147–148, 160–161
social justice, 4–5, 54
social reform, 63
social welfare services, 45–46, 56, 96, 123, 130, 201
socialism, 63–64
socio-economic disruption, 14
socio-economic liberalisation, 20
socio-political disruption, 14
socio-political transformations, 2, 7, 12, 16, 18, 114, 137
socio-political turmoil, 118–119
sodomy, 173, 175
Soli, Evie, 147, 159

Index

solidarity, 192–194
  against authoritarianism, 15–16
  with Palestine, 83
Somalia, 144
Sousa Santos, Boaventura de, 33
South Africa, post-apartheid, 175
'South Africa's Democratisation and the Politics of Gay Liberation' (Croucher), 175
State and Civil Society: Explorations in Political Theory (Chandhoke), 27–29
STI. *See* sexually transmitted infection
Stiglitz, Joseph, 45
strikes, 43–44
structural adjustment policies, 43–45, 64–65
student and youth movements, 36
sub-Saharan Africa, 19
Sunnism, 100–101, 143
supply-side approaches, 47–48
surveillance, 77–80, 158
Syria, 3, 143–144

takbir, 101
targeted advocacy, 81
terrorist attacks, ix
3C Etudes, 107
Tocqueville, Alexis de, 46–47
Torelli, Stefano, 143–144
trade liberalisation, 42–43
transitions, 12–14, 146, 168, 193, 203. *See also* revolution
  from authoritarian regimes, 8
  consensus and, 165, 190
  in Eastern Europe, 40–41
  expansion of space provided by, 168–169
  expectations for, 101–104, 118–122
  features of, 168
  generalities and specificities of, 14–21
  haziness during, 108–109
  indeterminacy of, 134
  instigation of, 9
  in Latin America, 40–41
  LGBT issues and, 185–186
  limitations on, 21–22
  Middle East and North Africa in periods of, 27
  sexual minorities and, 169
  stages of, 15
  transitological bias, 13
transitology, 12–14, 197
transphobia, International Day Against Homophobia and Transphobia, 176, 181, 188
'Troika,' 141, 146–147, 155
  formation of, 23–24, 100, 107–108
Tunisian Association for Justice and Equality, 176–177
Tunisian Association for Minorities, 178
Tunisian Association of Democratic Women (ATFD), 81–83
  surveillance of, 83–84
Tunisian Confederation of Industry, Trade and Handicrafts (UTICA), 192
Tunisian constitution, 1959, 63, 100
Tunisian Francophone media, 21–22
Tunisian Front of Islamic Associations, 101
Tunisian Human Rights League (LTDH), 21, 70–71, 76–77, 79, 81–83, 186, 192
Tunisian Islamist movement, 66–67
Tunisian National Dialogue Quartet, 192
Tunisian Order of Lawyers, 192
Tunisian state, 58–61
Tunisie: Etat, Economie, et Société: Ressources Politiques Légitimation Regulations Sociales (Ben Romdhane), 58
'Tunisie: Violences et Défi Salafiste' (International Crisis Group), 148
'Two Centuries of Participation: NGOs and International Governance' (Charnovitz), 49–50

Uganda, 171
UGTT. *See* General Labour Union of Tunisia
UN Conferences on Women (1975–1995), 51
UN Convention on the Rights of the Child, 51
UNAIDS. *See* United Nations Joint Programme on HIV/AIDS

UNDP. *See* United Nations Development Programme
unemployment, 19–20, 102, 146
UNGASS. *See* United Nations General Assembly Special Session
United Nations Development Programme (UNDP), 184–185
United Nations General Assembly Special Session (UNGASS), 179–180
United Nations Joint Programme on HIV/AIDS (UNAIDS), 179–180, 184–185
  Middle East and North Africa Regional Support Team, xii
United States presidential election, 2016, ix–x
University of Manouba in Tunis, 105–106
University of Zaytouna, 65
'The Uprisings Will Be Gendered' (Mikdashi), 102
Al-Usra al-Amina (The Secure Family), 148–149, 161–162
UTICA. *See* Tunisian Confederation of Industry, Trade and Handicrafts

vacuum in political power, 113
Velvet Revolution, 15
violence against women, 126
Voll, John, 136–137
voluntarism, 5–6, 39, 111–112
volunteerism, 114, 130–131
Voorhoeve, Maaike, 100

Waltz, Susan, 69–70, 72–74
Washington Consensus, 9, 44–45, 48

wealth gap, 43
Weffort, Francisco, 39–40
West Bank, 53
Whitaker, Brian, 174, 182
Willis, Michael, xi–xii, 58, 67, 138
women, 193
  Islamist, 103
  let down by revolution, 103
  marginalised, 5–6
  in National Constituent Assembly, 98–99
  political discourses concentrated on, 102
  Qur'anic education for, 147
  secular-liberal, 102–104
  status of, 132
  violence against, 126
  women's rights, 75, 80, 93–94, 125, 143
working classes
  agency of, 35
  marginalisation of, 54–55
  power of, 33–34
World Bank, 9, 64–65
  debt leveraged by, 42
  economic policies of, 41–43
  on Washington Consensus, 45

xenophobia, x

Yemen, 3, 16, 144
Yugoslavia, 37

zakat, 149
Zartman, William, 69
Zemni, Sami, 97–98
Zghal, Abdelkader, 66
Zwela (graffiti urban art group), 178

Made in the USA
Monee, IL
01 October 2025